SHATTERING THE STEREOTYPES

SHATTERING THE STEREOTYPES

Muslim Women Speak Out

EDITED BY FAWZIA AFZAL-KHAN

FOREWORD BY NAWAL EL SAADAWI

An imprint of Interlink Publishing Group, Inc.
www.interlinkbooks.com

For my loving and supportive husband and children: Babar, Faryal, and Naader.

First published in 2005 by

OLIVE BRANCH PRESS
An imprint of Interlink Publishing Group, Inc.
46 Crosby Street, Northampton, Massachusetts 01060
www.interlinkbooks.com

Library of Congress Cataloging-in-Publication Data
Shattering the stereotypes : Muslim women speak out / edited by Fawzia Afzal-Khan.
p.cm.
ISBN 1-56656-569-3 (pbk.)
1. Muslim women. 2. Muslim women—United States. 3. Stereotype (Psychology)—United States.
4. Muslim women in literature. 5. Women in Islam. I. Afzal-Khan, Fawzia, 1958–
HQ1170.S463 2005
305.48'697'0973—dc22 2004021771

Printed and bound in Canada by Webom

Cover Art: "Fleshy Weapons" by Shahzia Sikander

CONTENTS

FOREWORD

~Nawal El Saadawi

Today is Thursday, June 5, 2003. I am at home in Cairo. I am trying to write the foreword to this book by Fawzia Afzal-Khan and other Muslim women from the United States of America. On my desk lie the morning Egyptian newspapers, owned by the government and the political parties representing left to right wing tendencies. The so-called opposition parties in Egypt (created by Sadat) are not independent of the government. I call them legal or legitimate opposition, tamed by the power of the government. You cannot really distinguish between the governmental and non-governmental newspapers. On the first page I see G. W. Bush, whom we are trying to take to the international court for war crimes in Iraq (Fawzia is part of this group of international peace and justice activists); I see him smiling, raising his nose to the sky as a global god, coming to Egypt, to the Sharm El Sheikh summit, to tell the Arab governments what they should do to fight against terrorism. He considers the Israeli killer of Palestinian women and children (Mr. Sharon) a man of peace. Who are the terrorists then? He points with the tip of his nose to the Palestinian children who throw with their small hands tiny stones at Israeli tanks, who fight with their naked bodies the nuclear and mass destruction weapons of the American–Israeli army, or those adolescent girls and boys who explode their bodies at the checking points, when Israeli soldiers inspect their anus or vagina for weapons.

I spit on the first page. I close my eyes a minute. I imagine myself the Palestinian guerrilla fighter, Ayat El Akhrass, or Wafaa Idris; I imagine exploding myself in the face of G. W. Bush and all Arab leaders around him. Of course I lose my precious life, but they will all disappear with me, and the world will be better without them. I will be named "terrorist" by American and Arab media, but who cares about names after death?

G. W. Bush came to stop the intifada, the legitimate self-defense of the Palestinians. He came also to bribe more Arab leaders to be obedient to him and his imperialist neo-colonial war against us.

I see him on the first page by the Red Sea shore surrounded by obedient Arab leaders, who are smiling to him, bowing to his power, sacrificing the interest of millions of women and men in our countries for the sake of their interest or the little bribe they receive under the name of USAID and co-operational development.

I see him smiling to Sharon, defending the security of the "Jewish state" in Israel. He uses the word "Jewish state" to create more religious conflicts in our region. He did not say Israeli state. He said the Jewish state. It is very clear that neo-colonialism and religious fundamentalism are two faces of the same coin. You cannot exploit people without some sort of divine power or some sort of religion.

I see him standing on our land; I smell oil on his breath, in his nostrils, in his ears and fake tears, mourning the dead in the collective graves in Iraq. He buried more Iraqis than Saddam Hussein. He killed and is still killing more Palestinians, more Afghanis, and he threatens to kill more in Syria and Iran (and North Korea and others). The greedy capitalist military machine is not satiated. It needs more blood for more oil and other benefits.

Today I am trying to write the foreword to this book by Muslim women. The word Muslim or Islam on the cover of any book makes it a bestseller. I am critical of religious languages, or turning the political-economic and social conflicts into religious conflicts. But this book is different. It is useful for reinterpreting the Qur'an and prophet Mohammed's sayings. It corrects the distorted image of Islam in the Western countries. It clarifies that Islam is not the cause of terrorism or backwardness or oppression of women. It exposes the root causes of war and poverty embedded in the patriarchal capitalist system which has governed the world since slavery.

I enjoyed reading American Muslim women's stories and poetry in this book. The personal is the political. Fiction and facts are inseparable. Personal stories resist vague and generalized abstractions. They maintain the urgency, the intensity, the richness and vividness of the concrete. I hope many people read this book, perhaps because of the word "Muslim" in its title. But we have to keep in mind that what we need now is social, economic, and political dialogue, more than religious dialogue. Many of the pieces in this collection take the religious connotation of Islam or Muslim and deconstruct it to reveal precisely the intertwining of economic, political, and social issues that are tearing at the fabric of the entire world today, not just the Muslim countries. This is an important book to read because it helps the reader to understand how cynical the use of religion is and how the term "Islam" is being bandied about to cover up rather than to reveal the truth of the global injustices that have created a culture of violence on our precious earth.

I salute these women for their courage!

INTRODUCTION

Playing with Images, or Will the RE(A)EL Muslim Woman Please Stand Up, Please Stand Up?

~Fawzia Afzal-Khan

When I was growing up in Lahore, Pakistan, in the late sixties and seventies, I had no idea I was going to become a Muslim Woman after I migrated to that land of possibilities, the United States of America. I mean, the irony of having all those possibilities reduced to this one label is a bit mind-numbing, isn't it?

Of course, this label did not envelope me then as completely as it has of late, in the post-9/11 USA. When I first got here as a young woman from Pakistan, I attended graduate school in Massachusetts. Back then, I was merely "exotic," a "dark princess from a faraway land"—a role I did not altogether eschew, I must admit, since it conferred upon my person a certain cachet I otherwise would never have had. I played the role to the hilt when I wanted to seduce certain gullible young men or gain entry into the homes of the rich and famous who loved showing me off as their exotic find from the East—isn't she precious, dah-ling?—or when I wanted to get into exclusive dance clubs like the now defunct but then highly fashionable Studio 54 in Manhattan simply by going "native"—that is, by donning the embroidered togs, jingly ankle bracelets, and tons of silver jewelry on my neck and arms, with, of course, the requisite kohl eyeliner alluringly spread on my dark brown eyelids.

Alas, that was all before the fundamentalist craze got a hold of the imaginations of those gullible American boys and their mamas and papas, matched by an equally crazed mindset I have seen unfold in the country of my birth and elsewhere in the Muslim world. Growing up in Pakistan, I never thought much about Islam or my identity as a Muslim female, because although I grew up in an Islamic country (95% of the population is Muslim, the rest being made up of Christians and a very small percentage of Parsis and Hindus), religion was only one spoke in the wheel of our lives. Ethnicity was another (although not much remarked upon back then either), so we were Punjabis; we were also part of the urban, educated upper-middle class, equally at home in the English language as in our native Urdu and Punjabi.

As I began to mature I certainly became aware of patriarchal prejudices against women in our culture, but in my own home my mother was a professional, a professor of English at a local college for women, and she was always a model of independence and, indeed, a stronger personality in many ways than my father. Never the heavy-handed patriarch that the media in the West depict Muslim men to be, my father did pray five times a day back then, as he continues to do to this day at the ripe old age of 81, *ma'sahallah* (as we Muslims say whenever we remark on anything marvelous, such as the achievement represented by aging gracefully and well); but he never forced us to perform our prayers. Well, almost never. I do remember that one long, hot summer when he tried to yank me and my two younger brothers off our charpais (where we slept on the lawn to avoid our virtual oven of a house during the 106° F temperatures!) at the crack of dawn for our Fajr prayers. We complained so bitterly and said our prayers so sullenly that he soon realized the folly of forcing rituals down our throats and quietly gave up. But to this day, I admire his adherence to the rituals of his faith, which have never made him turn into the kind of self-righteous fanatic who insists his or her Muslim-ness is stronger or better than that of less ritually-inclined Muslims.

So then how did we get to the point of fundamentalist madness that is presumed to have led to 9/11 and its consequences? What happened in the Muslim world, in countries as varied as Saudi Arabia, Egypt, Iran, Algeria, Pakistan, Afghanistan, Iraq, Palestine (a country without a state)? Were we all the same "beneath the veil" (as U.S. and other western media would have everyone believe)? Were we all Muslims united by our faith despite vast historical and cultural and temperamental differences? Were Muslim women everywhere, including in the USA, the same? Other than our religion, what did we share? Were our views about Islam the same? Did we share a common "Islamic" culture? Temperament? World view? Politics? Clothing? Food tastes? Attitudes toward sex and sexuality? Common hatreds? Common prejudices? Common virtues? A common desire to become terrorists of the world? Why terrorism, and what did the word mean, really?

While such questions would occasionally addle my brain, they never became center stage. But now Muslims in general, and the Muslim Woman in particular, have suddenly been handed the starring role in the post-9/11 Drama of the New Century. Clearly, these and other questions are not mine alone, and neither is the angst over what it means to be a Muslim Woman living in America at this particular juncture of history. In the wake of the cataclysmic, world-altering events of 9/11, media pundits, scholars, activists, writers, and performance artists have taken to expressing their views not just on the horrific events of that day, but also on the global, historical, cultural, and economic issues within whose context those events and their significance can best be comprehended. However, media pundits, speaking or writing for mainstream media outlets in the United States, along with many scholars like Daniel Pipes (associated with conservative think-tanks in our country such as the Brookings Institute), and evangelical leaders of the Christian Right (such as Jerry Falwell and Pat Robertson) have not taken us very far on the path of true understanding of either Islam or the roots of terrorism—an understanding that I believe is crucial for a just and humane future for our shared world.

For many of us, particularly those of us who happen to be women, and Muslim women at that, this general expression of views has led to a process of self-understanding as well—a process meant to help us learn about and draw lessons from what happened with the goal of preventing terrorism within and without the Islamic world, as well as preventing "a war against terror" (a euphemism for a war against Islam) from becoming a permanent feature of our physical and psychic landscapes. Galvanized by 9/11, many of us have written, spoken, performed our outrage, our anguish, our fears, and hopes on airwaves, in essays circulated in the electronic and print media, at public rallies supporting our nation while questioning its militaristic policies, as well as in performances involving both the spoken and written word, be it song, poetry, drama, fiction, or non-fiction.

Having both participated in, and been witness to, many events and gatherings where Muslim-American women of different hues and ethnicities—along with other concerned citizens of the world—have been sharing their thoughts through creative work, I decided that it was crucial to put together some of this provocative and life-saving dialogue in a printed form. This dialogue in turn could reach many more people who might benefit from a collective sharing of wisdom borne of personal and political anguish and deep soul-searching. Thus, in this one volume—which I hope will be followed by many others—I endeavor to show a glimpse of some of the wonderful, illuminating, provocative, often heart-breaking, yet always uplifting, work of Muslim-American women writers, artists, activists, and scholars. In this book, I aim to weave together the different strands of conversation that have been taking place between women from diverse Muslim-American backgrounds since 9/11. Indeed, by bringing together and juxtaposing the various Muslim female voices we have heard over these past two years, I hope to bring these voices into dialogue with one another. I hope too that something new and dynamic can emerge from this recognition of a shared space and trajectory despite differences in outlook, culture, temperament, expression, and yes, the different relationship we each have to the concept of Islam and its place in our lives and identities. A second and crucial aim of this anthology, therefore, is to enlighten readers, both western and Muslim, about the wide array of thought and behavior embodied in the concept "Muslim Woman"—so that its monolithic quality may be shattered to reveal the complexities and variety that no such single label can justly contain.

For me—and I think for the women represented in this volume as well—a painful process of soul-searching began almost immediately after the initial shock of seeing the images of planes colliding into the World Trade Center towers and the towers' eventual collapse (only to be reactivated day after day by the relentless media coverage). I remember so clearly rushing to my Iranian-born neighbor's house the minute I learned of the attacks from—of all places—Pakistan (my mother called to inform me whilst I, in blissful ignorance, was busy packing for a plane out of Newark airport scheduled just hours after the third plane took off from there on its doomed flight). As I sat holding hands with my friend and staring, dumbfounded, at the TV screen's pitiless images of terror, the phone rang. It was her 16-year-old daughter, calling from her boarding school in upstate New York. "Why mama?" I could hear her loudly sobbing over the telephone lines. "Why did they do this horrible thing?" At this point no one knew who "they" were; no one had yet come forward to claim responsibility; no accusations had as yet been leveled or hypotheses offered. But of course I "knew." We all did. I screamed into my neighbor's ear, "Tell her it's because people are fed up—of oppression, of injustice, of what's been happening to the Palestinians with this country's blessings...." Even as the words came tumbling out, I knew there was no excuse. None. For the senseless slaughter of mothers. And fathers. And brothers. And sisters. And sons. And daughters. And all those on their life's journey to becoming part of humanity's relational web. Just as there were no justifications for all those "other" deaths that we somehow did not talk about nor question. Not often, anyway, and certainly not with the same degree of sorrow and horror. And those slaughters of innocents kept happening and had been happening, would continue to happen, in all those Muslim countries. One after another after another. Palestine. Sudan. Afghanistan. Iraq. Iran. Chechnya. Bosnia.

So, it was hardly an act of genius to connect the dots leading to Osama and the symbolic register he occupies for the malcontents of the Muslim world, whose number, clearly, has been increasing by leaps and bounds over the past several decades following the collapse of the Soviet Union and the concomitant rise of the USA as the world's only superpower. This, in turn, has fueled an unparalleled economic hegemony of the few over the many, a coup for the worst excesses of corporate capitalism, euphemistically referred to as "globalization." Religious fundamentalism, in this case of the Islamic variety (although there are others on the rise), is but a symptom of this deeper malaise of unequal power-sharing and imbalanced access to the world's resources.

The connections between economic and political oppression and injustice, the rise of Islamic extremism, and the cataclysmic world events now conveniently labeled in shorthand as "9/11" are teased out in all of its fascinating variety and complexity by just about every contribution you will read in this volume. Perhaps the most palpable documentation for this complexity is to be found in some of the journalistic entries by Barbara Nimri Aziz, a Syrian American journalist reporting from Iraq during our recent "War on Terror" there. This war is a direct and most unfair result of this nation's mourning for its own victims of the 9/11 tragedy, and of course it must remind us of our earlier terrorist behavior unleashed on Iraqi civilians since the Gulf War of 1991 (as a result of which over half a million Iraqi children have died in this past decade because of our unilaterally-imposed economic sanctions, unrelenting destruction of their water supply plants, and radioactive effects of depleted uranium weapons used by our forces). Reading Pakistani-American playwright and performance artist Bina Sharif's powerfully moving one-woman play, *An Afghan Woman*, we are reminded of the devastating consequences of never-ending war on the poor Afghani people, victims of the Great Game between the Former Soviet Union and the USA. The Taliban and Osama-bin-Laden connection is, as the play makes clear, one fomented and encouraged by our own government, and the price for our encouragement of this cruel fanaticism has been paid most heavily by the women of this sad, war-torn country. Has their plight really been improved by our precision bombing and regime-change operations in Afghanistan post-9/11?

Listening to the acclaimed Indian writer and peace activist Arundhati Roy recently in Albany, I was immediately struck by the accuracy of the questions she posed to the audience regarding 9/11, which directly challenge the naiveté and ignorance embedded in the most oft-quoted American response to that event: "Why did 9/11 happen?" or "Why do those people hate us so?" Instead of these questions, she suggested that the more accurate ones to ask might be, "Isn't it surprising that September 11 didn't happen earlier?" or "Why don't they hate us more than they do?"

Feroze Sidhwa, in a letter to the *New York Times* (June 4, 2003) asserts, "There is nothing complicated about the Muslim world's anti-Americanism. It is a product of Israel's occupation of Palestine, and now of our occupation of Iraq. What more reason could these people need than unprovoked usurpations of their territory?" This is an observation that pulls and gnaws at the psychic center of our being as we struggle, in our bifurcated identities as Muslim-American women, to take stock of the injustices that affect us on so many levels. How do we retain our dignity? Our humanity? Our sense of belonging *there*, but also *here*? Where is home? For instance, Rabab Abdulhadi's poignant essay in the first section of this book, "Where is Home? Fragmented Lives, Borders Crossings, and the Politics of Exile," describes the self-imposed exile of Palestinian-Americans like herself, and what it means to be "dispossessed" at a number of different levels—including the level of gender—so that concepts like "home," "abroad," and gendered identity can no longer be reduced to any comprehensible logic of "belonging" or nationhood. The fact is that in a post-9/11 New York, indeed USA, thousands of "Arabs, Arab Americans, Muslim-Americans are made to feel foreign at home.... [B]eneath the facade of liberal advocacy of multiculturalism lies an ethnocentric New York that continues to deny our existence except as bloodthirsty or suspect male villains, helpless female victims, and exoticized alien others." Criss-crossing vignettes of New York's response to the horror of 9/11 with memories of her own humiliating visits over the years into the ongoing horrors of Israeli-occupied Palestine, Abdulhadi painfully underscores the reality of the USA slowly turning into a giant Palestine-style refugee camp for many of its dispossessed Muslim residents.

While Abdulhadi's moving essay describes the bleakness of the current situation in no uncertain terms, it is also true that Muslim communities in the U.S. in general—and Muslim women writers, thinkers, and activists in particular—have faced this moment of existential and political terror with a blueprint for action and reflection that is cognizant of the need to mediate multiple identities. They have had to negotiate between reaching out to the American community at large with one hand and networking within diverse Muslim communities with the other. The latter imperative has required redefining the terms of the discourse emanating from "within," and renegotiating the power balance between Muslim moderates and conservatives.

Certainly, there are many examples of each of these courses of action from within Muslim communities across the USA; I myself, aided by an Egyptian-American Muslim woman neighbor and friend, organized a "teach-in" a few weeks after 9/11 at my local library, entitled, "Uniting for Peace: Muslim Neighbors in Dialogue with Other Neighbors in Westchester." It was a moving occasion, with the community room filled to capacity and an overflow crowd lining the hallway outside on a Wednesday night. All had gathered to hear from a panel of eight Muslim men and women and a 16-year-old girl (my daughter) about what they had been doing and thinking on 9/11 and what their reactions were to what had happened. While the question-and-answer session that followed showed how necessary it was for us to have taken this step in "reaching out" to the larger community, the event also underscored the point that, indeed, a renegotiation of the terms of cultural and religious discourse emanating from within our Muslim communities needed—and had now begun—to take shape. There were some Muslim women in the audience who had their heads covered, while the women on the panel, including my daughter and myself, did not. This difference was a visible marker of differing interpretations of Islam particularly concerning the politics of gender and dress. This diversity is possibly indicative of the fact—as one critic puts it—that "the Islamic identification of immigrant and first-generation Muslim-Americans is primarily cultural rather than religious."[1] It may also be a demonstration of a difference of opinion on the meaning of this sartorial identification within Muslims in this country—a mirror, possibly, of a similar religio-cultural split in the Muslim world at large today.

The rest of the essays in the first section elaborate positions and issues that resonate in some way and to varying degrees with those I've just enunciated. Eisa Nefertari Ulen's two essays assert her pride in an Islamically-identified sense of herself as a Black woman in the USA, while the legal scholar Azizah al-Hibri discusses the "reality" of Islam as a religion of good, not evil—a concept Muslims now have a burden to prove in the American context. Iranian-American scholar Minoo Moallem's "Am I a Muslim Woman?" questions the efficacy of the label "Muslim Woman" to explain anything other than an overdetermined reality that hampers genuine self-expression. My own essay, "Unholy Alliances: Zionism, U.S. Imperialism, and Islamic Fundamentalism," first published in December 2003 in *Counterpunch*, links the conservative ideologies holding sway in Jewish, Christian, and Muslim communities alike today, and I argue that it is important to situate the debate and obsession around "veiling" that engulfs the figure of "woman" in Muslim conservative discourse within an under-remarked alliance of politically regressive agendas shared by these seemingly unlikely bedfellows.

In a more humorous vein, Pakistani-American Humera Afridi's "Terrorist Chic" wryly underscores the stupidity now fully encouraged in the public sphere regarding the loaded term "terrorism"— a term so mindlessly associated with the world of Islam, but which, ironically enough, is on the verge of acquiring a certain "chic" status! The noted Pakistani-American historian Ayesha Jalal's essay, "A Letter to India in Manto's Spirit," is a brilliant "copy" of letters written by her now-dead uncle, the famous Urdu-language short story writer of India and Pakistan, Saadat Hasan Manto, to his "Uncle Sam," in the 1950s. In the inimitably witty style with which he wrote his original letters, he castigated the USA for its hegemonic control over the miserable lives of millions of Pakistani and Indian citizens. In a similar vein, Jalal addresses her "letter" to the Indian prime minister, Atal Bihari Vajpayee, and indirectly castigates the USA for its role in aiding and abetting India's vile pogroms against its Muslim citizens over the past few years—pogroms that have now been helped by India's adoption of similarly retrograde and undemocratic policies as the Bush government's "War on Terror" and the way that war was unleashed on American citizens and residents of Arabic and Muslim background. Her dire warnings of the increased possibility of nuclear holocaust—resulting from the dangerous convergence between Christian-fundamentalist USA, Hindu fundamentalist India, and the Muslim-fundamentalism taking increasing hold in Pakistan—deserve to be taken seriously.

The personal essays by Afghani-Americans Nadia Maiwandi, Zohra Saed, and Wajma Ahmedy all underscore the painful memories of war-torn Afghanistan that once again have resurfaced for these brave souls in an increasingly hate-tinged atmosphere against Muslims in post-9/11 USA—memories which must now be renegotiated against this new terror in their lives, so that they can somehow go on living with some honor and dignity in their American homeland. And the final essay in this section, "Must We Always Non-Intervene?" by Iranian-born scholar and Harvard professor Afsaneh Najmabadi, raises the provocative question of whether intervention by the U.S. government abroad, in this case in Iraq, is really such a bad thing, given Saddam Hussein's monstrous policies against his own citizens. What, she asks, would really help increase chances for achieving peace, justice, and democracy in the Muslim world today, following 9/11? A total hands-off policy by the USA or some form of intervention? Her essay, written before the war on Iraq took place, does not advocate violent intervention, but it does ask a provocative question meant to elicit pragmatic solutions to a global violence that she sees clearly increasing.

In organizing this volume, I thought that having non-fiction essays spanning the academic and personal terrain would be a good place to start, helping the reader get a sense of the lay of the land so to speak. However, I wanted to juxtapose this section with one in which poetry expresses similar concerns but in a completely different register that touches the heart as well as the mind—and indeed creates very different effects on a reader's sensibility. What to me is so remarkable about the women I have been fortunate to gather under the roof of this volume's house is that many of them move with equal ease between different modes of expression, gracing each genre with their distinctive voice and understanding. Thus, for example, we meet here the Arab-

American poet Mohja Kahf through her haiku-like set of poems entitled "Little Mosque," which are bold and beautiful in the extreme; we meet her again later, in Section Five, as author of an essay that unearths many little-known facts about Muslim women as religious and historical figures of substance—a fitting complement to the "littleness" of her own poems, which reveal quite the opposite in their substantiveness, courage, and wit.

Pakistani-American Maniza Naqvi is another writer represented in this volume whose creative expression takes the form not just of poetry but also of short fiction and playwriting. Her poems, like those of all the other poets represented here, address the intertwined complexities of politics and religion, culture and identity, war and humiliation, and anger and compassion felt by the dispossessed and the occupied of this unequal world of ours. In particular, the poems by Palestinian-born Suheir Hammad and Nathalie Handal make profound and startling connections between the suffering and humiliation of the Palestinian exile under Israeli Occupation and the suffering visited upon Americans of Arab and Muslim background since 9/11 in the presumed safety of their adoptive country. It's just one big concentration camp out there now, and as my own poem, Sham-e-Ali al-Jamil's (also Pakistani-American), and my daughter's "Terror" underscore, we are all victims of the injustice of language and history. Yet we draw strength from the resistance enacted through our own control of words that can and must weave connections between feelings and perceptions that do not readily yield meaning. Like Pakistani-American poet Mahwash Shoaib's marvelously economical and linguistically experimental poems demonstrate, we must build and reveal connections where none are easily apparent.

One of the fields in which Muslims are severely under-, and indeed, mis-represented, is the area of communications: the media, print, and non-print alike. It is therefore crucial to have women like Nadirah Sabir, Anisa Mehdi, and Barbara Nimri Aziz out there as journalists in print, radio, and television. They bring to bear their unique sensibilities as Muslim women of different ethnicities and perspectives on the topics they cover, so as to help counter some of the tired stereotypes and images about Muslims in general and Muslim women in particular that have redoubled in their circulation since 9/11 within the larger American society. I chose to begin Part Three with an epigraph from an Iraqi woman journalist, Nirmen al-Mufty, simply to show the connection between her angst and that felt by her American counterparts. We are indeed all part of the global village, the human family. Here we get the voices of the Muslim female segment of that family to help us realize that we crave, nay, *require,* the same basic amenities in life, and that we need the same compassion and love in order that the human spirit not only thrive but simply *survive* in its sojourn upon this planet. African-American journalist Sabir, writing in her daily column at the *Atlanta Journal* about her reactions to 9/11 as a Muslim woman, provides a communication link between Muslims and non-Muslims which, as we can see in the responses of various readers to her writings, is greatly appreciated.

Anisa Mehdi's essay records her shifting impressions of post-revolution Iran and women's roles there and elsewhere in the Muslim world, from Malaysia to Turkey to Algeria, where she and her TV crew spent several months pre- and post-9/11 to prepare a documentary entitled "Muslims" for the PBS program *Frontline*, which premiered on May 9, 2002. She discusses how her pre-9/11 project, to examine Muslims the world over simply living their lives, took on an even greater significance post-9/11, when all media attention suddenly became focused only on Islam's militant aspects. Her own journey through various Muslim countries, interviewing Muslims with a variety of viewpoints, helped her shed some of her own U.S.-media-inflected prejudices and reinforced her understanding of the just and peaceful Islam first imparted to her by her Iranian-born father, now echoed by the most progressive interpreters of Islam such as the leading Muslim feminist theologian of Malaysia, Zainah Anwar, whom she met and interviewed in Kuala Lumpur.

Veteran print and radio journalist, founder and host of WBAI's weekly Arab talk-show radio program *Tahrir*, Barbara Nimri Aziz concludes the section by bringing our attention back to the war against Iraq, which we can all see is anything but over. Whither is this War on Terror leading us, several years now after 9/11?

Section Five gives the reader a taste of Qur'anic exegesis and Islamic history as seen through the eyes of American Muslim feminists: Azizah al-Hibri, as an expert in Islamic law and jurisprudence, uses her knowledge of the Qur'anic scriptures to refute simplistic, ignorant views on Qur'anically-sanctioned misogyny. Mohja Kahf, as mentioned earlier, here presents the case for Islam as a religion that has produced and venerated women leaders in its midst and is not to be blamed for the vile and inhuman customs practiced today in different parts of the so-called Islamic world by tribal-minded men more interested in maintaining their patriarchal power than in creating the type of just societies envisioned by 7th-century Islam—a religion that gave property and other rights to women much before they secured similar rights in what we now think of as the progressive West.

This section concludes with an interview with Pakistani-American feminist theologian Riffat Hassan (chair of the Department of Religion at the University of Louisville), about a controversial essay she published in a leading English-language newspaper in Pakistan called *Dawn*. In that essay, Dr. Hassan had laid out her interpretation of the Qur'an, which she sees as a document that stresses justice and compassion as ideals for an Islamic society to strive toward. To arrive at her interpretations, she relies on the science of hermeneutics—studying the meanings of Arabic words in the Qur'an in their time-bound horizons—as well as what she calls "an ethical criterion." That is, if one believes, as she does, that the essential message of Islam is justice and compassion, then one cannot interpret certain passages as preaching control, subjugation, and other unequal treatment of women since to do so would be in violation of the egalitarian spirit of the Qur'an. She then takes to task two leading contemporary female leaders of Pakistan for their opposing yet inappropriate views about the role of Islam in Pakistani society, particularly in regard to the position of women. The first target of her critique is the religious scholar and "guru" Dr. Farhat Hashmi, who is at the vanguard of a conservative movement among upper-class Pakistani women preaching a return to the veil and traditional roles for women. The other is Asma Jehangir, the much-lauded human rights advocate and lawyer, who according to Hassan is much too enamored of a Western-style secularist approach to solving Pakistan's problems to be of much use in a country of believing Muslims. In the interview she essentially defends her views against criticisms leveled at her from different readers, and she reiterates her belief that Islam is a humane religion that needs a modern interpretative paradigm. Nevertheless, she proposes that the idea that Muslim societies like Pakistan might somehow jettison religion in the public sphere to adopt a secular culture is not a viable solution to conservative religious ideologies.

In Section Six, we meet fictional representations of Muslim womanhood as it clashes against —and simultaneously draws strength from—its spiritual roots, even as the figure of Muslim Woman transforms into its lower-case multiple selves as they go about their daily business in a post-9/11 America. Pakistani-American Farah Qidwai's story is a poignant encapsulation of a young Muslim-American woman's fears surrounding both a secret premarital relationship with a man she loves (a relationship not permissible under either strict Islamic codes or those of family honor, particularly when applied to female behavior), as well as the secret identity she now maintains as she goes about her daily business, especially when it requires airline travel.

"The Villa Orient," a story by Maniza Naqvi (whose poetry and play also appear in this anthology), is a slow-paced stroll through the streets and sounds of multicultural, multireligious Sarajevo, where the narrator is staying at a hotel undergoing expansion, the hotel from which the story gets its title. In this war-devastated city where various professionals representing international relief organizations such as UNCHR, the World Bank, and UNESCO (of whom the narrator is one) arrive and depart in their roles as aid-ministering transnationals, the unnamed narrator draws some comfort in her knowledge that as a Muslim, she can find sanctuary, a sense of belonging, in a city where *azans* mingle with church bells, where Serb and Muslim can still not be distinguished one from the other. What price, then, war? What sense, then, the hatred for another who is also the self?

Humera Afridi, whose non-fiction appeared in Section One, here treats us to two short and pithy stories about the terror of 9/11—and what that terror meant to New Yorkers of different ethnicities. The narrative voice in both stories is female, and we find echoes of similar immigrant anxieties and rebellions against gender-biased orthodox religious strictures and behaviors. But we also find an acceptance of those orthodoxies as a source of comfort in angry times when to be a Muslim is to be perceived and treated as an alien without rights, a potential terrorist to be humiliated and threatened not just by strangers but also by one's neighbors and friends.

Finally, Egyptian-American Amani Elkassabani's story, "Hanaan's House," captures the gamut of emotions coursing through Muslim-American veins since 9/11: desire to belong to the mainstream coupled with a fear of rejection by that mainstream and of being targeted for hate crimes; anger at being labeled terrorists; humiliation for their identification with a religion practiced by peoples and nations who have become the oppressed, the vanquished, the disenfranchised of the world; and victimization by the U.S. legal system, which since 9/11 has taken away their rights as American citizens and immigrants. Through the Arab-American Muslim female protagonist's eyes, we learn of the invidious passing on of prejudicial stereotypes from one generation to the next within all communities; we also learn of the ways that women, through informal networking in different neighborhoods, can (and do) try to challenge such stereotypes, which too often lead to hatred and warfare. Of course, this process of challenging the internal biases of one's community is not easy, as Hanaan finds out when she moves into a predominantly Jewish neighborhood in Maryland and her parents and best friend express their reservations about her moving next door to "those Jews"; yet, it is her encounter with one of her Jewish neighbor's expressions of enmity against Arabs that leaves her shaken to the bone and skeptical of achieving true reconciliation and mutual tolerance between the two.

The final section of this anthology is devoted to an art form that is particularly dear to me: drama. For as long as I can remember, I wanted passionately to be an actor. To become someone I wasn't, albeit temporarily, seemed to me to be the only realistic way in one lifetime to experience alternative trajectories and histories, to know what it feels like to inhabit another's skin. But it was not to be. At least, not while I was still living under my parent's roof, a young, marriageable girl growing up in a middle-class respectable Muslim home in a traditional society like Pakistan of the 1970s and 80s, where performing on stage in full public view was akin to prostitution for the fairer sex. Things have changed considerably since then, although it is still far from the norm for young women of my background to be allowed into the acting profession by their parents and guardians without some trepidation about the possible consequences (such as getting a bad reputation, which could lead to a paucity of decent marriage proposals).

In my own case, after I migrated to the USA and acquired both a Ph.D. and a husband(!), I found that I could now return to my native land, become involved with theatre groups that had sprung up since I'd left (mostly performing political theater focused on women's rights issues), follow my childhood dream of acting on extended visits back "home," and let my dramatic passion infuse my scholarship. Killing several birds with the proverbial stone, I began to write about the dramatic activities I had now embraced with gusto, with nary a peep from my parents—or my very Pakistani husband! While in the West, I also began to work with an American-French theater collective, *Compagnie Faim de Siecle*, that I helped to found in the late 1990s with a young Pakistani man, Ibrahim Quraishi. Prior to 9/11, we had already begun to work on material that explored the limits of multicultural liberalism so dear to Western nation-states like the USA and France; but it was only after 9/11 that I felt the need to sit down and explore in a play the many difficult issues that had become center-stage for me and for so many other Muslim-American women. That was the genesis of "Scheherezade Goes West," a playscript-in-progress, part of which some of our company members, including myself, performed for a largely Asian-American audience last fall in NYC at the Asian-American Writers' Workshop. It was interesting to see that the evening featured excerpts from dramatic works being written by a whole "new" category of playwrights to emerge and be accorded recognition in post-9/11 USA (the irony of which is almost unbearable): Muslim-American Women.

It was at this event that I first got acquainted with the work of one of the women whose plays are reproduced here: Bina Sharif, a Pakistani-American playwright. I had heard of Sharif's work earlier, but never had the opportunity to see any of it performed, and this evening she was reading some scenes from her recent play, which was to be staged the following month at the Theater for the New City. The play, provocatively entitled *Democracy in Islam,* which I did witness in its entirety later on, is both irreverently humorous and poignantly empathic in its portrayal of Islam as a way of life, while simultaneously satirizing the U.S. mainstream media's one-dimensional representation of both the religion and its billion-strong adherents of various nationalities, ethnicities, races, classes, genders, generations, and sexualities.

In this collection, however, I chose to print Bina's powerful one-woman play, *An Afghan Woman*, which was written and produced off-Broadway very shortly after 9/11 and ran to excellent, albeit scant, reviews. I had the privilege of seeing it and responding to it as a theatre critic and fellow Muslim Woman (!) at Ohio State University in 2003.

I was so moved by Bina's performance in this play that I also invited her to my own campus to perform it in front of a packed auditorium of students, faculty, and community members. It is a play that truly touches American audiences, non-Muslim and Muslim alike, through its remarkable portrayal of the terrorism of War unleashed on the innocent people of Afghanistan. It also reveals the way Afghani women have suffered from the double-whammy of fundamentalist oppression—forcing them to become faceless victims of a rigid patriarchy—and the Great Game of superpower geopolitical control—reducing them to the status of pawns as Western politicians manipulate their veiled images in order to justify armed combat against the men who oppress them in the name of Islam. 9/11 and the global injustices leading up to it and into our present times coalesce into an iconic moment whose complexities are hinted at through the multilayered perspective afforded us by the veiled protagonist of this play, the nameless, faceless Afghan Woman. We are unable to see her, but she is *not* silent.

Neither are any of the other female protagonists who become such memorable characters in the plays by Maryam Habibian, Maniza Naqvi, and Betty Shamieh. Naqvi's play exposes readers and audiences to Muslim women of Pakistani background living in New York who are navigating their way through very difficult territory in our particularly troubled times, all the while maintaining a sense of humor about the madness that seems to have enveloped us all post-9/11. In this play, we have intrepid and iconoclastic women who question traditional interpretations of the Qur'an, particularly as far as women's bodies and women's "proper" roles in society are concerned. The veil, or *hijab* to be precise, comes under intense scrutiny, and its adoption is revealed to be as much a badge of true faith as it is an ideological fad appropriated by women of dubious moral integrity vying for an easy way out of conflicting choices.

The obsession with women's bodies as markers of familial and societal honor surfaces also in *Chocolate in Heat* by Betty Shamieh, the only "non-Muslim" woman represented in this collection. Betty is a Christian Palestinian-American woman, and I decided to include her play, which is structured as interrelated vignettes, because it shows that the issues which are so important in the work of the Muslim women included here are not "Muslim" issues alone. Rather, they are rooted in the conditions of global injustice and oppression that have given rise to the terror women, but also men, are being subjected to from so many different fronts today.

Habibian's play, *Forugh's Reflecting Pool*, written and performed for the first time shortly after 9/11, is the only one without any direct reference to that fateful day or to the events leading up to or after it. As an Iranian-American choosing to tell the story of the leading Iranian feminist poet of the 20th century, Forugh Farrokhzad, Habibian clearly made an ideological choice to show contemporary American audiences a very different face of Muslim womanhood from the chador-covered women dotting the landscape of today's Iran as depicted in countless television, film, and newspaper images. Through a chronicling of Forugh's life, we get a glimpse of steely feminist resolve in the face of the patriarchal pressures of an Islamic culture. Like many of her more contemporary sisters, Forugh challenges blind adherence to society's traditional norms which render women as second-class citizens in the name of religion. (It was my privilege to play her under Maryam's direction in 2003.)

Through the concluding interview with these brilliant, humanity-loving playwrights, I hope to show readers the common struggles, fears, and joys shared by these women as they discuss the importance of crafting their concerns into a richly woven tapestry of character, plot, conflict, and, if not resolution, then certainly hope—a hope that arises when we witness the power of art, of creative expression, to transform our worst experiences into new knowledge and increased self-understanding. It is my hope that such new knowledge will lead to a more peaceful world, because the causes of ignorance and faulty reasoning will have been exposed more thoroughly than ever before. I believe that the multigenred, multilayered work of the women writers represented in this volume will contribute to the creation of such life-saving knowledge.

part one

NON-FICTION

Unholy Alliances: Zionism, U.S. Imperialism, and Islamic Fundamentalism

~Fawzia Afzal-Khan

Since 9/11, I have written and published several essays examining the reductive discourses that sprang up, mushroom-like, in mainstream media (particularly within the U.S.) to explain that apocalyptic moment in terms of an "Us/Them" binary. Many of these limited, and in my opinion spurious, analyses (written and promoted by the likes of Bernard Lewis, Daniel Pipes, etc.) need to be challenged for obvious reasons. The most important of these, as far as I am concerned, is that linking Islam to terrorism does absolutely nothing to vitiate the anger and resentment millions of Muslims around the world feel toward the West in general and the United States in particular for what are essentially *political* reasons: the economic lopsidedness of a top-down, winner-take-all globalization that serves to increase the wealth and power of the richer nations at the expense of the poorer ones. The egregious example of the state of Israel—supported unequivocally by the USA militarily and economically to serve as its watchdog and policeman in the Middle East whose oil resources continue to fuel (no pun intended!) its imperial interests and those of other western nations—underscores for the vast majority of third world peoples (of whom Muslims comprise a substantial portion) the connection between the maintenance of global hegemony and colonial usurpation of indigenous peoples' lands and resources and their concomitant subjugation and dehumanization.

The ire against Israel that is manifesting itself increasingly and vocally across not just the third world but within the heartland of Europe should thus be seen for what it is: not as evidence of a "rise in anti-Semitism" as supporters of Israel wish to paint it (including, unsurprisingly, prominent cabinet members of Ariel Sharon's right-wing government, which is busy erecting yet more settlements in the Occupied Territories on a daily basis), but as the legitimate frustration of the world's have-nots against the haves. Seen in this light, Israel is simply an example par excellence of the oppression and injustice upon which the contemporary world class system—the New World Order with USA at its head—is based. Insofar as the state of Israel proclaims itself to be a state for "Jews only," the expressions of anger directed against it (in its capacity as colonialism's last outpost) necessarily take on what appear to some to be the markings of anti-Semitism, but are, in fact, the ire of colonized and neo-colonized peoples against the colonial Master.

In two previous essays of mine, "Here are the Muslim Feminist Voices, Mr. Rushdie!" and "Islam and Identity," I critiqued Salman Rushdie for his abject willingness to mouth the most clichéd of colonialist rantings against the Islamic world: that there are no intellectuals worth their salt within Muslim societies, particularly no feminist intellectuals, since Islam is an utterly regressive and at bottom, profoundly anti-modern religion (are Judaism and Christianity profoundly modern, then?) whose followers are "anti-Semites" and whose critiques of Israeli state policies are labeled by Rushdie as "Islamic slander against Jews."[2] Such a sweeping indictment of Muslims and of Muslim societies is repulsive because it panders to the dangerous stereotype of Muslims-as-fundamentalist-terrorists, precisely the kind of stereotype that has gotten us to the apocalyptic juncture of world history we are so unfortunately witnessing today. Battle positions are now hardening on both sides: the avenging (yet seen in their own eyes as "liberating") Judeo-Christian armies of the West on the one hand, and the so-called terrorist Muslim barbarian hordes massing on the gates of "civilization" on the other. Such a dangerous but surely cartoonish division of the world into these simplistic binaries was popular only amongst the lunatic fringe, I used to think. However, that "fringe" has expanded since 9/11 to include most of the U.S. citizenry today, what with the various polls revealing high levels of support for President Bush up until very recently. (Even now, a majority of Americans support his "war on terror" despite angst over the mounting numbers of American dead and no evidence to date of WMDs; these folks still believe, as one of my students wrote in an angry response to an anti-war poem I had them read in class: "Just because we haven't found them, does not mean these weapons of mass destruction do not exist!")

What is interesting, and more than a little frightening to observe, is that this type of fanatical, extremist way of thinking, carving up the world into "Us" and "Them," has reared its ugly head on college campuses as well, those bastions of so-called "liberal thought" and "academic freedom." I would like to comment on a recent incident on my own campus, Montclair State University, that reveals the overlapping and intertwined agendas that are shared, paradoxical though this may seem, by right-wing neo-conservatives on both sides of the ideological divide. Even more frightening, however, is the fact that this neo-con agenda, which is increasingly being adopted by Zionist Jewish intellectuals as a way to serve the cause of Israeli state aggression against the Palestinians, is aided and abetted by the so-called fundamentalist Muslims whose extremist views on a host of issues (including the "proper role" of women) can be used as evidence of their overall regressive mentality leading to terrorist behavior. This is so clearly an apolitical, ahistorical analysis of the contemporary Muslim world that it continually astonishes me as to how anyone can believe it. Yet Israel supporters can, with the help of these conservative Muslim groups, "sell" the U.S. public the myth that Israel is a western-style democracy defending itself against Palestinian (read "Islamic," even though approximately 7 percent of Palestinians are Christians) terrorists hell-bent on destroying it through the pathetic acts of suicide bombers. Never mind that their Israeli victims to date number barely a fraction of the thousands of Palestinian civilians killed, maimed, and rendered homeless on a daily basis by Israeli tanks, gunships, and Apache helicopters all supplied by U.S. and engaged in state-sponsored terrorism against Palestinians whose lands have been and continue to be occupied by Israel in contravention of international law since 1967.

This type of analysis then extends itself as an explanatory prism through which to view ALL critics of Israel, especially if they happen to be Muslim, as potential terrorists. Indeed, such a way of thinking has already led Congress to pass a bill that would, in effect, police academics teaching in Middle Eastern and other area studies programs across the U.S. Michelle Goldberg, in a November 2003 article for Salon.com, explains:

> On Oct 21, 2003, the U.S. House of Representatives unanimously passed a bill, HR 3077, that, if passed into law, could require international studies departments to show more support for American foreign policy or risk their federal funding. Its approval followed hearings this summer in which members of Congress listened to testimony about the pernicious influence of the late Edward Said in Middle Eastern studies departments, described as enclaves of debased anti-Americanism. Stanley Kurtz, a research fellow at the Hoover Institution, a right-wing think tank, testified, "Title-VI funded programs in Middle Eastern Studies (and other

> area studies) tend to purvey extreme and one-sided criticism of American foreign policy." Evidently, the House agreed and decided to intervene.[3]

Clearly, if this bill passes into law, it will curtail federal grants to Middle Eastern studies departments and programs across U.S. universities unless they can prove that their faculty are not inspiring "terrorist" thinking in their students simply by teaching them to critically examine U.S. foreign policy in the Middle East and elsewhere. The bill, sponsored by pro-Israel lawmakers and inspired by an American-born Israeli citizen, Martin Kramer, wants to tie federal funding to an explicit mandate that heads of these programs hire pro-Israeli professors in their programs on the grounds that these programs are overstuffed with left-wing pro-Arab, pro-Islamic radicals, who constitute an intellectual fifth column in the country. That such a "deranged fantasy," as Professor Juan Cole of the University of Michigan points out, could be taken seriously as a basis for a Congressional bill is a scary thought. Most of the "experts" receiving Title VI grants, according to Cole, are pro-Israeli hawks: Leonard Binder, political scientist at UCLA, actually fought on the side of Israel in the 1948 war; others, like Ellis Goldberg at Washington University, Joel Migdal at Harvard, Marc Tessler at the University of Michigan, and Gary Sick at Columbia, are all supporters of Israel. Thus, it is indeed disturbing that the fast-approaching obsolescence of academic freedom is being promoted by Zionist academics who have tremendous power in this government and within academia and who are determined to prevent any criticism of U.S. foreign-policy regarding Israel and the Middle East from affecting the minds of the American people—the same American people who might then reconsider the "war on terror" from quite a different analytic angle, one in which Zionism, Islamophobia, as well as fanatical Islamicism and the capitalist oppression of "others" all conspire together to preserve a status quo that is literally driving the world into the abyss of annihilation.

So how are certain Muslim groups helping to further this conservative, capitalist agenda which supports injustice and oppression in the world as a fundamental precondition of its own power? The Muslim groups I am talking about in this particular instance are the various chapters of the Muslim Students Association found across the USA today. Most of these attract young immigrant or first-generation Muslims looking for an identity to hold onto in the midst of confusing times. Unfortunately, it is the most regressive variety of Islam that holds sway in these organizations. So, for instance, the students who are office bearers of the MSA at Montclair are men who sport beards and name themselves in Saudi/Arab fashion (since Arab Islam, particularly of the Saudi variety, is seen as the "authentic" version by conservatives), even when they happen to be of different ethnicities and backgrounds. (Case in point: The president of the MSA is a young man from India, who calls himself Anwar bin Omar—an appellation that has no roots in India but is in fact an Arab construction). Women similarly present themselves in the most conservative way possible, heads covered in Arab-style hijabs, often wearing long coat-like garments to conceal their bodies.

To these young men and women, Islam is essentially a conservative ideology that can help resolve life's contradictions in a consumerist, inegalitarian, capitalist society—where everything, including the female body, is a commodity in the marketplace—by "restoring" the balance between men and women that has been disrupted by modernity (delinked from a class analysis). According to this logic, if women stay home and defer to their men, in a gesture mimicking subservience to God, all will be well. And of course an important part of that subservience has to be in the form of dress, since to expose the body is tantamount to creating *fitna* or chaos, an idea that is misogynistically linked to women's bodies and women's sexuality under the patriarchal class system common to all religious ideologies, including Islam. Thus, this conservative reading of Islam serves the ideological purposes of pro-Israeli cohorts on U.S. campuses and elsewhere (including the Christian right-wing groups of which Jerry Falwell, Billy Graham, Tom Delay, and indeed the entire White House staff appear to be a part of), since it is a short logical step to connect the "oppression of women" endemic to the philosophy of such groups to their penchant for violence in other arenas. Indeed, in her review of Jessica Stern's book, *Terror in the Name of God*, Isabel Hilton points out the similarity between fundamentalist Jews and fundamentalist Muslims by quoting one of the former as reported by Stern:

> Here in Israel, we don't like to say this very loudly, but the radical right Jewish groups have a lot in common with Hamas. Both, Stern goes on to add, have twin political and religious objectives and both use selective readings of religious texts and of history *to justify violence over territory* [my emphasis].[4]

As we see here, controlling women's bodies—conceived as the territory or possession of men—is a form of violence similar to that enacted against the inhabitants of Occupied Territories. In both cases, such violence is naturalized through discourse—religious in the case of the former and nationalist/Zionist in the case of the latter. What is elided in both cases is that such ideological ruses (even when they are adopted by victims claiming "freedom of choice," as in the case of Muslim women who insist their covering of themselves is a "happy choice") ultimately paper over the real issue of oppression of the many by the few. In other words, such an ideology serves to keep the status quo of a capitalist patriarchal world order intact, with ruling-class men, be they named Bush, Sharon, Saddam, or Osama, doing their best to keep the world in a perpetual state of war. As Orwell so presciently foretold in his novel *1984*, this practice is the only way to keep the elite in power in their palaces and the rest of us disenfranchised and hungry to one degree or another.

My attempts, then, at finessing the links that I see between "Islamic" terrorism and Israeli/U.S. terrorism, between the oppression of women and the oppression of the poor, the disenfranchised, and the homeless (epitomized by Israel's inhuman treatment of Palestinians) are basically aimed at deconstructing the links between Islam as a religion hijacked to serve the ends of western imperialism and Muslim patriarchal control and Islam as a political rallying cry for those fed up with the new forms of colonialism—the globalization-from-above paradigm—being forced down their throats. Yet, this de-linking—or re-linking of patriarchy, religion, and realpolitik, if you will—has had equally unsettling effects on my liberal colleagues at Montclair, including the women's studies faculty on whose advisory board I have served for many years, as well as on the Muslim students. I have become a persona-non-grata with the Zionists on campus in this and other organizations, with the religious Muslims, and with those affiliated with neither camp who are more often than not afraid to speak up and defend positions like mine, because they are afraid of "insulting" people who inhabit/identify with either extremes. Thus, when a number of organizations on campus—with the Global Studies Institute spearheading the initiative, led by an ardent promoter of Israel, followed by women's studies, the Women's Center, the Department of Religion and Philosophy, and the MSA—decided to plan a year-long series called "The Many Faces of the Muslim World," they quite deliberately left me out of their planning sessions. Nor, unsurprisingly, did they deign to invite me as a speaker at any of their listed events, despite the fact that I am perhaps the only faculty member on campus who is both a Muslim and a scholar of Islamic feminism—with many published works in the area. A Muslim woman who says what I say is anathema to all these groups since I can neither be marshaled as evidence of Oppressed Muslim Womanhood, nor as a mouthpiece for pro-Israeli, anti-Islamic rhetoric, nor as an apologist for Islam. If I don't inhabit a binary position, I don't exist.

I would like to conclude this essay simply by suggesting that there is a dangerous convergence, not just of right-wing forces representing all religious ideologies, but (perhaps worse) of scared intellectuals in various disciplines who are supposed to be committed to speaking truth to empower (Women's Studies being one of these supposedly exemplary fields). In the latter, the conspiracy toward silence around certain "sacred cows" such as the topic of Israel outweighs the need to speak out unequivocally against injustice wherever it occurs. Such a convergence and its contributions to a pervasive culture of fear must be challenged if we are to reclaim our integrity—not just as academics and scholars, but as human beings committed to finding just solutions to the problems and inequities of the world we live in.

The Burden on U.S. Muslims

~Azizah al-Hibri (September 11, 2002)

The ripple effects of the attacks on the United States a year ago continue to unfold. At first there was the enormous loss of life, the malicious destruction of American symbols, and the somber and grief-stricken nation huddling together in unity, defiance, and anticipation. At the Washington National Cathedral, President Bush invited an imam to join him in the National Day of Prayer and Remembrance. In many American cities, non-Muslims protected neighboring mosques from the wrath of the misguided. They instinctively understood that we were all in this together and that Muslims were victimized by the attacks alongside their compatriots. After all, missiles do not inquire about one's religion.

A year later, consequences continue to build up. Those in charge of our safety inform us that another attack will surely occur, and when it does it will be another horrific one. We feel helpless, angry, and exposed. Yet we go to work every day trying to rebuild the pension nest egg we lost because some corrupt executives cheated the nation out of its delicate recovery. We continue to act as if tomorrow will be just another day.

It is getting harder for Muslims to act that way. Unlike their compatriots, they have had to bear multiple burdens. They suffered human losses and will again. They suffered from growing suspicion about "sleeper cells" in their midst. They suffered government raids on their homes and their educational and charitable institutions. There were secret detentions, profiling, and secret evidence used against many of them; devices that stretched our constitutional limits to accommodate urgent security concerns.

Then, when no one thought things could get worse, they did. In July a member of the U.S. Civil Rights Commission reminded Muslims of the possibility of their internment if there is another attack on U.S. soil. Those comments were rejected by the full panel. But that was only the beginning. An attack from the "religious right" followed soon after. It maligned everything the Muslims held sacred. Those who were known for their vehement opposition to intolerance and incivility in the public square tepidly objected. The situation started to resemble that of America in the 18th century, when Islam was freely referred to as a "false religion" and our prophet as a great "impostor."

Muslim regimes then as now restricted freedom of speech, and they were recklessly viewed as the embodiment of Islamic principles.

It may not be a known fact that some minority leaders have blamed Muslims for the recent erosion of civil liberties. Some Muslims have blamed others within their community because they came from the same ethnic background as the terrorists.

Those blamed are in a daze. They have not yet fathomed the horrendous events and refuse to own them. Why should they? After all, how many Christians owned the Oklahoma City bombing?

In the midst of their pain, American Muslims know that they cannot prevent another attack. No terrorist asked for their opinion in the first instance; nor did the terrorists of 9/11 seem to have had the welfare of American Muslims at heart. Otherwise, why would hundreds of Muslims perish in the World Trade Center? Why would the terrorists expose American Muslims to a catastrophic backlash just about the time that Muslims were beginning to find their own voice within this society?

So let us be very clear: These attacks were not about the world of religion and spirituality. They were about the assertion of a brute worldly power, power that willfully harms and destroys people, symbols, and our peace of mind.

The America I knew and loved should not become the casualty of 9/11. I am not afraid of internment if God chooses it for me. Nor do I have children whose future needs to be secured. When I arrived in this country years ago I read about the McCarthy era, the Japanese internment camps, the forced conversion of enslaved African Muslims, and the genocidal wars against the natives of this country. As time passed, I saw a mature country struggling to get out from under this painful heritage into the sun of true liberty and remarkable diversity, and I loved it, warts and all.

My country was never perfect, nor will it be, but at least I have the constitutional right and the caring heart to try to make it so. I will not let any terrorist take that away from me or from you. God willing, I shall succeed.

9/11 and the Afghan-American Community

~Nadia Ali Maiwandi

I was barely rubbing the sleep from my eyes when at 8:54 am the message, "In response to all the anti-middle eastern bullshit rhetoric we are sure to be inundated with over the course of the next few weeks, let me just apologize now on behalf of america. love, lisa," came through my email account.

What could it mean?

I headed downstairs and noted the blinking light on my answering machine: My mom, nervous and stuttering about what she had just seen on TV. I caught something about twin towers falling before the machine cut her off. I called and got the details. Thousands dead, she told me, the towers are gone. She was terrified, wanting me to be careful and stay home if possible, for fear of falling planes from the sky, even in Portland, Oregon.

I didn't have a TV and couldn't check the news for myself. I got ready and numbly drove to work, trying to sort over the secondhand details in my mind. I entered the office to find my co-workers gathered around the television set. All very kind people who I have known for years, and yet I could feel them peer up at me as the words from the news reports "Osama bin Laden," "Taliban," "terrorists," and "Afghanistan" merged to become one.

I didn't stop to watch.

In the first ten days after the World Trade Center bombings, I had seen only about five minutes of the coverage. Perhaps that amounted to what some called my "insensitivity" to the tragedies. It wasn't that I was insensitive, but that my mind was somewhere else other than New York. While everyone around me wanted to know my thoughts on the World Trade Center, I talked about the starving people in Afghanistan, the kind of oppressions we will never know here, and the 23 years they have had like our day in New York.

This sentiment won me no favors, nor fan mail. But what I never would have guessed is the anguish I felt would be better received in my American circles than in my Afghan circles. While the majority of Afghans were supportive—especially my Afghan sisters, it seemed—a few blasted my vulnerabilities, questioned my right to express myself and my right to live in America, the place of my origin.

It was a confusing time for all Afghans, to say the least. For years a foreign element had invaded our home, taken it hostage, and exploited its grounds to train human killing machines and warp the minds of the young. Now that element had struck out to attack our new home—a place we had run to escape similar brutality. The Afghan-American community, like any other, was grieving the loss of life on September 11 and the weeks following, and grief strikes people in different ways.

No precedent could be applied to such a fantastically unusual tragedy—the Afghan community had to wing it. But a two-decade precedent of an Afghan community further dividing against itself had been well established. The early two-camp dynamic, Communist vs. non-Communist, had mutated during 20-plus years of war to multi-camp divisions based on ethnicity, geography, religion, political affiliation, organizational affiliations.... The Afghan-American activist movement was plagued by infighting and a lack of trust across divisions. With this history and the deep emotions behind it, it was barely surprising September 11 would not bring about the unity some hoped.

Some lines between schisms blurred following September 11, while others were newly born. Throw into the mix of already-instituted divisions those who wanted the U.S. to retaliate quickly, harshly, and at any cost, those who wanted more calculated operations, those who wanted peace.... It seemed there were more opinions than there were Afghans.

Perhaps expecting less tension in the Afghan community—or any community that had undergone so much—was illogical in light of these calamities. Shock and numbness had not yet worn off when Afghans began to fear for their own safety. The days and weeks following September 11 jeopardized the well-being of every Afghan or Muslim in America. Some Afghans claimed Greek, Italian, or Hispanic heritage to prevent abuse and hid their "Allah" pendants under their clothes. American furor swelled to a permitted violence; people were hurt and businesses burned. Even non-Muslims and those not of Middle-Eastern/Central-Asian descent found themselves in danger: Indian Sikhs were killed for having long beards and turbans, and a Cherokee woman was run down and killed as her assailant screamed, "Go back to your country!"

A few Afghans responded to the looming backlash and their fears by demonstrating their American patriotism, hanging flags from their porches, and backing any U.S. efforts to destroy the Taliban and Osama bin Laden, even if their own people were going to be sacrificed meanwhile.

But in the midst of all the tension, a tremendous thing started to happen: The level of activism in the Afghan-American community grew exponentially. The community had been suffering from low participation in activism; the work was tiring and debates exhausting. Donor fatigue overwhelmed do-gooders who saw it as an insignificant drop in a vast, endless ocean. An occasional rousing talk from a senator or star-studded charity event failed to generate long-lasting support. No one was listening to the Afghan-Americans, and we felt powerless in generating a movement.

But with the world's attention to the September 11 events, people not only listened, but started *asking*. Afghan listserves, some barely active, grew to accommodate quickly increasing numbers and adopted many American activists seeking information and looking to help. September 11 demonstrated in the most graphic way what Afghanistan was being used for, and this was completely unacceptable to those who had called it home. The American mainstream media covered the plight of the Afghans with more sensitivity in the passing weeks, and Afghans in the West were seeing—many for the first time—graphic images of what was going on in their homeland.

We came together to see what we could do to rid our country of an invasive and terrorizing element and related to each other's fears in feeling unsafe. We discussed our anguish at hearing people call for the deaths of Afghans and dreaded what might happen next. Afghans joined existing groups, created new ones, and became first-time activists, granting interviews and taking to public speaking to get the word out. We swallowed our nervousness and put our suffering people in front of ourselves.

Since September 11, thousands of Afghans have returned home to help or to reclaim their homeland. It's incredible to be able to return after not having the choice for so long, and devastating for some when they see what they are returning to.

With the world's spotlight on the country grows new hope for a long-awaited peace. It seems the prayers of the Afghan people may soon be answered.

Perhaps the Afghan community is not united in words or ideologies, but maybe this is not a reasonable expectation for a people torn apart by 23 years of war, dozens of conflicting leaders, and countless murdered loved ones. These latest events sparked an interest that old-time Afghan activists could only dream about, and it's vital to our survival as a people and a community that we hold onto it. Our coming together, whether in debate or solace, is the first step in a long road to recovery and the healing of war wounds.

Fragments from a Journal

~Zohra Saed (September 2001)

September 20, 2001

One week after the destruction of the World Trade Center, I take the 6 train to the downtown Manhattan area with my Afghan-American friend, Shekaiba. Since the Wall Street station has been shut down, we pass by in seeming slow motion and emerge out of the Bowling Green stop. Shekaiba and I don't know what to expect after we have seen so many images of this area on television—a place reserved for grieving families, eager journalists, and heroic firefighters. I unwrap two surgical masks from inside a Bounty paper towel. My mother had tucked this into my hands as I was leaving the door, a precaution against the potentially toxic air. Shekaiba and I come out to a section of the city that has more police officers than pedestrians. One six-foot tall officer gives directions to a woman two feet away from him through a bullhorn. Yet she doesn't allow the force of his triply amplified voice to distance her from him. She hangs by so close that her face is crinkled from discomfort.

Shekaiba and I are lost in this new labyrinth of yellow tape and police blockades. As we walk toward Wall Street, what strikes us as especially sad is not the dusty streets—I expected this, so I wore my boots today—but the dust on the store awnings. It looks as if a dam broke loose and crashed its way through a narrow urban canyon. The acrid smell makes my eyes burn and the sides of my nose, even beneath the mask, sting. It is unlike anything I have ever smelled before in my life—is it melted steel? Our heads ache and throb. Yet people are here going to work and standing outside smoking cigarettes, a mute collection of faces still raw from an immense shock.

They look at Shekaiba and I as if we are the rookies on the block. Apparently, everyone else has already given up wearing their masks, except for a few. We may be passé, but we refuse to remove ours; the air is too thick. Everything seems normal, that is if I don't catch my reflection, and if I avoid noticing the military presence at every other intersection. Here is a scene I never imagined: two Afghan-American women walking around with surgical masks just around the corner from the mall on South Street Seaport and asking directions from soldiers. No one checked for our IDs—although I had three forms of picture ID ready, just in case.

Tuesday, September 11

While crossing the Manhattan Bridge on the Q train, I along with other straphangers see the Twin Towers burning. Following New York train etiquette, I take only a few looks from under a woman's arms then return to my book, just as everyone else has returned to their newspapers. No one guesses the magnitude of what is to follow.

Early in the afternoon, I walk from 34th Street across the Manhattan Bridge into Brooklyn with a mass of other displaced workers. Rather than following everyone in their migration to the north of Manhattan, I go south, away from the shadow of the Empire State Building, to Dekalb Avenue in Brooklyn. Alone and frightened, I am convinced that New York City is going to crack beneath me like an egg. As a little Afghan girl, growing up on films of the threats or aftermath of geothermal nuclear war, I used to have nightmares about the end of the world. In my childhood nightmares, the fear came not from death but the separation from my family. After seeing the Twin Towers burning from the Q train, which passes over the Manhattan Bridge, these old sensations return.

Before I leave the City University of New York's Graduate School and Center, where I am a doctoral candidate, I run into a Turkish friend of mine in the chaos of people out on the street. She tells me that a suicide bomber attacked a police station in Istanbul. I inform her that on Sunday, suicide bombers, disguised as journalists, assassinated the anti-Taliban opposition leader, Commander Ahmad Shah Massoud. Both of our lips turn even paler from fear. A faraway threat has come to our town.

For three hours, I am unable to get any phone connection to Brooklyn. Until then, I make friends with a post-doctorate fellow. I am calmed by her reassuring voice, the only voice that hasn't become thin and shrill from fear. She advises that we go downstairs and carry a radio with us. So we end up downstairs, walking for an hour aimlessly in and out of the building, wondering if it is safer inside or outside, and taking turns holding a portable radio with the plug dragging around on the floor. We can't find any outlets and we do not have batteries. Yet we cling to the radio as if it is some form of security blanket. We spend a few hours together, walking north, eating pizza, and discussing Bollywood films to distract ourselves from the events.

Several times on my walk across a bridge littered with empty film canisters and Red Cross water cups—I suppose a moment of crisis in NYC calls for water and snapshots—I look over my shoulder, incredulous that something like this could strike New York. It is something out of a science fiction novel. Hollywood and fantasy fiction is our only reference to such an act. I pray with the others crossing the bridge that no one will attack us. Then, at the very end of the bridge, humanity resurfaces and offers water, kind words, restrooms, and warm support for us—a mass of disheveled and frightened workers finding our way home. It is these acts of kindness that give me faith that the world is not over.

After the longest, most frightening walk of my life, I come home to death threats from people who have grown up with my younger siblings. I come home to cold stares on the streets—this from acquaintances, since, like many Afghans, I have ambiguous racial features. I am not attacked on the basis of my face, only for the sake of my name and where I was born, Afghanistan. Luckily these are only verbal threats and harassment, although it is enough to put me under virtual house arrest.

Already, there are reports that drip through the phone lines of physical violence and vandalism of property against visibly Muslim, or South Asian, or Middle Eastern Americans. "Be careful," I hear this word more and more as the day progresses, a warning not only for my safety as a New Yorker, but as a Muslim Afghan New Yorker who lived in Saudi Arabia for four years before coming to America—a combustible combination in these days when fear has dug so deeply into our hearts that it threatens to congeal our blood.

Saturday, September 15

After four days of remaining under self-imposed house-arrest, I venture out with my family. We go to Flushing, Queens—the heart of the Afghan-American community in New York—with the pretense of going to stock up on ethnic groceries. In actuality, we go to check up on our community, but we are afraid to admit that it needs to be checked up on. To admit this would verify the rumors we hear through the insulated walls of our home in the midst of Sheepshead Bay—a mix of newly immigrated Russian, Albanian, and Turkish families, set upon an older layer of Italian-American and Jewish-American families—all of whom we grew up playing with on the streets. As in many places, here we are one of the few Afghans anyone has met.

I don't know what we expect to find in Queens, after hearing so many stories about Arab, Afghan, and Pakistani stores being attacked, but the Afghan shops still seem intact and people are smiling and overcharging us lovingly. We check the Kouchi (Nomad) Market on Kissena Boulevard, the Bakhtar Market on Main Street, and the Ariana Halal Meat store on Main Street near the Queens Botanical Garden. All are fine. All refuse to talk about any incidents. Everything is fine, so say the large flags on their windows and their neatly compressed smiles. Afghan etiquette is difficult to pry through for a young female equipped with a fragmented Dari trying to break into the heart of the matter. My parents refuse to ask for me. Instead, they walk over to the nearby Hindi video and music shop, which displays not only an American flag, but an Indian flag as well, to avoid being misrecognized.

Main Street, which is usually filled with Muslims in *hijab*, is now empty of ladies perfuming the air with a spill of ornate languages. I see three women in total—and women who have come out in a group of three, with large men accompanying them. Everyone has flags up, but it seems part of Muslim-Americans' survival to carry one prominently. One Afghan woman in an Indian shop is dressed modestly in Western clothes. When her two blonde-haired boys speak to her in Dari, she shushes them and speaks to them in English. The English language winds around them throughout the store—a young mother protecting her two boys, who can potentially pass as white Americans.

All of these women I see are out only to shop. The nearby Queens Botanical Garden, once filled with families taking their children out for strolls amongst the flowers, seems reserved for wedding parties. My family and I are avid picnickers. We keep a rolled up carpet in our trunk for impromptu picnics. The park behind the Botanical Gardens is empty, except for the ice-cream truck with his rather grossly out-of-place music. The day is tinged with autumn, so to keep warm we huddle next to each other to nap under the sun. Lying like this, so far away from the pain of the past few days, makes me feel so fortunate to be alive and so fortunate to be able to love. As a little girl, I was always tucking myself in between my parents as they slept, and I would feel like a pearl between them.

One of my last memorable images of Queens is a South Asian man, strolling by himself down a quiet street with cardboard American flags stapled together to make a hat. He looks funny to my sister and me. A little farther down, there is a group of white American men waving flags with signs that say, "GOD BLESS AMERICA"—God should bless America. In these days of simplifications and Us vs. Them, do I have the right to claim America as my own in order to bless? The men are average lower- to middle-class white Queens residents. Their beer bellies look ready to bust at the seams from so much patriotism. A frenzy of beeping cars and shouting men confuse us. They smile broadly at us and shake their fists in the air, a sign of unity. I wonder if they would be so happy to see us if our car weren't fluttering with little flags, or if my sister and I had veils on. But it is not fair of me to assume what they would assume. Then I remember that man in the American flag hat and realize that it wasn't funny at all. It was more sad than anything.

On the Belt Parkway, we see smoke fill the red horizon, reminding us of the deep wound in Manhattan.

Tuesday, September 18

In downtown Manhattan, sadness looms over these streets, which are cluttered with heavy generators. The sound outside is not the usual New York noise pollution. There are no snippets of conversations, or car horns, or streaming voices from radios. The loud noise of the area is a crescendo of generators outside of each building that has survived. Yes, here even the buildings sag from the weight of witnessing such a tremendous loss. Monstrous machine sounds and smells rule the streets. This keeps Shekaiba and I quiet. As we struggle to find the radio station on Wall Street, we realize that we have lost our sense of direction, until we see Trinity Church and behind it, a gauze-like memory of smoke emanating from the destroyed buildings.

Finally, we find our way into the building, stepping over layers of extension wires. Upstairs, we find that everything is out of sync—the phone connections are bad because of the explosion and the guests haven't been interviewed. Shekaiba and I come into a studio that is frantic with attempts to replace the interviewed guests. Shekaiba reads poetry by Afghan-Americans who recount their childhood memory of Afghanistan. I read poems about growing up in Brooklyn. Of course, such childhoods seem so distant from what we have only recently experienced, but then it makes more sense as the program goes on. It adds a different dimension to the words Afghan and American. Certainly, they aren't as flammable together as the world has believed in the past week. Perhaps, this will pass on the idea that we are Americans and have grown up here and aren't what they see on the television.

During the show's question-and-answer session, I come face to face with the average American listener. Some are trying to change their ways of thinking, while others are just there to spew more hatred. I notice that at the very navel of this anger and backlash is fear. There is a deep wound within us that needs to be healed—and this can be done through conversation.

My Earliest Memories

~ Wajma Ahmad

These are the images I carry with me to this day... the sky immensely dark, Russian soldiers floating to the ground in parachutes, carrying machine guns, monstrous military tanks crossing the streets of Kabul, powerful piercing pain vibrating in my eardrums, the sounds of bombs exploding outside my grandmother's home where I spent nights without my parents. This is when the Communists invaded Kabul and began massive bombing raids. As a four-year-old child, I remember tightly pressing pillows over my ears to block out the harsh noises. Years later, as I walk across the University of California San Diego campus, I cringe at the sound of F-16's flying above me. The Edwards air force base is located nearby the campus.

Fleeing

My last memories of Afghanistan are of fleeing war. We left in an open bed truck in the stillness of the night, the stars cradling our passage, Allah watching over us. In my memory, this truck is packed with mostly men. I ask myself: Were most refugees that fled the war males? Years later, as my father narrated the details of our escape, I discovered the facts: Five or six men including my father were lying down in the cargo bed, their bodies and faces covered by rice and potato sacks. Women and children from four different families hid in the front of the truck where the driver sat. This is also where my mother, sister, brother, and I hid.

I remember squishing my little body into the sharp angles and curves under the driver's seat. I was only four years old at the time, but I knew I was playing a dangerous game of hide and seek—a familiar game, one in which I knew if I got caught, we would get killed. A few things I can remember vividly: A scary soviet tank crossed in front of our truck and then an equally scary soldier walked up to the truck. I thought it was the end of us. I ducked under the seats as my mother breathed these words into my ear. I felt my heart beat rapidly to my mother's. I was so scared I peed in my pants! The soldier let our driver pass. We stopped only once in the early morning to do namaz before we entered the Pakistani border.

Pika

My uncle Jameel picked me up from daycare in Kabul. I was so excited to see him! He was my favorite uncle because he spoiled me. As the middle of three children, I rarely received attention from my parents and siblings. It was from my mother's family, my uncles and aunts, that I actively sought attention. They were equally as important as my parents and siblings in shaping my world as a young girl. My uncle had a chair on the back of his bike where he placed me. We rode past bazaars where I could smell my favorite foods, *rut* and *bolanee*, being cooked. One day, as he was riding past a display, I saw a beautiful *pika*. There was one in particular that caught my attention: a semi-circle shaped mirror fan with bright colors and a magnificent *parwana* painted on it. I wanted it so badly that I cried until he stopped the bike. I didn't know it at the time, but the *pika* reminded me of my best friend. Her name was Parwana. The image of the *parwana* is my flight from the war and the best friend I left behind.

My First Encounter with Jail

My favorite uncle who picked me up from daycare in Afghanistan came to the states illegally as an immigrant some years after we had arrived. He was placed in a jail with other immigrants who also came illegally. They also came from countries affected by war. As a nine-year-old child, I was scared of what would happen to my uncle. Would he be sent back to Afghanistan? The INS detention center looked like a scary warehouse. There were steel doors and windows. It was impossible to see what was going on inside. From the inside, it looked like an apartment complex like the one we lived in in Germany with other refugees. The apartment doors of the third-story building faced a courtyard area, where the visitors met the inmates. I remember this courtyard filled with voices of children giggling and talking during visiting time. My uncle shared a room with two other men; I wasn't allowed to enter the room but wondered how it looked. Did he share a bunk bed with his roommate like my younger brother and I? Did he have posters or pictures on the walls? It was a foreign idea for me to think that my uncle was living amongst strangers and in exile. I was nine at the time and was scared of my uncle's situation. My uncle embraced me when we met him inside the complex. He tried to appear happy, but I could see he was exhausted. He had lost weight; he looked so different from the chubby and happy Jameel I remembered as a four-year-old. When I saw my uncle in shackles as a prisoner, I lost the freedom I felt as a child riding in his arms.

Our Musdoor

I was born in Mazar-e-Sharif two weeks late. A midwife and my father, who was a doctor, delivered me in our home. I always thought it was an important fact that I was delivered at home and not in the hospital. I was eager to see the world. This home is where I remember spending time as a young girl running in the backyard, through freshly sun-dried clothes with my friend Parwana. The laundry was washed by our *musdoor*. Parwana and I competed to gain the most attention from our *musdoor*. She worked for both of our families and we spent a lot of time with her. I was jealous of the relationship she and Parwana had; I thought that the *musdoor* favored her.

The *musdoor* was relatively old, in her late forties to early fifties. She wore *paran-e-tombon* and a chadar. The chadar fell midway from her head onto her back, where she gathered it around her long braid. Walking low, hunchbacked, it seemed as if she had a back problem. I watched her as she washed clothes, banging the pieces of clothing against the wide metal pan. I remember feeling her insignificance and pain; I knew that she was looked upon as inferior to us. I sensed it even in the way my parents treated her; she was not one of us. She was called the clothes washer, but she was much more than that to me. She was my companion when I had no one to play with; she provided comfort when my mother wasn't around. The veins on her hands emerged as pulps of blue color along the dark, dirt-stained hands. They were continually occupied, either by clothes washing or by holding our hands. Parwana on one side, me on the other. She had warm, healing hands and I held onto them, feeling like I knew a secret no one else did.

Years later, the memory of her came vividly as I was looking at a painting in an small art gallery in La Jolla; it was an oil painting of a woman's hands, cupped together holding peas. The piece was called "An Offering."

War had made the *musdoor* another loved one I left behind, a loss I could never reconcile in my mind.

Tapping Our Strength

~Eisa Nefertari Ulen

I walk with women draped in full-length fabric. We swirl through the delicate smell of incense and oil filling air around the mosque. Even as the mad Manhattan streets overflow with noise, we sisters rustle past the crisp ease of brothers in pressed cotton tunics and loose-fitting pants, past tables of over-garments and woven caps, Arabic books, and Islamic tapes. Our scarves flap and wave in bright color or sober earth tones above an Upper East Side sidewalk that is transformed, every Friday, into a bazaar—the sandy souk reborn on asphalt.

Worshippers walk through a stone gate, along a path, and into a room unadorned yet filled with spiritual energy. Women and men lean to remove their shoes where rows of slippers, sandals, heels, and sneakers line the entrance hall. White walls bounce light onto the high ceiling. Men sit in rows along the carpeted floors, shifting in silence as we file past them, up the stairs and to a loft where other women sit and wait. "As salaam u alaikum." "Wa alaikum as salaam." "Kaifa halak—how are you, sister?" "Al humdilillah—praise be to God—I am well."

Soon the imam's voice begins to resonate in the hushed rooms. Contemplative quiet focuses communal piety. The cleric speaks in Arabic, then in English, building ideas about a complete way of life. About an hour later, when he concludes, a chanting song, lyrical poetry, calls the Muslims to prayer. We women stand tall, shoulder to shoulder, forming ranks, facing Mecca, kneeling down and then forward in complete submission to Allah, our faces just tapping the prayer rug.

And our ranks are growing. Islam is the second most popular religion in the world, with over one billion Muslims forming a global Umma (community) that represents about 23 percent of the world's population. In virtually every country of Western Europe, Islam is now the second religion after Christianity. There are approximately six million Muslims in the U.S. today, and about 60 percent or so are immigrants. About 30 percent of the remaining American-Muslim population are African-American, with U.S.-born Latinos and Asian-Americans making up the 10 percent difference. There are now more Muslims in the U.S. than Jews, and the numbers of new shahadas and Muslim immigrants continue to rise. Islam is even changing the way the United States sounds, as the azan converges with church bells, calling

Muslims to prayer five times a day. Words of worship are filling the air with Arabic all across America. This country will increasingly need to explore gender, generation, politics, and plurality from an Islamic perspective. The veiled lives of American Muslim women, so often garbled into still passivity, pulsate with social ramifications.

So how will pluralistic America shift and groan under the weight of this new diversity? What happens when uber-girrrl in spiked heels and spiked hair turns the corner on her urban street and peers into the wide eyes of a woman whose face is covered with cloth? What happens when uber-girrrl's daughter brings home a friend who has two mommies—and one daddy? Under what terms do we launch that dialogue of encounter? Are women who insist on wearing hijab unselfconsciously oppressed, or—particularly in the land that gave birth to wet T-shirt contests—are they performing daily acts of resistance by covering their hair? In the West, where long blond tresses signify a certain power through sexuality and set the standard for beauty, are veiled women the most daring revolutionaries? In workplaces, where anything less than full assimilation is dismissed, are women who quietly refuse to uncover actually storming the gates for our own liberation? Is liberation possible within the veil? American feminists would do well to engage these and other questions, and then again to engage what may seem the easy answers.

I am peering outward, clustered with sisters in scarves. And I am also aligned with women sporting spikes. I am a Muslim woman. I am also a womanist, a feminist rooted in the traditions of Sistah Alice Walker. I run those mad Manhattan streets, contribute my own voice to the cacophony; I also sit in focused silence, shifting space to embrace the presence of my many-hued sisters. I celebrate the sanctity of vari-colored flesh, of difference, that is celebrated in Islam. And I am also an ardent advocate of Black Empowerment, of Uplift, of Pride—I am a Race Woman.

When non-Muslims ask how a progressive womanist sistah like me could convert to Islam, I tell them Muslim women inherited property, participated in public life, divorced their husbands, worked and controlled the money they earned, even fought on the battlefield—1,400 years ago. When Muslims ask how a woman who submits to Allah like me could still be feminist, I tell them the same thing and add that modern realities too often fall short of the Islamic ideal. The Qur'an was revealed because Arabs were burying their newborn daughters in the sand, because Indians were burning their wives for dowry, because Europeans were keeping closet mistresses in economic servitude, because Africans were mutilating female genitals, and because the Chinese word for woman is slave. Obviously, these forms of violence against women continue, very often at the hands of Muslim women and men. The presence of patriarchal, sanctioned assaults against women and girls anywhere in the global Ummah horrifies me, particularly because I recognize these atrocities as anti-Islamic.

Contrary to popular opinion among non-Muslims, the Qur'an rejects the sexist propaganda that Eve is the first sinner who tempted Adam and led him to perdition. Both are held responsible for their exploits in the garden. Muslims believe Islam is the perpetuation—the refinement—of monotheistic religion and admonishes the persecution of people on the basis of gender, race, and class. Non-Muslims often confuse sexist individuals or groups with an entire religious system—and a cross-racial, multicultural swath of the world's population gets entangled in the inevitable stereotypes.

This political irresponsibility is dangerous especially because Islam is the sustenance more and more women feel they need. Indeed, while American women were publicly calling for more foreplay a few decades ago, Islam sanctioned equal pleasure in spouses' physical relationship—again, 1,400 years ago. Muslim men actually receive Allah's blessing when they bring their wives to orgasm.

Knowing many Muslim women are cutting their daughters, I celebrate Islam and teach to raise awareness about the culturally manifested, pre-Islamic practice of female genital mutilation, which is falsely considered an Islamic practice worldwide. I feel the same passionate need for widespread truth and empowerment when I read about women across this country knifing their breasts and hips and faces in the name of Western-inspired beautification. Fellow feminists too often allow difference to impede a coalition based on these virtual duplications, on this cross-cultural torture. My Muslim sisters too often think feminism is a secular evil that would destroy the very foundations of our faith. This is all a waste. While we allow difference to divide us, women everywhere are steadily slicing into their own flesh—and into the flesh of emergent women around them.

Any concerted efforts to link and liberate on the part of American feminists must proceed from factual knowledge of the veiled "other." Immigrant Muslim women must begin to align themselves with non-Muslim-American women, even as they maintain their *deen* (religion) and their home culture. Increasing conversion in this country demands U.S. citizens interested in women's freedom begin to understand why women like myself have chosen Islam.

I became Muslim because the Qur'an made sense, because my mind and spirit connected. Islam is a thinking chick's religion. Education is more than just a privilege in Islam; it is a demand. Qur'anic exhortations to reflect and understand highlight each Muslim's duty to increase in knowledge, a key component of this *deen*, this religion, where science especially supports a better understanding of spirit. Islam makes no distinction between women and men and access to knowledge, though some men would deny women's Islamic right to education, just as men in America have historically denied women the opportunity to learn.

The more I think about feminism and Islam, the more compatibility emerges from the dust of difference, and the more potential I see. I want to reconcile the great gulf that all my sisters—American non-Muslims who can't get past the *hijab* and American Muslims who can't get past secularism—see when they peer (usually past) "the other." I understand my Muslim sisters' trepidation, because first wave feminism's relationship with African-Americans lacked a cohesion born of acute commitment and fell victim to white supremacist techniques. Likewise, second wave feminism fell victim to the science of divide and conquer. Daring individuals pushed past division, though. They leaped over the great gulfs system controllers contrived to separate abolition and suffrage, Black Power and Women's Lib, and embraced a decidedly universal freedom. I am still slightly shocked when Muslims and non-Muslims claim I can not be both Muslim and feminist. I am leaping the great abyss dividing submission (to Allah) and resistance (to patriarchy) in this increasingly complex place called America. We must build bridges.

We must build cross-cultural, multi-ethnic bridges. Now, especially now, I ask my African-American sistahs to remember our legacy of domestic terrorism, of white sheets streaking by on horseback, of strange fruit, of Black men burned alive, of four little girls. Now, more than ever, we must remember the centuries of domestic terrorism in this country, but we must also remember this: that countless white women were our sisters in fighting the horror and pain their fathers and brothers wrought. We must remember this, too: We must remember the white men appalled by the terrorism of white supremacists, the white men who battled their own souls. We must allow these memories to help form a link connecting non-Muslims with Muslims in the country today. I am asking women to remember today. I am asking you.

I am ready to do this important new work. Islam fuels my momentum. I empower myself when I wash and wrap for prayer. I transform out of a space belonging to big city chaos and into a space conjuring inner peace. I renew. With the ritual Salaat, I generate serenity. I can create and channel strong energy as I pray.

Although I only cover for prayer, I deeply admire women who choose to outwardly manifest their connection to the Divine within. I want more non-Muslims to understand veiled Muslim women and respect them for celebrating Islamic creed, for resisting overwhelming economic forces in this country, for not succumbing to the images captured in high fashion gloss. By living in constant alignment with faith, they challenge the misogynist systems that compel too many Western women and girls to binge, purge, and starve themselves. For these pious sisters, plain cloth is the most meaningful accessory they could ever wear. To me, American Muslim women who choose to cover undeniably act out real life resistance to the hyper-sexualization of girls and women in the West. In the context of consumerist America, women who cover express power of intellect over silhouette, of mind over matters of the flesh.

Because I move in non-Muslim circles, I hear too many of my fellow feminists focus on *hijab*, urging complete unveiling as the key to unleashing an authentic liberation. For them, scarves strangle any movement toward Muslim women's emancipation. I ask them to just imagine 1,400 years—generations—of women moving without bustles, hoops, garters, bustiers, corsets, zippers, pantyhose, buckles, belts, pins, and supertight micro-minis. The way I see it, Western men wear comfortable shoes and slacks while women are pinned, underwired, heeled, and buttoned to psychological death. We American women still strangle ourselves every day we get up and get dressed for work.

Ah, you say—but even in their loose garb, Muslim women are still, so, so… passive. But Muslim women are not silent, not sitting still. We do not require American pity. We take the very best America has to offer. We are moving our bodies. As American women wow the world with unleashed athletic excellence in the WNBA, women's soccer, bob sledding, and pole vaulting, Muslim-American women are running and kicking along that mainstream—in full *hijab* or not. For Muslim immigrants who hail from nations that denied women access to physical movement, this country has freed them to pilot their own bodies. Many American Muslims are destroying the cultural forces that chained them while remaining true to the essence of Islam.

I remember hearing Sister Ama Shabazz, a bi-racial Muslim educator and lecturer (her mother is Japanese-American and her father is African-American) urging a large group of Muslim women to take swimming classes and learn CPR to satisfy the Shariah (Islamic law) not to defy it. (Anecdotes can be so helpful sometimes.) A friend of mine, whose mother immigrated to this country from Colombia, wears long loose clothing to the gym three days a week, then washes to cover and go home. An African-American girlfriend of mine rollerblades through her Bedford Stuyvescent neighborhood, full *hijab* blowing through her own body's wind.

These women fiercely assert Islam even though they have felt American hands tug at their clothing, especially since 9/11. They are obviously Muslim even though non-Muslims hurl offensive epithets or gestures at them. They do not cower. "It takes a warrior to be a Muslim woman," says another friend, a New Yorker born and bred Dominican. I agree with her.

Yet there is so much promise in the future: I know two Muslim high school students of mixed Iraqi/Indian heritage who play tennis in traditional whites and have earned black belts in karate. One even coaches the boys' basketball team. Interestingly, their immigrant mother could not wear blue jeans because her father forbade it. Certainly some men are still using women to assert a political agenda via Islam. I recoil when I see young Muslim girls in full *hijab* while their brothers skip beside them in shorts and t-shirts. I think about the women I know who cover themselves and their daughters for the wrong reason, and then I remember I know some women who wear push up bras for the same wrong reason: to please men.

We must recognize that the similarities in our oppression as women far outweigh the differences in the ways that oppression manifests. And to do that we must fuse our stories. Like African-American women who have fought to wear locks and braids and naturals on the job—or have fought to use relaxers without the ultra-righteous disparaging them as loser sell-outs—Muslim women have had to fight to wear *hijab* here. For everything from job security to an American passport photo, Muslim women have been asked to uncover. At root, we are all denied our right to represent an authentic self by these predominant cultural and social forces.

The last place we women of all faiths need to suffer the indignity of judgment based solely on outward appearance is in the company of other women. Right now, half of American non-Muslim women encourage other women to be free by being naked, and the other half desperately tries to get women and girls to cover up. Meanwhile, the men simply get dressed in the morning. Likewise, Muslim women who wear *hijab* are automatically considered unhappy, while men who wear turbans and long loose clothing are just considered Muslim.

Non-Muslim women need to stop telling Muslim women their traditional Islamic garb symbolizes oppression. Muslim women need to open themselves to coalitions with women in mini-skirts. Only then will we work successfully toward a world where all women can truly wear what they feel. Ultimately, societies grant men much more freedom in clothing. Perhaps this is the point from which our discussion should launch.

We must begin to think more critically, and honestly, about media representations of all women. While Muslim immigrants need to reconsider the East's portrayal of American women as loose and wild, feminists need to check their sweeping generalizations about the seemingly inherent violence and suppression the media projects as Islam.

Since the 1970s America has slowly shifted evil empire status from the former Soviet Union to the site of underground power, where black, slick, liquid energy fuels America's Middle East policy. Americans have been taught to fear the Arab world so that America can easily justify killing Arabs. Images of Middle Eastern men in the state of *jihad* demonized the people of an entire region. But the only legitimate Islamic war is a war waged in self-defense—the other guy must be the clear aggressor. And the direct translation of *jihad* is struggle, while the primary focus of that struggle is within. We must remember this as we watch our evening news, as we watch bombs fall from U.S. planes. We must remember this as we vote.

American feminists should not join the Pentagon and media in denigrating veiled women and our faith as archaic, out-of-touch, regressive. This is part of the propaganda of fear America needs to perpetuate in order to maintain world dominance. This country takes the very universal problem of sexism and often presents it as if it were exclusively a Muslim issue, as when non-Muslims degrade Islam for allowing men to marry up to four wives, even as American men practice their own kind of polygamy—via mistresses, madams, and baby's-mammas. Who are we to judge? After all, while the United States has never had a woman president, Pakistan, Turkey, and Bangladesh—all Muslim countries—have had female heads of state.

Of course, as Jane Smith of the Hartford Seminary says, "I think you'd have to be blind not to see things going on in the Islamic world—and in the name of Islam—that are not Islamic." Muslim women would do well to remember that the Hadith (sayings of Prophet Muhammad) have been interpreted to give men powerful social advantages over women, and that there are men, and women complicit in their own oppression, who use Islam as justification for misogyny.

Certainly the 9/11 attacks were not Islamic. Islam means peace. We greet each other with peace. Islam is no more violent than Christianity. Yet there have been American Christian networks formed to throw bombs—at abortion clinics. When have you ever heard the term Christian terrorist? We Americans do not profile white men with crew cuts, but a white man in a crew cut bombed the federal office building in Oklahoma City. Certainly we should not denigrate Christianity—and Christians—because of the few who would use their faith as a justification for violence. Why has it been easy for white Americans to turn on their own darker brothers?

Maybe we simply need to understand each other. Certainly America needs to begin the work necessary to understand Islam. El Hajj Malik El Shabazz said in his letter from Mecca, "America needs to understand Islam, because it is the one religion that erases from its society the race problem." Back at the Islamic Cultural Center in Manhattan, when the congregational Jummah prayer concludes, chatter fills the once hushed room as women and men prepare to leave. They step off the carpet, slip on their shoes, and the women readjust their *hijabs*. Vari-colored Indian and Pakistani sisters toss beautifully brilliant cloth sari-style. Olive-skinned Arab sisters check the pin securing the cotton scarves underneath their chins. Deep brown African sisters toss oversized lightweight cloth in their handbags, revealing their artfully wrapped gelees. And some women—of all colors and nationalities—take their *hijab* off completely, now that prayer has ended. This dynamic diversity might just be what the next wave of American feminism needs.

Muslim women and men are active forces in many different struggles, just as Western feminists struggle against misogynist forces. As a Muslim brother of mine once reminded me, race is just a smokescreen. Gender is just a smokescreen. Religion is just a smokescreen. These are tools of the oppressor used to separate and slay as he takes.

We have so much work to do. I chose Islam for the wonder of the word, because I believe in the five pillars of the faith, because I love Allah and justice. I have been blessed to bear witness to women's realities in what people think of as two different worlds, and I have seen that those realities are essentially the same.

I bear witness to the woman beaten by her lover in the street outside my Brooklyn apartment—and to the woman tied to a Nigerian whipping post. I bear witness to the woman forced to strip to survive in Atlanta—and the woman forced to cover to survive in Afghanistan. I bear witness to the ever-increasing legions of women caught in this country's prison industrial complex, often because of their associations with husbands and male lovers—and I bear witness to the women struggling against inequity in interpretations of the Shariah in Islamic courtrooms. How do we measure a veiled woman's pain? Does it weigh more or less than the trauma in an American woman's eyes? Should we compare and contrast the horror, brutality, and hard smack against a woman's cheek?

I simply ask that we warrior women, Muslim and non-Muslim, stand shoulder to shoulder, forming ranks, bending forward to carry all our sisters, Muslim and non-Muslim, tapping our collective strength.

Am I a Muslim Woman? Nationalist Reactions and Postcolonial Transactions

~MINOO MOALLEM (FEBRUARY 2002)

The question "Am I a Muslim woman?" sounds like a simple one. Yet it has been a very complex and almost impossible question for me to answer. The complexity of the question and the impossibility of an answer has prompted me to echo Gayatri Spivak, when she said that we need to pay attention to "the new making visible of a success that does not conceal or bracket problems." My intention here is to investigate the vast systemic work of violence that precisely underlies modernist institutions of education as they are characterized by colonial discourses, first world hegemonies, and the centrality of the humanist subject as a universal subject.

The institutionalization of race and gender cannot be separated from the conditions of "neo-colonialism," which derives from an unexamined identification with, and benevolence toward, the oppressed—my spirituality versus her religiosity, my militancy versus her passivity, my sophistication versus her naiveté, my location outside the class system versus her middle-class background, my consciousness versus her internal oppression. In October 2001, a question-and-answer with a reporter from the *San Francisco Examiner* on Muslim feminism brought me back to the question of cultural essentialism, Islam, and its racialization in the U.S., as well as the absence of a discursive subject position that enables one to talk about this racial formation and its consequences for the issues of women of color as well as the issues of race, gender, and sexuality in academia.

Of course, in the last decade a few scholars, among them Joanna Kadi and Ella Shohat and myself, have tried to engage with the issue of racialization of Arabs and Muslims, that is, Middle Easterners in the U.S., by expressing dissatisfaction with the disciplinary framework of area studies and their lack of engagement with ethnic studies, as well as the absence of engagement within ethnic studies with the racialization of Middle Easterners. Kadi has proposed the category of "West Asians"; Shohat argues for "multicultural feminism"; I have found a productive space at the limit of each one of these disciplines.

However, the absence of a dialogic space created for "women of color" did not help my conversation with the *San Francisco Examiner* journalist. Neither has it helped me to transgress the dichotomy of "foreign" versus "U.S. born" woman of color in the encounters that happen in the corridors of academia. Having been described in the article as a transnational Muslim feminist, I asked the reporter why she added "Muslim," since during the interview I did not describe myself in those terms. She responded by saying that she did not know that I was "not practicing Islam anymore."

The reporter from the *Examiner* has not been the only one or even the first to make such a remark. A few years ago, in a job interview at a respectable Canadian university, the faculty member who was driving me back to the airport finally managed to ask me the pressing question: whether I was "a practicing Muslim." Obviously, this could only raise in my mind a number of questions, such as: Why did my opinion need to be checked against my religious practice? Was it at all possible for me to talk as a woman coming from a Muslim culture without revealing my religious beliefs? Where was the secularist framing to protect me from this journalistic or academic intrusion? Do we ask all feminists who talk about women's issues in the U.S. and elsewhere in the world to identify their religious beliefs? Isn't it unacceptable in a job interview to ask someone if she does or does not practice a particular religion? Should a true representative of Muslim women wear a veil? And if this sounds like a ridiculous question to be asked of anybody, then what is peculiar about Islam which makes it impossible for us not to think of it in "fundamentalist" terms?

In a sense, it is ironic to see that the greater the challenge to fundamentalist Islam a plurality of interpretations and positions in the Muslim world presents, the more we become attached to imagining Islam and Muslim women as foundational and fundamentalist entities. It is time for us to question the representation of Muslim women at this particular conjuncture. The trope of the Muslim woman as the ultimate victim of a timeless patriarchy defined by the barbarism of Islamic religion and in need of civilizing has become a very important component of Western regimes of knowledge. The need to engage pedagogically with gendered Orientalism is no longer a flourish of postcolonial criticism but a sine qua non, since it is under the sign of a veiled woman that we increasingly come to recognize ourselves not only as gendered and heteronormative subjects but also as located in the free West, where women are not imprisoned.

We are still justifying our civilizing mission which began in the age of colonial modernity and continues to give meaning to our contemporary world. In the post-September 11 period, it is not hard to see the persistence of what I would call civilizational thinking in the representation of the Other in the hegemonic moment of the articulation of an American multicultural nationalism that relies heavily on Orientalism and Eurocentrism. The dichotomies—civilized/barbaric, east/west, veiled woman/unveiled woman—are indeed very important components of colonial modernity and postcolonial formations. It was in the name of the "mission civilizatrice" that French colonizers justified the occupation of Algeria; it is under the banner of "high tech humanism" ("bombs with food") that we legitimized the war on Afghanistan.

Of course it is not hard to understand that neither Islam as a religion nor Muslims as a community are unified and homogenous categories. They constitute a complex web of relations between social subjects and economies, political structures and cultures, across a range of geopolitical locations, in which religion is only one element. In addition, entering the realm of Islam requires a detour through colonial and postcolonial representational regimes of knowledge and power, including old and new forms of gendered and sexualized Orientalism characterized by the grotesque othering of Islam in the West—by, for example, the placing of Islam completely "outside history." It is only by way of such a detour that we may enter at all into the world of Islam and Muslim women. To enter the discursive universe of Islam since the 19th century has been made possible through its portrayal as a world of unchanging traditions, immoral and perverse sexualities, and the irrational bonding of barbaric men and obedient women in need of Western civilizational disciplining. That is to say, it is impossible to understand Islam without locating it in the context of old and new forms of globalization, colonialism, postcolonial formations, including modernization and Westernization discourses and practices, nation-state formation, nationalism, and citizenship. Furthermore, it is important to understand Islamic discourses and practices in the modern era, because modern religious discourses are radically influenced by (a) their connection to the sovereign power of the state that possesses, according to Michel Foucault, the right "*a faire vivre et à laisser mourir*" (to make live or let die) in the name of religion, and (b) their connection to a medico-military scientific constitution that establishes a fundamental adversarial power between good and evil as well as normal and abnormal.

The failure of secularism to protect me either in the media or on the campus brings to mind the importance of "civilizational and counter-civilizational thinking" that constantly mobilizes and dichotomizes both secular and religious universalistic and fundamentalist impulses. They are sometimes spatial (West/Islam), sometimes temporal (modern/archaic), and sometimes moral (good/evil), and they have become hegemonic since the Enlightenment. Is it because the culture cannot be separated from the religion of the "other," or is it because the very idea of religion only applies to the others that we are facing this situation? Or is it simply that a Muslim can only announce or renounce her/his religion if she is to be a legitimate citizen of the modern world? Is it easier to fit into the category of Arab, Iranian, Turk, etc.? After all, isn't it the case that these categories are themselves by-products of the modern history of colonialism and postcoloniality? Or is it in the assimilatory process of such determinations that the "Other women" enter the discursive spaces of "race" and gender? What, after all, is religion as a unitary category? Whose religion? Whose understanding? Where? How? By whom? Are we on the point of falling into postcolonial amnesia? When something made in time is treated as timeless, as trans-historical, there is a problem. What is it that we are making out of Islam and Muslim women? What is it that Muslims and Muslim women are making out of Islam? What is the relationship of the academy to the specific cultural and historical context and the conditions of postcoloniality? What is the relationship between the academy and the privileging of "identity" such that someone is believed to be in possession of the truth? What is the relationship of the academy to the "truth-making" apparatus of modern education? How do we participate in its reproduction? Theorizing resistance in the subjects of the "education" process is a crucial project, but what are the modes and occasions of resistance in the context of "postcolonial civilizational" thinking? What are the new "itineraries of silencing" of those subjects who are written off/out? What are the textual possibilities of voicification that are not assimilatory, not liable to re/appropriation or cancellation by the dominant modes of engagement? Isn't it important at this particular time to look at the transactionality and complicity of postcolonial "negotiations" with the dominant regimes of power and knowledge? What are the possibilities of preventing postcolonial struggles from lapsing into fundamentalist politics?

If the predicates—"Muslim," "Iranian," "woman"—are not innate but subject positions discursively constructed, the neocolonial forces and the epistemic violence constituting the postcolonial subject are undeniable. The term "Muslim" as it circulates in modernity cannot escape its appropriation and use within colonial discourse. The tendency toward a "fundamentalist" conception of non-Western Muslim women of course reveals the paradoxical nostalgia of colonial discourse for the "barbaric other" in need of civilization. The West is now claiming once again the liberation of the rest of the world as its responsibility. Likewise, the "coming into voice" of women and subaltern classes through the legitimate and civilizational tropes of the West.

I am concerned that some of the counter-hegemonic categories are being recuperated as a civilizational trope. I am not of course talking about the idiotic white man; I am talking about my fellows of color for whom the question, "How do we keep the ethnocentric subject?"—which is able to selectively define an "Other"—has become irrelevant. That is, it is a question lost in a celebratory moment of imagining a space beyond the ruses of power. Am I a Muslim woman? Even to answer this question is to enter the discursive spaces of race and gender in the conditions of postcoloniality. Or to put it another way, I am faced with the impossibility of transgression since either I am required to submit to the "itinerary of silencing" by refusing to answer the question or to adopt a subject position that makes me "pass."

Terrorist Chic

~Humera Afridi

All over New York City, there are signs of a startling new fashion—"terrorism" is becoming trendy. My first sighting of this peculiar phenomenon happened a month ago in Hiroko's Café on Thompson Street in SoHo. Sipping my kiwi juice, lamenting the fate of this mysteriously unappreciated new neighborhood eatery, I was delighted when an exuberant young woman waltzed into the restaurant from the snowy night. She appeared to know the owner—I gathered this, as I eavesdropped, from her ecstatic narration of her recent shopping spree. She deconstructed her outfit, filling in details of the location of the vintage store; waxed lyrical on the wonderful winter sale at Barney's; and, finally, shared her feelings for what she was wearing, starting with her fur-lined boots, embellished with turquoise beads and suede trimmings, and finishing with her fuchsia hand-knitted woolen cap whose flaps framed her cheekbones.

"Doesn't this make me look like a terrorist?" she asked as she primped it snug over her scalp for emphasis. "It's so cute. I adore it!"

Moments later, she tripped into the snow-shrouded street and, with the courage of a freedom fighter, fought the blustery wind on her way to BOOM.

There is something about the urban psyche that is enticed by the outlawed and the condemned. Though not in the articulate manner in which PLO red-and-black checkered scarves became a fashion statement, references to accessories ostensibly worn by terrorists are, nevertheless, entering the popular vocabulary. The problem is that although Dubya is exhorting American citizens to notify authorities of all suspicious or "terrorist type" people or activities, no one really knows exactly what a terrorist looks like, wears, and what he or she—is it even probable to say *she* when referring to a terrorist in America?—ought to be doing in order to qualify. Hence, the collective imagination of the city is inflamed by the lure of the elusive and fueled, additionally, by the curious disjuncture between the established threat of terror and any concrete presence of terrorists and their activities.

Color-coded in pumpkin-orange and with its own special corner on the CNN screen, the alert for domestic terrorism has been at a persistent and unprecedented high. It sits there numbly like an allergen report of the atmosphere. How long until this shade of orange becomes the hot new color for leather jackets, branded by avant-garde designers as "terrorist-orange"?

The word "terror" has never before enjoyed so much attention in American usage—in newspaper headlines, as the subject of cover stories and in ordinary conversations, it inhabits various parts of speech, proving itself grammatically versatile. "Terrorism" is also rather rapidly developing an extra dimension. By a syntactic ruse employing stealth and repetition, the word terrorism has become conflated with Islam and now, by extension, every Muslim is a potential terrorist in America today. Thus, as we engage in the new American pastime of terrorist-spotting, we shouldn't overlook the resurgence of baubles bearing "Allah" in Arabic calligraphy that went into brief hibernation following September 11. Those who were hesitant to display their faith in the furor that followed the Trade Center attack are now vehemently sparkling with jewels boasting Arabic calligraphy. Are these accessories to be read as a sign of defiance, a symbol of terrorism? Or as signifiers of resistance and subversion of the popular notion of a terrorist? Are they deserving of attention at all?

Posturing as a terrorist in order to recreate the aura of the terrorist or as a form of sympathy for the invisible enemy may also be becoming de rigueur. A fortnight ago, at Bar Pitti on Sixth Avenue and Bleecker, as I was savoring the marrow of a succulent capretto, the heated overtones of a conversation happening two tables down caught my attention, in part because the buzz word terrorist was being tossed liberally. I listened shamelessly. "I was fuckin' suicidal when I was sixteen," the twenty-something woman of indeterminate origin was saying. "You think if I could attempt it living the bored, privileged life I had, I would even for a moment hesitate blowing myself up for the benefit of my community if I was forced to live a depraved, disenfranchised life in a fuckin' Palestinian camp?" The man sitting across from her was visibly uncomfortable. He squirmed and cast discreet glances around him. Several diners simulated conversations while focusing on the young woman's diatribe. "They think they're doing us a favor by only asking for the men to be fingerprinted. You think my eighty-year-old grandfather who escaped genocide is capable of being a terrorist if he visits this country? I. . . *I* am more likely to be a terrorist on the loose than him. But they're not fingerprinting me! Hah! What imbeciles!"

But just as soon as a new trend emerges, the Canal Street knock-off also simultaneously and stealthily infiltrates the streets such that to the untrained eye, the world is democratically designer, and even the scornful connoisseur's confidence in her ability to discern the genuine article in a swamp of fakes is seriously challenged by the often meticulous quality of the reproduction.

So it was that in the beautifully appointed PoggenPohl and Hastings showroom off Union Square, the woman jerked her head back and said, "Oh… But you are so modern!" She tucked her chin into her neck and held this peculiar, unnatural posture as she studied me with a furrowed brow. I cleared my throat in anticipation of the price of the stunning embossed basin displayed in the shop window. But the woman was evidently distracted and she seemed disappointed somehow by my answer to her question, *Where is that accent from?*

The saleswoman's eyes roamed liberally over my body, swallowing my woolen cap, my beige Banana Republic quilted jacket, chocolate corduroy pants and magnetic Nike sneakers while her fingers began to frantically sift the pages of a folder that balanced on her lap. "It's *very* expensive," she said and again her indigo-penciled eyebrows puckered. Her face was a mold of dismay and disapproval. "I haven't found the page just yet but I can tell you it's *extremely* expensive." She then directed her gaze upon my husband.

The sibilance of rustling paper filled the room. Outside the night was cold and the city glimmered. It was Martin Luther King Day. I thought, even in Manhattan, one ought not to walk into boutiques unless one is appropriately attired and accessorized, especially if one can be mistaken for a terrorist. My fingers felt naked without my Ceylon sapphire; I regretted my sneakers. (We had taken our dogs for a walk through Washington Square Park, then dashed out to window shop for our loft renovation before stores shut for the day. There'd been no time to change but then that's what I loved about New York City: the unspoken tolerance of sartorial anarchy, an unwillingness to read people exclusively by their clothes.)

"You're really from Pakistan? *Really*? I'm surprised they let you into the country, you know, with the kind of terrorism you have there?" She emerged from her folder, nullifying forever all possibility of learning the price of the sink.

"Why wouldn't they *let me in* the country? Pakistan is an *ally* in the war against terrorism," I countered in a well-honed pacific voice. "Have you considered your own home-grown terrorism? Remember Oklahoma?" This was my post-9/11 mantra.

"Yeah, we have our weirdos in Mississippi, but God they're not like the terrorists you have in your part of the world. That's the problem with this country. We let everyone in. I mean, I'm here because my grandparents came from Europe." She clutched her black pashmina shawl tightly around her. (I wondered if hives would be induced if I notified her that her pashmina hailed from the land of "terrorism.")

"I'm sorry. I don't mean to question your right to be here, but look at all the beautiful things America offers you." She gestured extravagantly at the showroom. "Look how we treat our people in America! That's why they want to come here. I'm saying we've created problems not being careful who we let in."

I wondered: had she sampled chai at Starbucks? Was she aware that Kashmir was more than just the exotic code name for the multi-colored slate that is a popular choice for contemporary American kitchens and bathrooms? And the invisible labor that went into my clothes, her products... but I was getting carried away. This is what jingoism does. It makes you take sides that you don't necessarily want to be on or even defend.

"We didn't come here to talk politics with you...," my husband started.

"Listen, you two look like real intelligent people and so modern," she said in a conciliatory tone. Don't take it the wrong way, I mean, it's just with all this stuff going on in the world. Anyway, you surprised me when you said you were from Pakistan; you sure don't look like you are."

The equanimity of many Americans is ruffled when the appearance of a potential terrorist is disarmingly ingenuous, pedestrian even. Panic ensues when a possible terrorist looks like just another ordinary city-dweller sans *hijab* in the case of women, sans hirsute, dun exterior in the case of men. And when the ostensible victims of terrorism think they've spotted their perpetrator in a crowd—based on a hunch, based on an inarticulate fear—and they brand that person a terrorist—a person who, it turns out, is innocent—then one has to question the validity of their sense of themselves as victims. By wreaking havoc in the life of the misidentified "terrorist," have they not been the ones to terrorize and to have created a victim in the process? As bewildering, arbitrary, and awkward as it may be to hunt out a terrorist in a crowd, many New Yorkers, emboldened by the president's words, still feel compelled to do so in defense of their city.

Equally discombobulating is the experience of being mistaken for a potential terrorist. To know that I have the absurd capacity to terrorize a saleswoman and render her incompetent at her job terrifies me! And yet in the current political atmosphere, I would be lying if I said I was entirely averse to the seduction of this strange and ambiguous power. There is bitter appeal in witnessing someone's confusion as she trips over my identity, as she wonders how I, a Muslim woman from Pakistan, and by default, a potential terrorist, could look so ordinary and at the same time hail from that feared region—how I could blend into the crowd and yet have an accent that betrays my roots.

Meanwhile, "terrorism" in its various permutations is here to stay; it has found its way into pop culture. There is something cutting edge about recreating the aura of a terrorist for those who have the luxury to dabble in the exercise from the safety of Caucasian exteriors. But unlike other trends—nose-piercing and tribal tattoos—appropriated from other cultures, terrorist chic may be the most egregious one cast in the deepest ambivalence.

A Letter to India: In Manto's Spirit

~Ayesha Jalal

Uncle Sam

At the height of the cold war when America was about to sign a deal by which, in return for military assistance, Pakistan would commit itself to combating communism in Southeast Asia and the Middle East, the great Urdu short-story writer, Saadat Hasan Manto, who lived in Lahore, wrote a series of facetious letters to "Uncle Sam." In one of these letters written on February 21, 1954, Manto wrote:

> Regardless of the storm India is kicking up, you must sign a military agreement with Pakistan since you are seriously concerned about the stability of the world's largest Islamic state. And why not. Our mullahs are the best counter to Russian communism. Once military aid starts flowing, these mullahs are the first people you should arm.
>
> They would need American-made rosaries and prayer-mats.... Cutthroat razors and scissors should be at the top of the list, and also American hair colouring formulas. That will keep these chaps happily in tow. I think the only purpose of military aid is to arm these mullahs. I am your Pakistani nephew and can see through all your moves. Anyone can now become too clever by half, thanks to your style of politics.

"Once these mullahs are armed with American weapons," Manto predicted, "the Soviet Union with its communist propaganda will have to close shop in this country." He could visualize the situation clearly: "Mullahs, their hair trimmed with American scissors, wearing pajamas stitched with American machines in conformity with the *Sharia*... and possessing American made prayer mats too. Everyone would then quickly fall into line and read only your name on their rosaries."[5]

In a previous letter, the nephew had asked his respected uncle for a tiny atom bomb so that he could emulate America's "good work" in Hiroshima by hurling it on the mullahs and having the pleasure of seeing them go up in smoke. Since such a gift might raise suspicions in India, Manto took care to suggest that America should sign a military pact with New Delhi as well. They could then dump all the discarded arms and ammunition from World War II on the two countries. That would keep the American defense industries in productive business. Like Jawaharlal Nehru, he too was a Kashmiri, but thought Nehru should be sent the proverbial Kashmiri gun, which would go off by itself in the sun, while he, being a Kashmiri Muslim, deserved an atom bomb.[6]

When, despite assurances about no first-use against India, the gift failed to arrive, the disappointed nephew noted that his American uncle was unlike uncles in Pakistan who loved their nephews more than their own fathers. But that was not the only difference between America and Pakistan, where exciting things happened all the time. Ministers were changed on a daily basis in Pakistan. Someone claimed to be a new prophet and his follower became foreign minister; disturbances against such strange happenings came to nothing. Even commissions set up to determine the cause of the troubles were directed by higher authorities.

Nothing remotely as interesting as all this ever occurred in America. As for military aid to Pakistan, he hoped Washington would not change its mind in view of Jawaharlal Nehru's criticisms in an effort to win India over to the anti-communist camp. By courting both India and Pakistan, America no doubt wanted to keep the lamp of freedom and democracy burning in the two countries. It could do so not by blowing on it but by pouring lots of oil over it so that there was never any lack of that all too scarce commodity in the subcontinent. America wanted Pakistan to stay independent only because it loved the Khyber Pass from where the subcontinent had been repeatedly invaded for centuries. The Khyber Pass was very beautiful, but then, what else did Pakistan have? He had also heard that the United States had made a hydrogen bomb so there could be lasting peace in the world. Manto had complete faith in his uncle since he had eaten American wheat. Yet he wondered "how many countries will need to be removed from the face of the earth" for "this lasting peace to be established." His niece asked him to draw a map of the world for her. He told her that he would draw the map after consulting with his uncle to "find out the names of the countries that were going to survive."[7]

Survival was a real issue for a man who was slowing committing suicide by drinking the dreadful local liquor sold in Pakistan—the only kind he could afford. Hard up for funds, he was unable to pay his house rent nor buy postage stamps for some of the letters he had so diligently written. When despite repeated requests for an atom bomb, good quality whisky, American pin-ups—if not Elizabeth Taylor herself—or, at the very least, a healthy stipend, his American uncle failed to respond, Manto did not lose heart. In his ninth and final letter to Uncle

Sam, Manto promised never again to ask for American whisky. He was content to continue drinking the poisoned local brew, which was available despite the government's prohibition. This was ostensibly in response to the hue and cry raised by the mullahs. In fact, many mullahs had a weakness for alcohol. That was insurance enough that alcohol, however deadly the indigenous variety, would continue to sell in Pakistan. Anyone could obtain a permit if he could pay a doctor to verify that he would die if deprived of alcohol. Putting the survival of the country before his own, which he realized was coming to an untimely end, Manto maintained that so long as American military assistance continued to flow to Pakistan, he would be happy and so too would his God.

Mant and Nehr

In August 1954, Manto wrote yet another facetious letter, this time to the Indian prime minister, which he turned into the preface of a book of short stories called *Untitled*. He introduced himself to Nehru as a fellow Kashmiri, even though he had never had the privilege of seeing the whole of Kashmir. There were other differences between the Indian prime minister and Pakistan's leading Urdu short-story writer. Nehru's family name implied that they had originated in a place near or *nehr* a river. By contrast, Manto's name came from the Kashmiri word *mant*, which means a stone weighing one and a half seer—or roughly three pounds. He admired the Indian prime minister and, given their common ancestry, took pride in his style of politics, which involved saying something one day and contradicting it the next. "No one can beat us Kashmiris in wrestling," Manto opined, "and who could get the better of us in poetry."

Nehru's writing and oratorical skills showed that he was a true Kashmiri. Yet the only time Manto heard Nehru on the radio, he had been taken aback when the prime minister switched from English to Urdu. It seemed as if a Mahasabhite had drafted the script; Nehru was retching as he spoke and, now Manto had learnt, Urdu was being done away with in India altogether! But amazingly enough, publishers in India were continuing to publish Manto's Urdu short stories illegally. How could Nehru let such unethical things happen under his rule?

As far as Manto was concerned, India could keep Kashmir if it solved the problem of rampant poverty there. However, he doubted very much whether Nehru had any time for such things. He was too busy helping useless men like Bakshi Ghulam Muhammad to lord it over the hapless valley and its downtrodden people. And Manto knew only too well that Nehru was so emotionally attached to Kashmir that he was thoroughly preoccupied with fanning Indo–Pakistani tensions. But what had come to him as a complete surprise, because it was so uncharacteristic of Kashmiris, was that Nehru was thinking of closing down Pakistan's share of river water. This was plainly unfair. India's control over Kashmir did not entitle it to stop the flow of the river water to Pakistan. Manto often yearned for the fruits of Kashmir, especially its delicious pears.

But he was happy to let a scoundrel like Bakshi keep them all. Water was another matter. If he had weighed a few hundred tons, he would thrown himself into the river, forcing Nehru to spend considerable time consulting with his chief engineers to find a way of getting him out. Given the discrepancy in their relative power, how could Manto willingly drown himself into the Nehruvian river? The best course for Nehru to take was one of sweet reasonableness, since both of them were chips of the same regional brick.[8]

As early as the fifties, Manto in his inimitable way was able to convey to both Uncle Sam and Pandit Nehru what Pakistan's many uniformed masters and mostly disgraced elected leaders have tried in vain to get across for more than five decades. Fully aware of the importance of his communication skills in a country where the people have no real voice, he never ceased keeping an eye on Pakistan even after his tragic death in January 1956 at the age of 43. Gifted with a profound imagination in life, Manto after death spent much of his time refining the art of putting the supernatural to good use. In the following letter addressed to the Indian prime minister, Atal Behari Vajpayee, mysteriously communicated, he offers a spirited assessment of the most recent standoff between India and Pakistan, peppered with rare insights that have always been his hallmark.

Mant and Atal

Dear Uncle Vajpayee,

While I would have been much older than you had I lived, it is best that I call you "uncle" because that is how everyone thinks of you in the subcontinent. You are an elderly statesman, a reputed poet and a paragon of moderation, though I am sorry to see that of late you have been sidelined by your top party hawk, Lal Krishna Advani. Maybe that is why you are beginning to sound more and more like an American eagle and less and less like your good old former self. In any case, dear uncle, I am sending you this missive from on high—with no return address for you to bother sending a response—because the situation in the subcontinent has slipped out of control, and we up here are not so sure whether anyone in your great secular democratic country knows who is running the show—you, Advani, or the Sangh Parivar. In Pakistan, there is always the controlling hand of Almighty Allah, the would-be mighty Army and, since September 11, 2001, the not-nearly-so-mighty America, which is just as well because Uncle Sam let me be poisoned to death through sheer heartlessness.

But dear uncle, do you have a heart or did you lose it in the Pokhran blast? Or was it the Bombay blast? What I wanted to say is that there have been far too many blasts in the subcontinent of late and a lot of blustering too. What possessed you to conduct a nuclear explosion in 1998? It only strengthened your old foes in Pakistan, who have now become too big for their boots. They will very soon have to cut off their feet and stand on stilts instead—though I am not sure what will cost poor Pakistan more, new boots or stilts. I know you would prefer for it to have no legs to stand on at all. But that may cost you dearly, because then those *jihadis* you hate and fear so much will spread like locusts into India and there may not be anyone left to blame in Pakistan.

I have heard all the long mantras about your efforts to improve relations with Pakistan. It was cavalier of you to go on a bus all the way to Lahore, my hometown, and a very hospitable place too. Lahoris love Indian visitors, you know; it gives them a real sense of satisfaction to hear firsthand just how immense a loss the city has been for Indians, especially Punjabi Hindus. But your coming to Lahore was special, even though the Jamat-I-Islami goons tried to spoil your show. You so kindly visited the Minar-I-Pakistan, said you were reconciled to Partition and wished Pakistan well, and even shook hands with the military top brass who were none too happy to see you there. All very creditable. But why are you shying away from discussing Kashmir, which—it's an open secret everywhere except in your country—is the source of all the problems between India and Pakistan? The Kashmir issue, and then

American military assistance and all the strings that came attached with it, gave Pakistan's army the space it needed to dig its heels deeply into the country's fragile body politic. Now the heels move the country. Small wonder that Pakistan has barely moved in over fifty years, except of course in a downward direction. By forcing the Pakistan army to expose its heels on Kashmir, you might actually give a much needed breathing space to the country's frustrated democrats. I am telling you all this because I know that being the prime minister of the world's largest democracy, you really care about democracy in Pakistan. Hasn't anyone told you that there can be no democracy in Pakistan until you neutralize its army on the Kashmir issue? And the only way to do that is to open the Kashmir issue to full-fledged public discussion, both in Pakistan and also in India where such debates are supposed to take place because it is not only great but also democratic.

Instead you are letting the Pakistani army keep its Kashmir cards close to its chest. Don't you remember what happened when the Indian National Congress let Quaid-I-Azam Mohammed Ali Jinnah get away with that tactic? Your government will need to do your homework before you can outwit the Pakistan army on Kashmir and help pave the way for democracy there. Take Kargil for instance. You and your government have been harping on Pakistani duplicity and pointing your fingers at General Pervez Musharraf. But it is well known in Pakistan that the plan to infiltrate was no brainchild of Musharraf's. It had been there since at least the mid-1980s. Even the symbol of Pakistani democracy-gone-wrong, Benazir Bhutto, has publicly said that the plan was placed before her twice, but she refused to give her consent. All that Musharraf did was to exploit the opening you provided by conducting the nuclear tests. Securing Nawaz Sharif's approval was easy. As Musharraf briefed him, Sharif nodded his head off and was dreaming about ways to make a killing on all the deals he could strike with India, when the general saluted him and walked away. It was just your luck that Pakistan had a prime minister like Sharif. He was so delighted at becoming the leader of a nuclear country that his attention span dropped from fifteen to five minutes. Is that why the two of you got on so famously?

Dear uncle, I don't want to be disrespectful, but your intelligence agencies did botch things up. If Kargil brought Pakistan disgrace, India's military machine was caught napping along a line of control where nibbling of territory by both sides is a routine affair. That gave those ranting and raving mullahs—all *jihadis* by vocation—their moment in the sun. You did well to whip up hysteria in India and in the world against Pakistan. Isolating Pakistan internationally serves you well domestically. But it does not win you extra points in the political battle for Kashmir. And it certainly does not help you achieve the goal that is so dear to your heart—a democratic and peace-loving Pakistan. As I told Panditji several years ago, winning the hearts of Kashmiris requires tackling widespread poverty and creating conditions for the emergence of a popular leadership that is not alienated and hostile to your wonderful country. Everyone's uncle, these are hard truths, but truths nonetheless. I think you've become too complacent, much as American eagles are prone to become, with the manufacturing of consent by your very free and very fair press on your government's tough stance on Kashmir and Pakistan. Could it be that democracy dulls the mind?

Pakistani minds are far too restive to become dull and its army thrives on tensions with India. I know you are very gracious. But what was the point of giving General Pervez Musharraf a royal welcome at Agra and that too when he was under fire in Pakistan for assuming the office of president unconstitutionally? India was the first country to recognize the commando's self-elevation as legitimate. So many Pakistanis have been banging their heads at your consulates for years, trying to get visas to see the Taj Mahal in Agra just once in their lives. Do you know what a risk a Pakistani takes in applying for an Indian visa? They are interrogated by members of the various intelligent spying institutions that flourish in Pakistan without let or hindrance, files are opened against them, and they are forever doomed. To add insult to injury, they are denied visas by your consulate while their dictator is given a suite at the Amar Singh palace so that he can get a million dollar view of that exquisite monument to love from his bath tub. How can that help democracy in Pakistan? Several young men rushed to volunteer for recruitment to the Pakistan army, seeing it as the only way to realize their dream of seeing the Taj Mahal.

As long ago as 1954, I had wanted to send the mullahs up in smoke. But my American uncle, who is now your bosom pal, refused to gift me an atom bomb. Now you have gifted Pakistan an atom bomb! I mean, why else did Pakistan build it, if not for the Kashmir dispute and its congenital rivalry with your democratic and peace-loving country? I would have kept mine hidden for use at the right time against our common enemy. Now you have forced it out of the Pakistani closet, and no one can say when, where, and how it might be used, except that its sole target is your country. The subcontinent is in danger of getting vaporized, and I fear the Taj Mahal may vanish—what with you and your Agnis and Trishuls and Musharraf with his Ghaznavis and Ghouris just waiting to set everything alight. It will be the most spectacular fireworks ever in the world. Only there will be nobody applauding.

Dear uncle, matters have come to such a pass that I appeal to your uncommon sense to save the subcontinent from going to further wrack and ruin. Please solve the Kashmir problem, whatever it takes. Those Pakistani *jihadis*, created by the country's premier intelligent spying institute, are determined to force their innocent compatriots to commit collective suicide—they call it *shahadat*, though no one up here can identify the verses in the Qur'an that equate suicide, far less murder, with martyrdom. Rest assured, God is great in His infinite mercy and justice, but even God is fed up with India and Pakistan for failing to solve their problems. He allowed the attack against your august parliament to take place to show that playing with fire does come back to haunt. But you took the easy way out and pointed the finger at Musharraf, who is hated by all the *jihadis* because for them he ceased being a Muslim the moment he hitched his wagons to America in the war against terrorism. They now call him Bush-arraf! These *jihadis* are plotting several other attacks on your country so that you are forced to fight a war with Pakistan, thereby creating a situation that would allow them to get rid of Musharraf and seize power in Islamabad.

You ought to have seen through this subterfuge. Instead you upped the ante by sending your forces to the Pakistani border. Worse still, you played straight into the hands of the *jihadis* by suspending all forms of communication, air, rail, or otherwise, with Pakistan. Even more than the government, the *jihadis* want the people of Pakistan to have no contact whatsoever with Indian infidels. Your misguided decision so rattled Musharraf that he in turn banned all Indian television channels in Pakistan, heightening the misery of an already depressed nation for whom the ridiculous fantasies that are the trademark of your Hindi film industry is the only form of cheap entertainment available. (When I wrote good film scripts, there was only Hollywood and no imitation called Bollywood.) There has been a dramatic increase in the suicide rate in several Pakistani cities, and you are contributing to this by keeping tensions with Pakistan at fever pitch.

A full-scale military mobilization, now in its eighth month, is bleeding Pakistan financially, when it desperately needs to revive its economy so that its youth are gainfully employed, not uselessly dead. This is grist to the *jihadi* mill!

Dear uncle, Pakistan is internally so troubled that your fire and fury only ends up aiding and abetting your main enemies there. Surely you cannot be in league with them; otherwise you would not be chanting so loudly about the need for a democratic Pakistan? Or are you doing the American number in Pakistan as well—talking democracy but assisting autocracy! The tougher India gets with Pakistan, the tougher the army gets with its people, and the less prospect there is for democracy. It's an old chain reaction; only now it's on the verge of exploding. With no sign of a cessation of hostilities with India in sight, the military regime is tightening the reins of control. There has been a monsoon of (un)constitutional amendments in Pakistan, thanks to India's playing weather vane. And we now hear that the general may postpone the promised elections for another six months. If he does that, such protests as do take place will eventually die out with the proverbial whimper. With the enemy ogling at the border, and Americans crawling all over the place in search of al-Qaeda and its associates, I fear that an emergency in the national interest may be invoked and dissent put down with an iron fist, reviving memories of the darkest days of General Zia-ul-Haq's rule.

I trust that you will take serious note of all that I have said and cool-headedly plan your next moves. The situation is so precarious that one false move on your side will bring a flash of lightning on the other, completing the downward spiral that has been the fate of the subcontinent—and Pakistan in particular—ever since independence. I expect to see you up here before very long. But please don't come too soon. There is an overflow of dead people here—victims of the September 11 attack and violence in the West Bank and, closer to the subcontinent, thousands of angry Afghans killed by American bombs, petrified victims of the Gujarat pogrom, and any number of defiant Kashmiris, including many terrorists who perished at the hands of your security forces. As they await their turn to go to heaven or hell, they are holding street corner meetings on the subject of terrorism. These often degenerate into scuffles between those who call themselves *jihadis* and others who accuse them of causing their premature deaths by taking up cudgels against state terrorism. Your presence here will create total mayhem.

Take good care of yourself, especially your knees. Which reminds me—you of all people should be able to empathize with those who have no real legs to stand on! So do recall your forces from the border and flush out the Pakistani dictator on Kashmir. He is getting so bogged down under the combined weight of pressure from you, America, and his own homegrown *jihadis*—now in league with several dissident political parties—that he may need an express stretcher from up here. That will not serve the cause of democracy in Pakistan, I am afraid. What will help is if he is provided a democratically-oiled Pakistani wheel chair so that he can drive himself out of the corner into which he has painted himself with the connivance, I am sorry to say, of my own dear uncles.

—Your very sincerely concerned nephew,
Saadat Hasan Manto

Where is Home? Fragmented Lives, Border Crossings, and the Politics of Exile

~Rabab Abdulhadi

For the politically exiled, "going home" means more than taking a journey to the place where one was born. The ability to go, the decision to embark on such a trip, and the experience of crossing borders to one's "native" land involves an "interrogation"[9] of the make-up of the individual and the collective self; a definition and a re-definition of the meaning and the location of *home*; and a reexamination of one's current and former political commitments. In the Palestinian case, *going home* assumes further complications, especially in view of the Israeli Law of Return, which bestows automatic citizenship on Jews arriving in Israel while denying the indigenous Palestinian population the right to return to the homes from which they were uprooted in 1948. For the Palestinian exiled, *going home* brings back memories of one's worst nightmares at international borders: interrogation and harassment, suspicion of mal-intent, and rejection of one's chosen self-identification. For exiled Palestinian women, the case is further complicated by gender relations at home and abroad—two concepts that shift depending on where one is situated at any particular moment. Add to the pot the problematic meaning of such notions, *going home* ceases to be just about traveling to where one was born to collect accessible data—if that ever were the case; instead, going home is transformed into a politically-charged project in which the struggle for self-identification, self-determination, freedom, and dignity becomes as salient as the physical and mental safety of one's "informants" and the power differential in the production and reproduction of knowledge. "Where is home?" is a question that lies at the center of the Palestinian's precarious experience.

Do We Belong? Home Is a Safe Space

When life under Israeli occupation became worse in Palestine, my siblings and I began a campaign to convince our parents to leave. We felt that they should relocate either to the United States, where I lived, or to England, where my sister, Reem, is based. My parents would refuse again and again. Whenever pressed, they would invariably say: "*illi waqe' 'ala nass waqe' aleina*," (our fate is not different from others), or "*who ihna ahsan min ennas?*" (Do you think we are better than others?) When we persisted, they would respond by invoking Palestinian dispossession, "*ma hada be-eid illi sar fil 48*"—no one will ever think of repeating what happened in 1948!

My brother and sister-in-law shared my parents' sentiments. They were nonetheless contemplating a relocation to give their daughters a better education, a safe environment, and an innocent childhood. Nasser and Lana felt that they had to make the sacrifice and risk their residence in Jerusalem. The "situation on the ground," as Palestinians refer to their reality, was becoming unbearable: Israeli tanks were holding Palestinian towns under siege. Violence was on the rise. And Palestinians were criminalized for being Palestinians or just for being.

Nasser, Lana, and the girls never left Israeli-annexed Jerusalem. With the closure of U.S. borders to immigrants from Middle East origins, it did not look like they would make it to New York any time soon. But I did. On August 27, 2001, I came back from a year in Egypt where I had taught at the American University in Cairo. I returned "home" to this anonymous city to take in its cultures. To thrive in its rhythms. To disappear and reappear in a sea of accents, tongues, cultures, and lifestyles. Two weeks later, my life came to a standstill and so did the lives of hundreds of thousands of Arabs, Arab Americans, Muslim-Americans, and Central and South Asians.

Besides the fear for our loved ones whom we could not locate for several hours on that infamous day, we no longer feel safe: No longer can we draw on New York City's rich, vibrant, and diverse cultural scene, and no longer can we enjoy the anonymity of this city as we enjoyed it before.

We rationalize things to make ourselves feel better. We think to ourselves: We are alive; our loved ones are alive; this is more than what many other New Yorkers could say. We should be grateful. My mother's words ring in my ear, "*illi waqe' ala nass waqe' aleina*"—whatever happens to other people will happen to us. We are not *alone* in this!

True, we are not alone. Along with thousands of New Yorkers, we feel miserable, sad, hurt, and wounded. But in more profound ways than one, this similitude is not so: What affects us and how it affects us is very different. My mother's assurances do not apply here—we *are* alone, very much so!

The experience of diasporic and fragmented lives in which our souls and concerns are split between here and there is a major difference that sets us apart: we who have a particular skin shade, a particular accent, a certain last or first name, or markings on the body that betray some affiliation with the enemy.

Be careful if you happen to be named Osama, or even if you own a restaurant named "Osama's Place"!

You do need to worry if your last name sounds like an Abdul, an Ahmad, a Mohammad, or a Masoud!

Change your name if you can, from Mohammad to Smith!

Americanize!

Be thankful that winter is upon us for it allows you to wear a heavy long coat and a big hat. It allows you to hide your beliefs from the public space that is supposed to accommodate all beliefs: If you are a Sikh man or a devout Muslim woman, do not parade your convictions in public—the public has no space for you!

Do not speak up a lot. Save your words. Try not to use words with a "P" if you are an Arab. You may mix it up with a "B," causing someone to ask, "And where are you from?" You do not want to answer this question—avoid it as much as you can!

Try to avoid situations in which you have to present an ID: Do not drive a car. Do not use a credit card, pay in cash: Money laundering is not a priority for law and order now. No one will check if you present big bills.

Avoid as much as you can Being You!

Pass if you can!

Melt in this melting pot!

Do not cry multiculturalism and diversity! This is not the time… better save your life!

Better yet: "Go home," foreigner!

What if you have no home to go back to? What if this is your home?

Dual loyalty? Split personality? Divided? Not a real American? But who is? How many "real" Americans are still left around?

Crossing Borders: Passing and Passing Through

September 11, 2001

I am stuck on 96th Street and Lexington Avenue. I cannot get home. No trains are running. I desperately need to hear Jaime's voice, to know that he is alive. I cannot reach him. A long line is getting longer at the phone booth. I begin walking aimlessly, hoping to find an available phone to call my mother-in-law. Right in front of me, a woman pushing a baby carriage starts to cross the street. She is covering her head with a scarf. I am debating whether to say something. Finally, I decide to approach her: "Go home!" Immediately I realize how awful I must have sounded. She looks at me with a mix of fear and resentment, too polite to ask me to mind my own business and probably too afraid to fight back. I come closer and declare a part of me I thought I would never claim: "I am a Muslim like you! Go home now. You cannot run with a baby. When they realize what has happened they will attack." I am already bracing myself for the battle between "us" and "them."

My hand instinctively goes to my neck to hide the chain with the Qur'anic inscription my students, Ghalia and Hedayat, gave me before I left Cairo. Luckily, I had forgotten to put it on today. My split lives are on a collision course again: I feel like such a traitor for *passing*. But wouldn't it be better to *pass* today? Do I want to identify with "them"? Do I want to escape the collective guilt-by-association, the fate of my fellow Arabs, Palestinians, and Muslims? Should I renege on my roots? There is this nagging feeling that I need some sort of a symbol to shout to the world who I am. I want so much to defy this monolithic image.

Better tread lightly, I conclude! Today is not the time for bravado! "Don't be foolish. It is not about courage," I tell myself. The thought of what will happen to women wearing a *hijab* sends shivers down my back. It won't leave my mind. "But we all make choices," one part of me says. "Not always as we please," the radical in me shouts back.

Passing is a survival mechanism.

Lay low until the storm has passed and hope for the best.

I find a Caribbean taxi driver who agrees to take me home. Four white businessmen jump in on 125th Street. We are on our way home. As the only passenger who knows the back roads around blockaded bridges, I begin to give him directions. Then I begin to worry that someone may notice my accent and ask where I came from. I am not sure I want to deploy my activist identity and use this occasion to try to explain the plight of the Palestinian people. A passenger next to me says, "So this is how it feels to live with terrorist bombings." I am certain that he is referring to Palestinian suicide bombings in Israel. There is no way he could be relating to how Palestinian towns are being bombarded every day. I almost say something about the value of Palestinian life. I want to share what I have personally experienced this past year alone but I am not sure that this is such a good idea. So I keep my mouth shut and try to *pass* for a professional "American" woman. Another passenger, I realize from his accent, is Iranian. But we sort of make a silent pact not to tell on each other. We both pretend not to notice each other's accents. At least this is what I think.

Police cars are stationed at the bridges and on different checkpoints along the highway. I should be calm. I have seen this before. But West Bank memories add to, rather than alleviate, my anxiety: What if they stop us now to check our ID's? They *will* surely notice my last name. Will I be safe? What if a cop becomes trigger-happy? Would it do me any good if they were to apologize to my family afterwards?

I shudder to remember Nasser and Lana telling me about a "road incident" they experienced. A few months before Yasmeen's first birthday, they were driving from Israeli-annexed Jerusalem to our parents' home in Nablus with the baby in the back seat. At an Israeli checkpoint, a large rock flew at them out of nowhere, shattering the windshield and almost killing them. Twice privileged for having a Jerusalem ID and for being employed by a UN agency, Lana got out of the car full of rage and lashed out at the Israeli soldiers who controlled the human traffic in and out of Palestinian controlled areas. "It is not our fault!" yelled an 18-year-old soldier. "It was the settlers. What am I supposed to do?" was all he could say, shrugging away Lana's fears and contributing to her sense of helplessness.

For Nasser and Lana and the 3 million Palestinians living in the West Bank and Gaza, "road incidents" are a daily routine. There is no ordinary travel. If you live under Israeli control, you never know whether you will make it to your destination alive. "You were given a new life," Palestinians say to each other whenever one succeeds in making it home safe across the never-ending checkpoints.

It was what happened on a recent drive to Nablus that finally convinced Lana and Nasser that it was time to make the move to the U.S. During my visit to Nablus in July of 2001, Lana was bringing the girls over to see me. As they were about to get out of their Jerusalem apartment, 4-year-old Yasmeen asked her mother if she could bring along their kitten, Nadia, named for her youngest sister. It was not the request, rather the way Yasmeen asked it, that broke Lana's heart: "Do you think the army will let her pass through, Mama?"

September 13, 2001

I am working at home. No one is allowed below 14th Street in Manhattan unless s/he can prove a legitimate reason, the mayor of New York City declares. I am so grateful that I cannot get to work. I still do not have a valid ID. September 11 was the day on which my NYU paperwork was to be completed. I am spared the trouble of having to go through checkpoints or to reveal my identity.

A police car stops in front of the house. I begin to think that they have come for me. Maybe someone had called and said that a Palestinian lives here. Maybe it is because our house has no flags. The neighborhood is full of flags: Our next-door neighbor has two flags on the front of her house, two on the back porch, one on a planter, and two on her car; her husband has three flags on his van.

The only public symbol of Palestine we could speak of is a sticker my dad had given us with the phrase, "Palestine in my heart." It was made in 1994 when Palestinians thought that they would soon have a state. Better remove it immediately. The next day, Jaime says, "I am glad we removed the sticker. There were so many road blocks. The car was searched twice. They even asked me to open the trunk." My sense of security is wiped out. This *home* is becoming so similar to what happens *back home*.

I share this experience with friends but I sense the skepticism in their eyes. At least a flicker of disappointment. I should not jump to conclusions, they seem to be cautioning.

May 14, 1998 (Another Road: "Back Home")

I am leaving Ramallah on the eve of the 50th anniversary of Nakba, or Palestinian dispossession. My cousin's children ask if I want to hoist a Palestinian flag with the slogan of the occasion, "So we will not forget," on the car. "Sure, why not?" I say, not really thinking things through. I exit Palestinian controlled "Area A" and drive through "Area B" with joint Israeli–Palestinian patrol (Palestinians control the population while Israel controls everything else, according to the Oslo Accords) to catch the highway to Nablus. All is well. It is a beautiful summer day. I should make it home in 30 minutes or so. At the fork, one direction leads to Ofra, a Jewish settlement built on hilltops sparsely covered with olive trees. The other to which I am allowed passage leads to "Area C" (total Israeli control) and *'aber samera*. 'Aber Samera, or the Samaria (the name

Israel assigns to the West Bank) bypass, is a modern highway carved out of the mountains by then Israeli minister of infrastructure, Ariel Sharon. The road links the network of West Bank Jewish settlements whose villas have red tile roofs, lush gardens, and children's playgrounds. Winding through Palestinian towns and villages, the highway, a short commute to Tel Aviv and West Jerusalem, allows the 120,000 settlers to bypass the constant reminder of the 1.8 million Palestinians whose land was seized to construct these privileged gated colonies.

Along the highway, electric poles are covered with Israeli flags. It is Israel's 50th birthday as a state and as a haven for diasporic refugees escaping discrimination, intolerance, and the Holocaust. But there is no space in this celebration of Jewish diversity for Palestinians. My lonely flag is not welcomed here. Cars with Israeli license plates full of settlers honk in annoyance and make obscene gestures at me. Palestinian drivers veer away from this provocative car.

Passing is a survival strategy!

September 24, 2001

A day before traveling from New York to D.C. to speak at an anti-globalization teach-in, a scholar of a certain descent reserves the ticket over the phone wondering while being put on hold whether her name is being checked by the FBI.

She begins packing, going through her wallet—cleaning it up. She finds a Home Depot receipt which she sets aside lest an unexpected search raises questions as to why certain tools were bought! She takes out her U.S. pass-port (a passport is for passing through). With a name like hers, a driver's license and a faculty ID from a major university may not be enough to prove her "Americanness"! After all, equality does not mean total equality; it only means that some of us are more equal than others.

She goes through her briefcase. Should she take her laptop along? Would it be searched, causing a delay and humiliation in front of other passengers? She does need it. It is a few-hour trip. She has a lot of work to do. Take it but better leave early to avoid embarrassment. Better ask someone to go with her to the station: What if she is held? Someone needs to notify the organizers of the teach-in; someone needs to call a lawyer!

She arrives at the station one hour early. She approaches the window to pick up her ticket. She slips in the credit card and driver's license under the glass ever so discreetly, hoping that the clerk would not address her by her last name. It is taking a while to print the ticket. All the while, she is wondering whether a camera high up is taking her photo. She is convinced that it is there. She picks up the ticket—no incidents. She goes to the tracks. Five policemen are standing there on the platform looking directly at her—she is convinced. She begins rehearsing what to say when approached—not *if* but *when* approached: what she is doing here, why she is going to D.C. "Did I bring the formal invitation on the official letterhead?" she wonders. Acting like a criminal, she treads ever so lightly, moving away from the eyes of the cops burning her back to the center of the station. She is getting more nervous and starts babbling away. Her companion warns, "You are attracting attention. Relax! Stop it!" to no avail.

The train pulls into the station. She gets on and finds a seat. Now the conductor will come to check the ticket. Is he going to give her looks once he sees her name? She opens the briefcase to take out a paper to read. *Al-Hayat*? You cannot read *Al-Hayat* here! She puts it away before anyone notices the Arabic script. She turns on the laptop. "Can the passenger behind me see what I am working on?" Like a little 3rd grader who guards her work from cheaters, she wraps her arms around her laptop before she gives up and puts it away.

The train arrives. The D.C. station is full of security personnel. Will anyone pull her aside for questioning? Nothing happens! She is free to go where she wants. Why does she, then, feel this way? Is this paranoia? She has not done anything wrong. "I am not a criminal."

Her mind travels to another time, another place, and another continent a few months earlier.

June 10, 2001

The plane is approaching the airport. Butterflies in the stomach: excited to arrive, soon to be "home"—soon to see parents and the fifteen nieces and nephews. She disembarks and gets on the bus. A short distance and they are at border control. Standing in line for "holders of foreign passports."

Butterflies in the stomach. Fear and anxiety. "Did I clean up my wallet? Did I remove all business cards from the briefcase? Is my calendar clean? White-outed of suspect dates?" "What should I say if they ask about the letters from the kids in Shatila to their friends in Dheisheh?" She rehearses her story, reminds herself to only answer with a yes or no, no need to elaborate: This is where they try to trick you—it only prolongs the interrogation. Do I smile or keep a straight-face, rude or docile, which image to present to the world here today? What do I do when asked again and again the same question?

Here it comes, here we go again...

King Hussein Bridge, July 1994
Going in/Ben Gurion Airport, July 2001—Getting out—"Rabab, what is the purpose of your visit to Israel?" A young Israeli woman behind the counter. I am a bit annoyed for being addressed by my first name, almost wanting to say, "Do I know you?" but I bite my tongue and maintain my calm. I respond that I am visiting the Palestinian areas to see my family. She asks again: "You have family in Israel? Where?" I answer, "In Nablus." She retorts, "Shekhem?" (The Hebrew name Israel assigned to my hometown). I calmly say, "Nablus, yes." Now, I am directed to step aside so that my luggage will be searched. I remember—a bit too late—that I should have said that I was staying in Jerusalem or Tel Aviv to prevent the hassle of luggage search. I am taken, along with my luggage, aside.

A young man in civilian clothing approaches me and states that he is from Israeli security. He wants to ask me a few questions—this is being done for my safety, he says. Having been through Israeli borders so many times before, I do not bother to question or correct his concern about my safety. I am too tired. I just want to get *home*. He, along with a young female soldier, search my bags. They take everything out and spread my stuff on a table. My underwear is there for everyone to see. An elderly Palestinian man is being searched at the next table. We pretend not to notice each other's intimate belongings, but my face is getting very, very hot with embarrassment. They go through all my stuff, waving an electrical device over it to (I am guessing) detect explosives. Having found nothing, they attempt to put things back as they found them, but it is not possible to replicate the manner in which I packed my stuff or to restore my dignity.

Exile and Exclusion

October 5, 2001 (Home)
News Bulletin: *"Reconstruction of the downtown area is being discussed."*

Who moves back?

Who goes home?
Who returns?
And who is left behind?

June 2001 (Back home)

Beirut is a City reconstructed—beautiful, fashionable downtown. The "Paris of the Orient" is resurrected!

Shatila is a miserable place. It is a crowded area of one square kilometer on which 17,000 people live and where expanding the livable space is not an option. People in Shatila, though, are resourceful. To make space, "they buy air," says Nihad Hamad, director of the Shatila Center for Social Development. I first dismiss it thinking that she is just joking. "Move along; do not dwell on it!" I think to myself. But then she just repeats it. So I ask. It is very simple: There are more people than land. The only choice left for camp residents is to expand vertically: Buy the roof of a house and build another house on top of it—the towers of Babel without the glory! The geography of dispossession in action!

The streets of Shatila—alleys would be more accurate—are narrow and dirty. Sewage is open for the eye to see and the garbage is piling up all over the place. In the winter, rain and cesspools flood the alleys, and in the summer the acrid smell of the garbage threatens to suffocate you. If you lived here, you would probably want to escape too!

The people of Shatila have nowhere to go. The only place to which they want to return is a home no more: Erased from the map, not from memory—collective, alive, and painful. But the borders are closed today.

September 21, 2001 (Home)

News Bulletin: "Artists, developers, and families discuss how to memorialize 9/11 victims."

July 2001 (Back home)

We are walking toward the mass grave. This is where most of the victims of the massacre are buried. A sign at the gate announces: "Here lie the martyrs of the Sabra and Shatila Massacre." We enter through the gate. A lone man is watering the plants: Adnan, the custodian, is not a Palestinian; he came with his family from the South of Lebanon to escape Israeli incursions. With little access to resources, Adnan's family could only afford to live in the Palestinian neighborhood, viewed as a ghetto in dominant Lebanese discourse. Their fate was not much better than that of their Palestinian neighbors. Thirty-eight members of Adnan's family, the Miqdadis, were slaughtered during the 1982 massacre. To honor them and other victims, Adnan has planted flowers and greeneries but "not the tomatoes," he said. "I did not plant the tomatoes; they grew out all on their own."

October 20, 2001 (Home)
Mobile phone messages with the last words are saved. Cellular companies offer them to families free of charge.

July 2001 (Back home)
We are sitting in the living room of Maher Srour as he remembers what happened to him and his family nineteen years ago. He speaks matter-of-factly, a ghost of a smile comes across and slowly disappears on his face as he tells us how 15-month-old Shadia, his youngest sister, was ordered to stand and put her hands up in surrender, like the rest of her family members. "'But she cannot walk! She is still crawling!' We told them. Their leader said, 'Yes, she can.' Sure enough, she walked. It was her first time walking... Shadia walked just like the rest of us. She stood in line with her hands up and walked. They shot her and she fell right there between the bodies of my mother and my father. You see? Right there on the floor. That is Shadia," Maher points out to the TV and the homemade video he assembled from newspaper cuttings and fading copies of family photos, exhibited to remember Palestinian refugees killed in the 1982 massacre at Sabra and Shatila camps on the outskirts of Beirut.

We are all sitting around. Tears are flowing down our cheeks; none of us can stop. Each one is trying very hard to stop, but it is impossible as Maher re-members, or tries to re-assemble, to put together, memories of family members who are gone forever—the only remaining memories are faded photos and a broken heart. As Maher remembers, my mind drifts to another setting. Ciraj Rassoul, a co-founder of the District 6 Museum in Cape Town, recounts how this community was completely razed to the ground by Apartheid's Group Area Act, save for a mosque and a church. "Remembering," Ciraj says, "is re-membering, putting together. District 6 Museum is all about re-membering our community, putting it together."

A video of faded pictures here, a museum there: People remember. People memorialize.

Whose memories are valid?

For whom memorials are built?

Does your life count if you are a person dispossessed?

October 25, 2001 (Home)

"478 people are confirmed dead at the World Trade Center."

New York grieves for people with a mix of last names, cultures, professions, lifestyles, religious beliefs, and family arrangements.

Grieve, New York, Grieve!

Grieve for the Pakistani man who died in INS detention center of a heart attack while awaiting deportation: Prisoners are not entitled to adequate healthcare!

Grieve for the Egyptian who moved to New York in search of a safer life...

Grieve for the West African who used to pray in the Bronx...

Grieve for all those anonymous beings whose labor no one credits, names no one remembers, and bodies no one dares to claim...

Grieve for the mothers and fathers, the daughters and the sons, the lovers and the beloved, the friends and the co-workers...

Grieve for shuttered dreams, for lives lost, for closed possibilities...

Grieve for a loss of human life and Remember!

Remember, New York!

Remember Iman Hajou, a 15-month-old baby girl whose brains were splattered on the back seat of her father's car as he went looking for help. No hospital for Iman. No passing through: The "road situation" is bad today.

Grieve for Mohamed el-Dura, whose father could not protect him from death, bullet after bullet after bullet—a Palestinian Amadou Diallo?

Grieve, New York!

Search your heart!

Is there a space to grieve?

Grieve, if you will, for the Afghanis whose screams of pain no one seems to hear...

Grieve!

Where is Home?

I once believed that the restoration of my dignity was possible in New York. In theory at least, people are supposed to be equal before the law. I am not naive: I am fully aware of subtle and not-so-subtle systems of domination and discrimination. But no one is pretending any more that equality before the law applies to us.

As we continue to be ethnically and racially profiled, thousands of Arabs, Arab Americans, Muslim-Americans, and Muslim-Americans are made to feel foreign at home: No longer do we feel welcomed nor do we feel safe. Call it what you want but the melting pot theory fails as "America" refuses to grind the course kernels of our foods, name them what they are and accept them on their own terms: garlicky, spicy, strong, and fulfilling. Beneath the facade of liberal advocacy of multiculturalism lies an ethnocentric New York that continues to deny our existence except as bloodthirsty or suspect male villains, helpless female victims, and exoticized alien others. Our cultures are erased, our lives flattened to fit neatly in the folds of "Americanness." No longer can we draw on New York City's rich, vibrant, and diverse cultural scene: Red, white, and blue may be a safety blanket to some, but those colors symbolize exclusion to the rest of us. Safety in this anonymous city is a precious commodity achieved only by those who *pass* for something other than the multiplicities and complexities in which we are embedded.

Rationalizing things to feel better may help; a band-aid solution to dull the pain. But when 1,000 are detained and 5,000 are not-so-voluntarily interviewed, New York and indeed the U.S.A. feels suspiciously like the occupied West Bank. But this is not the West Bank, though, where most Palestinians are subject to the same misery and terror as my mother would say: "*illi waqe' 'ala nass waqe' aleina*"—we are very alone here: our diasporic lives are fragmented. Our souls are split open. It is perhaps time to go home, but back home exists no more.

Must We Always Non-Intervene?

~Afsaneh Najmabadi (2002)

Though this piece was written in August 2002, before the U.S. military intervention began in Iraq, Najmabadi's challenge to those in the U.S. opposed to the war to make room in their discourse for the voices of the Iraqi people who call for change (perhaps even intervention) is as relevant today as it was when the war began. The question today is no longer whether *to intervene, but how to conclude our intervention.*

The prospect of a possible change of regime in Iraq has brought the dispersed forces of the opposition together to work for a unified vision of a federated democratic Iraq "on the day after." Despite repeated previous bitter experience with the U.S. government, these forces consider the possibility of a change in regime as an opportunity to get rid of Saddam Hussein—something that they know their force alone is too weak to accomplish, given the brutal atomization of the Iraqi society under the Ba'ath. With no illusion over their strength, nor over any direct influence on the interests that drive the U.S. policy and would decide the course of action that the U.S. government may take, they are committed to attempting to redirect U.S. policy away from replacing one dictator with another and toward a commitment to building a democratic Iraq. So far they have succeeded in getting a public U.S. government pronouncement to this effect. Such stated commitment, they feel, may also affect the kind of action that the U.S. would take. Perhaps it would reorient it toward supporting Iraqi forces of opposition rather than a direct military attack, with the hope of minimizing civilian damage, and making the task of a democratic reconstruction less difficult.

The dissident voices in this country (at least the ones with which I have engaged) have met this prospect with an orientation that could be summarized as: Oppose and Expose. This is a similar orientation to that taken toward the two recent American engagements with this part of the world: the Gulf War of 1990–91 and the campaign in Afghanistan against the Taliban. In both cases, this dissident American position came to be in conflict with those of the people who have lived and suffered under these regimes and who in both instances welcomed (and at times begged for) outside, including American and including military, interventions. The kind of social disintegration that the Ba'ath or the Taliban had produced meant that internal forces opposing these regimes knew all too well that they were too weak on their own to get rid of them. No outside intervention meant continuing to live with (and die from) the intolerable brutalities of these regimes indefinitely. The American dissident position, therefore, was received by these forces (and is received currently by the Iraqi opposition) as worse than irrelevant: It is tantamount to criminal non-intervention. What here may seem the honorable position of opposing the war machine and military adventurism of one's own government, in this configuration, came at the price of other people continuing to suffer with no end in sight.

In all these instances, the opposition to war has been linked to another stance, that of exposing the U.S. government's history of prior support for the very forces that it then has set to overthrow, the Taliban and the Iraqi Ba'ath. In the extreme, the Taliban and the Ba'ath become mere creations of the all-powerful U.S. government—something verging on racist denial of any agency on the part of the people of the Near East to be able to even produce their own dictators. In any event, even if one were to agree on the total responsibility of the American government, that responsibility could just as easily and in fact more logically be invoked for a U.S. intervention to set these past bad deeds to good for a change, instead of a non-interventionist stand. Why should Afghanis and Iraqis continue to suffer the consequences of terrible U.S. foreign policy instead of expecting that government to take responsibility for its bad judgments and do some good? Without an interventionist orientation that is centered on the interests of the people of these regions, the exposition of prior U.S. foreign policy by the voices of American dissidence over the war is received by Afghanis and Iraqis as hollow moralism at their expense. While they have been repeatedly betrayed by U.S. government policies, Iraqi dissidents feel they have no other option but to seek its support for their struggle. Similarly, the great fear of Afghanis today is lack of long-term commitment by the U.S. government (and other international forces) to stay in Afghanistan and help their post-Taliban reconstruction. Why shouldn't the dissident energies in this country be focused on *the kind* of American intervention rather than on a policy of non-intervention?

Historically, non-intervention has not always been the stand of dissidence. One can mention the Spanish Civil War and the different positions taken toward the Second World War as immediate examples. I am not suggesting that the current situation in Afghanistan or Iraq is equivalent to either, though I do wonder if it is the colonial burden that makes an intervention in a non-European context unthinkable, whereas intervening to help Europeans fighting a Hitler or a Franco was acceptable, even morally obligatory. Intervention, moreover, does not always and only mean military intervention. A progressive internationalist perspective would advocate policies on the basis of solidarity with what Afghani or Iraqis are struggling for, though decidedly not on their behalf in the old missionary style. An internationalist interventionist orientation would also make it possible to build alliances with forces in Europe and the Middle East who resist U.S. militarism while being concerned about the future of Iraqi and Afghani people.

The problem, however, arises from elsewhere. We live in a world in which there may be a conflict of interests between, to put it most simply, what is good for the Iraqis and Afghanis and what is good for American people. This is particularly the case in the post-September 11 period, where the war-against-terrorism policies of the U.S. government have meant the most frightening infringements on civil liberties and on the rights of immigrants and travelers, especially those of Arab, Middle Eastern, and Muslim backgrounds. The cases of large numbers of people who have suffered over the past year as a result of these policies are widely known, and there is no question that these policies need to be resisted as strongly as possible. Moreover, the current military orientation of the U.S. government would in all likelihood result in further strengthening the conservative forces in this country. All this is quite frightening and cannot be ignored in any discussion of "Responding to Violence."

Under this seemingly conflicting set of interests, one may have to consider the terrible possibility that a policy that may be wise for internal U.S. developments may not be good for Iraqis and Afghanis. One may have to openly say: Sorry folks, but we have to abandon you. Yet I am not convinced that this desperate position is necessary, at least not until we have considered other options. I do not believe that opposition to the attack on civil liberties and immigrant rights necessarily have to be linked with a non-interventionist policy. This is a link that the most hawkish and right-wing forces in this country have worked hard to forge in the post-September 11 political landscape: the you-are-with-us-or-against-us mentality. It is critical to break apart this link. There is no reason why opposition to internal U.S. developments cannot be linked with an interventionist policy that puts demands on the government over the terms of its interventions and the consequent responsibility beyond the military aspects of intervention.

In such a framework, it becomes critical to know what is going on elsewhere in this world, and to learn the complexities of local alignments. It becomes vital to connect with Iraqis and Afghanis, for instance. It becomes critical not to assume we already know what is good for other people, and if "they" have illusions about what they may get from the U.S. government, our sole task is to expose the prior history of this government and disabuse them of their naiveté, as if they didn't already know all too well and hadn't suffered from such policies. The Iraqis who are now struggling to effect a re-direction of U.S. intervention against Saddam Hussein know better than all of us here what price their society has paid for all those prior U.S. policies. Yet they also know that they need outside help to get rid of Saddam Hussein. This is what underlies their attempts to push U.S. policy in a direction more attuned to their aspirations. Should our advice to them be: Don't be fools? Or should we rethink our own orientation from one of non-intervention to one that attempts to affect the terms of intervention in a direction that breaks apart the intimate link currently established between intervention and a right-wing agenda internally or globally?

part two

POETRY

first writing since

~Suheir Hammad

1. there have been no words.
i have not written one word.
no poetry in the ashes south of canal street.
no prose in the refrigerated trucks driving debris and dna.
not one word.

today is a week, and seven is of heavens, gods, science.
evident out my kitchen window is an abstract reality.
sky where once was steel.
smoke where once was flesh.

fire in the city air and i feared for my sister's life in a way never
before. and then, and now, i fear for the rest of us.
first, please god, let it be a mistake, the pilot's heart failed, the plane's
engine died.
then, please god, let it be a nightmare, wake me now.
please god, after the second plane, please, don't let it be anyone
who looks like my brothers.

i do not know how bad a life has to break in order to kill.
i have never been so hungry that i willed hunger.
i have never been so angry as to want to control a gun over a pen.
not really.
even as a woman, as a palestinian, as a broken human being.
never this broken.

more than ever, i believe there is no difference.
the most privileged nation, most americans do not know the difference
between indians, afghanis, syrians, muslims, sikhs, hindus.
more than ever, there is no difference.

2. thank you korea for kimchi and bibim bob, and corn tea and the
genteel smiles of the wait staff at wonjo—smiles never revealing
the heat of the food or how tired they must be working long midtown
shifts. thank you korea, for the belly craving that brought me into

the city late the night before and diverted my daily train ride into the world trade center.
there are plenty of thank yous in ny right now. thank you for my lazy procrastinating late ass. thank you to the germs that had me call in sick. thank you, my attitude, you had me fired the week before. thank you for the train that never came, the rude nyer who stole my cab going downtown. thank you for the sense my mama gave me to run. thank you for my legs, my eyes, my life.

3. the dead are called lost and their families hold up shaky printouts in front of us through screens smoked up.
we are looking for iris, mother of three. please call with any information. we are searching for priti, last seen on the 103rd floor. she was talking to her husband on the phone and the line went. please help us find george, also known as adel. his family is waiting for him with his favorite meal. i am looking for my son, who was delivering coffee. i am looking for my sister girl, she started her job on monday.

i am looking for peace. i am looking for mercy. i am looking for evidence of compassion. any evidence of life. i am looking for life.

4. ricardo on the radio said in his accent thick as yuca, "i will feel so much better when the first bombs drop over there. and my friends feel the same way."

on my block, a woman was crying in a car parked and stranded in hurt. i offered comfort, extended a hand she did not see before she said, "we're gonna burn them so bad, i swear, so bad." my hand went to my head and my head went to the numbers within it of the dead iraqi children, the dead in nicaragua. the dead in rwanda who had to vie with fake sport wrestling for america's attention.

yet when people sent emails saying, this was bound to happen, let's not forget u.s. transgressions, for half a second i felt resentful.
hold up with that, cause i live here, these are my friends and fam, and it could have been me in those buildings, and we're not bad people, do not support america's bullying. can i just have a half second to feel bad?

if i can find through this exhaust people who were left behind to
mourn and to resist mass murder, i might be all right.
thank you to the woman who saw me breaking my cool and blinking
back tears. she opened her arms before she asked "do you want a hug?"
a big white woman, and her embrace was the kind only people with the
warmth of flesh can offer. i wasn't about to say no to any comfort.
"my brother's in the navy," i said. "and we're arabs." "wow, you
got double trouble." word.

5. one more person ask me if i knew the hijackers.
one more motherfucker ask me what navy my brother is in.
one more person assume no arabs or muslims were killed.
one more person assume they know me, or that i represent a people.
or that a people represent an evil. or that evil is as simple as a
flag and words on a page.

we did not vilify all white men when mcveigh bombed oklahoma.
america did not give out his family's addresses or where he went to
church. or blame the bible or pat robertson.
and when the networks air footage of palestinians dancing in the
street, there is no apology that hungry children are bribed with
sweets that turn their teeth brown. that correspondents edit images.
that archives are there to facilitate lazy and inaccurate journalism.

and when we talk about holy books and hooded men and death, why do
we never mention the kkk?

if there are any people on earth who understand how new york is
feeling right now, they are in the west bank and the gaza strip.

6. today it is ten days. last night bush waged war on a man once
openly funded by the cia. i do not know who is responsible. read too
many books, know too many people to believe what i am told. i don't
give a fuck about bin laden. his vision of the world does not include me
or those i love. and petitions have been going around for years trying to
get the u.s. sponsored taliban out of power. shit is complicated, and i
don't know what to think.

but i know for sure who will pay.

in the world, it will be women, mostly colored and poor. women will have to bury children, and support themselves through grief. "either you are with us, or with the terrorists"—meaning keep your people under control and your resistance censored. meaning we got the loot and the nukes.

in america, it will be those amongst us who refuse blanket attacks on the shivering. those of us who work toward social justice, in support of civil liberties, in opposition to hateful foreign policies.

i have never felt less american and more new yorker—particularly brooklyn, than these past days. the stars and stripes on all these cars and apartment windows represent the dead as citizens first—not family members, not lovers.

i feel like my skin is real thin, and that my eyes are only going to get darker. the future holds little light.
my baby brother is a man now, and on alert, and praying five times a day that the orders he will take in a few days time are righteous and will not weigh his soul down from the afterlife he deserves.
both my brothers—my heart stops when i try to pray—not a beat to disturb my fear. one a rock god, the other a sergeant, and both palestinian, practicing muslim, gentle men. both born in brooklyn and their faces are of the archetypal arab man, all eyelashes and nose and beautiful color and stubborn hair.
what will their lives be like now?

over there is over here.

7. all day, across the river, the smell of burning rubber and limbs floats through. the sirens have stopped now. the advertisers are back on the air. the rescue workers are traumatized. the skyline is brought back to human size. no longer taunting the gods with its height.
i have not cried at all while writing this. i cried when i saw those buildings collapse on themselves like a broken heart. i have never owned pain that needs to spread like that. and i cry daily that my brothers return to our mother safe and whole.

there is no poetry in this. there are causes and effects. there are symbols and ideologies. mad conspiracy here, and information we will never know. there is death here, and there are promises of more. there is life here. anyone reading this is breathing, maybe hurting, but breathing for sure. and if there is any light to come, it will shine from the eyes of those who look for peace and justice after the rubble and rhetoric are cleared and the phoenix has risen.
affirm life.
affirm life.
we got to carry each other now.
you are either with life, or against it.
affirm life.

First Bombing

~Nathalie Handal

For Suheir

Sitting in my small chair
at the Longacre Theatre
New York City
a trembling inside me
the first bomb
Baghdad
and all I see
to keep me safe, keep me sane
is you, sister
all I want to see
is that familiar face,
your eyes that remind me
of my mother's eyes—dark deep beautiful
your desert color like my father
who gives the earth color,
my father
who told me so many times—
that's power—it kills—
but I choose to believe in
another power tonight

the power
rocking the stage
telling the world
we exist
look at us
pronounce our names
remember us.

Ten O'Clock
the music's off
the words
packed inside of us...
I look for you
the only one I know
who feels the way I do
we hold each other
our lives questioning
our tears falling
and I know
we are the civilized ones
no space between us
we hold each other tighter
we cry in this basement
on Broadway
knowing that
the worst is yet to come.

Eleven O'Clock
I get home
close the door
a new trembling
in our world—
the sins we will commit
the shadows that will
grow in our silence
in our sleep
and
the words the dead

will keep
to remind us
of our deceits.

The Conflict

~Nathalie Handal

They came as if I was not there—
thirty-three, one hundred and twenty-five
long hair, brown hair, blue eyes
lines on the sides of my mouth
yellow skin

They came while I was out buying bread,
not knowing that I walk
outside the house
without myself

It is not morning yet—
two ambulances, three fire trucks,
twenty-four cars passed in eighty-two seconds,
and they came

They came with death on their uniforms
perhaps we are not meant to understand everything,
so we try to understand
where we are from, where we are going,
what we look like
They came with a picture of a subway ticket
half a bottle of juice,
told me I can leave,
as if I need their permission
as if I am in the wrong place,
told me I wouldn't shiver when I sleep
or dream of moist earth
as if they knew me,
told me I didn't need to follow

misery at every corner
didn't need to see my sidewalks bleeding
as if that will change my mind

They came to tell me that
I do not understand the place I inherited
so they will help me leave,
and I realize—we are far from each other,
and grow farther still, smaller still
like broken glass shattered in our throats,
our breath abandoning God.

Baladna

~Nathalie Handal

We are who we are,
and a home is a home
to keep us warm
to keep the seasons dreaming
to remind us of the small things—
ahweh, zaatar, houbiz, kaak

I am no longer sure what I see—
a field of wheat or a field of olive trees,
a herd of sheep or a burning mountain,
not sure if it even matters
now that I stand alone
at the corner of a small road
somewhere between my grandfather's past
and what seems to be my present…
And I think—am I as old, as young,
as sad, as torn, as strange, as sorry
as those I have lost.
I try to remember all that has been offered to me—
wrinkled bed sheets, library passes, old passports
ports we once stopped at for an hour or a lifetime…
we are who we are, are we who we are?

We write a ballad to celebrate ourselves, *baladna*
and wonder if that's
what it's like to dance in Arabic…

The Lives of Rain

~Nathalie Handal

The old Chinese man
in the health food shop
at 98th and Broadway tells me
that the rain has many lives.
I don't understand what he means
but like the way it sounds.
I wonder if he tells everyone the
same thing or if this is something between
us, wonder if he fought any wars, killed
anyone, wonder if he ever fell in love,
lost a house, lost his accent, lost a wife or
a child in the rain, wonder if he calls for
the rain when he stirs his daily soup,
wonder what hides in his silk cloth—
rice, pictures, maybe memories of rain.
Rain he tells me, carries rumors of the dead,
of those with suitcases and epidemics.
Rain carries the memory of droughts,
of houses gone, rain like lovers
comes and goes, like soldiers go
and sometimes return to a life
no longer standing.
The Chinese man waits for me to ask
for more. I stand, outside is the rain—
who really knows how many lives to come.

I Never Made It to Café Beirut; Nor, I Heard, Did You

~Nathalie Handal

You told me that I should wait
at the Lebanese border. You told me not
to fear the Hezbollah, the gunshots,
the missiles or grenades, told me
that I would not see the shadows of corpses
in the stained gray clouds, would not see
the refugees and the UN trucks waiting for God.
You told me that no one would

be singing war songs, or speak of
liberation, Saddam, Bush, the Israelis.
You said nothing about the trumpet of flames,
the shattering glass.

You insisted, meet me at the Lebanese border,
told me to bring my favorite poems
of Baudelaire and Gibran, my dreams
wrapped in my dyed black hair, and my questions—

the ones you could not answer at the time,
the simple facts—your real name, age, nationality—
and also why the night was held in siege,
why the souks were so quiet, the mountains

so quiet and the dead still struggling.
And why I had to meet you at that border.

War

~Nathalie Handal

A cup of empty messages in a room of light,
light that blinds & blinded men lined up
the young are unable to die peacefully, I hear a man say.

All is gone: the messy hair of boys, their smile,
the pictures of ancestors, the stories of spirits,
the misty hour before sunrise
when the fig trees await the small hands of a child.

Now the candles have melted
and the bells of the church
no longer ring in Bethlehem.

A continued past of blood,
of jailed cities
confiscated lives
and goodbyes.

How can we bear the images that flood our eyes
and bleed our veins: a dead man, perhaps thirty,
with a tight fist, holding some sugar for morning coffee.

Coffee cups full
left on the table
in a radio station
beside three corpses.

Corpses follow gunmen in their sleep, remind them
that today they have killed a tiny child,
a woman trying to say, "Stop, please."

Please stop the tears, the suitcases, the silence,
the single man holding on to his prayer rug,
holding on to whatever is left of memory

as he grows insane with every passing day...
listen, how many should die before we start counting,
listen, who is listening, there is no one here, there is nothing left,
there is nothing left after war, only other wars.

Rachel's Palestinian War[11]

~Nathalie Handal

To Rachel Corrie, American peace activist

Maybe hopefully one day
as you would say,
the world will
know what you know—
that small Palestinian children
know too much about
inhumanity for their age,
that Sharon's
assassination-during-peace-negotiations / land grab
is on full force,
that life in Palestine is about
checkpoints explosions digging roads,
about vegetable farms gardens orchards greenhouses
fruit trees after years hours, of care of work, bulldozed—
but I don't think you realized yet
that you would only be hearing
Ali's name—
the eight-year-old shot, killed by an Israeli tank—
only a little while longer,
that even if you thought
one day you could see the
ocean again, go home again,
that coming to Palestine
meant no longer having a choice again,
that you came from Mud Bay to Rafah
and became our Olympia
The night is warm and cold
and I can't stop crying
as I sit and write to you
I want every line to celebrate you
to caress your soul
your small body
Bulldozed

and once again Bulldozed
difficult to say to believe
even as I repeat...
Your shape
stains Rafah's earth
reminds this place
of its crimes

Your family
still questioning—why?
but in Falestin, the question is why?
the answer—why?

Tonight and every night
you will dance inside all of us—
Rachel's *debke*[12]...
We will remember how you loved
barnhair sesamees Lincoln School
how you loved Nidal Mansur
Rafat, your Palestinian Grandma
We will remember the fragility of life
as your voice travels through us:
Mama, I have nightmares
of tanks and bulldozers
outside our house,
you and me inside
Mama, Love you, really miss you
Mama, the place is shrinking
Mama, life is shrinking
Mama, it hurts... to witness how
awful we can allow the world to be.

Detained

~Nathalie Handal

For Mourad and all those unjustly detained
in Palestine and elsewhere, and to Ghassan

Over a cup of Arabic coffee
back in nineteen ninety nine,
on a balcony in Ramallah,
we spoke of the *situation*,
how we survive, *we don't* you said.

We had more coffee
your hand trembled
your trembling revealing
your fears the years
you never saw go by
the wait jailing you
your wife and child…

Three years later
you are detained…
I imagine a cell as tall as you—
five foot eleven inches,
as wide as you—
twenty-one and a half inches,
your life reduced to your body
and your memory of light,
your wife's whispers slide
under the slim opening of
the iron door to remind you
that you must not forget these hours
who you were, are—
we forget too easily
keep changing back to ourselves…

But brother, don't be jealous
of another's memories,
don't be jealous of your memories,

just remember what they
have done to themselves—
that the darkness they have planted
in our bones will cripple their bones,
that detainment is their life sentence,
that their blood staining our graves
is a stubborn witness.

Billy Bush Sam-ton

~Fawzia Afzal-Khan

Osama
Sam A
Uncle Sam

will you
defend me
against that SOB
who fondled my breasts
and squeezed my ass

he said Lie
through your tongue
baby it's okay
you're defending the
integrity of your
Man
-ly Nation hood
Not
hoodwinking but

upholding the
Truth (of)
Justice
Law
Democracy

That's why
It's okay
to nukefry
those damn boys
in Af-ghan-is-tan
　　and Su-dan
I-raq
and I-ran

barbarian chauvinists
not like us oh no
MONIKA

don't be disappointed
I've vindicated your
Honor
see by striking
those afroasian Breasts

so very different from
your soft White ones
I am a
Real Man now
are you Proud
of Me

Expert

~Sham-e-Ali al-Jamil

dusty desire
to suspend her in
a make-believe past.
traditional
customary
time warp.

instruct her
on her plight
you,
ventriloquist voyeur
telepathic authority
who climbs the bones of her spine
to get a better view.

expert of delusions
speaking of silhouette apparitions
draped in black,
non-entities restricted
to fantasy private spaces.

ponder over this "kind" of woman.
grade A specimen B
displayed in glass case #5
scurrying about natural habitat
imaginary woman
indiscernible invisible kind of woman
distorted contorted
shadow woman.

but despite desperate wishes
you can't claim her blood
healed wounds, heart
can't explain what you don't know
indispensable life-force

gut essence, dignity
unable to contain
nucleus incandescent spirit
substance, survival
who exists
in this modern present,
living being.

An Everyday Occurrence

~Sham-e-Ali al-Jamil

stopped at airport security
again
metal detector buzzes
conveniently
when I walk through

doesn't matter that
I spent time to empty pockets of
change and gum wrappers
remembered not to wear
the belt with the buckle
the metal barrett

futile attempts to avoid
this ritual,
pulled to the side
eyes scanning with suspicion
beeping wands
scouring my body
unwanted touching

I imagine their profile:
look for veil
headscarf
cloak
stop immediately

for our security
like clockwork they
peer under hijaab
unbutton expose
insert prod
pat and feel
when necessary
take to curtained booth
and I must comply.

where is my security?
with arms outstretched and
legs apart
only
humiliation and anger
violation and violence
an every day assault
my fear of flying.

Seeing Ourselves

~Sham-e-Ali al-Jamil

No matter,
that I was told to
devalue
her,
Resilient with
kaleidoscopic
beauty
flourishing
even without
nourishment.

Told to
embrace
apologies for oppression
or pull the frayed edges
of fabric we have woven

holding our tale
in our words.

How do I see you through the
tangled caricature?
Us?
sharing story
over dinner as we
carefully weave
soul strands together
or the serenity of your smile,
as you wish me peace
on the subway platform.

Paleontology of Occupation

~Maniza Naqvi

That we should get away, at every place,
As always, the exonerated.
As though we've had no other part to play.
Viewers from outside.
The insiders, outside.
Through destruction
Picking our way, where War's aftermaths
Leaves marked, the mirroring clues.
For us who claim
We're Passing through,
With parts of peace-keepers left to play.
Amongst tortured architectures/landscapes,
That offer in choked whispers,
To the same old interrogation,
The same old confessions.
A paleontology of occupations
Of humiliations.
Lenin no longer beckons,
Outside the Opera house, in Dushanbe
Where disoriented refugees set up camp
In "800 years of Moscow" Square.

Nor do those cartographers breathe,
Whose lines like jagged teeth,
Map many a nation's pain.
The age of Crusaders, and Janissaries,
of Emperors,
Has long slipped away
Yet the hills, the shooting galleries
Of Sarajevo, continue to echo
Their awful sound every day.
Nor does the wall in Berlin
Stand
For whose demise,
A million Afghans died and
Yes, where the Buddhas,
At Bamiyan, are no longer keepers
of peace
And an eternal plan.
That we should get away at every place
As always, the exonerated.
As though we've had no other part to play.
Viewers from outside.
The insiders, outside.
Through destruction
Picking our way, where War's aftermaths
Leaves marked, the mirroring clues.
For us who claim
We're Passing through,
Just parts of peace-keepers left to play.
That we should get away at every place
As always, the exonerated.

Time and War

~Maniza Naqvi

Three themes
Three lines
Lie threaded

Through time:
Before the war.
During the war.
After the war.
Three Lines one point:
War.
Preceded by hate.
Trailed by sadness.
Three lines, one point, a pause.
A time to live?
Without question. In War.
A simple time.
Of Clarity.
That thing, called peace,
Just another term for defeat.
A broken spirit.
Three lines
Lie threaded
Through Time.
Three lines, a point, a pause.
Before the war
During the war
After the war.
Time.
How did its adjectives,
Manage to blame the ultimate constant noun?
Qualify it, subjugate it,
Take possession of it?
Last time
Lost time
Waste of time
Running out of time
Managing time.
Right time
Wrong time.
Bad time
Good time.
Time is time.

It is.
And we,
At least,
At worst,
At most,
At best
Its adjectives.

The Time of Last Things

~Maniza Naqvi

This is the time
Of last things:
Last bottles of wine,
Last chocolates,
Last lumps of sugar,
Last bread,
Last meat,
Last nail polish,
Last batteries,
Last hair color,
Last grapes,
Last tea,
This time of last times:
Last smile,
Last kiss.
Last we,
Last us,
Last dance
Last song
Last stroll.
Last trust.
Last time the sky was just the sky
Last time just stars
Last time for any other
Lasting memories
This time of war.

War Is Terrorism

~Maniza Naqvi

Terrorism:
Violence by states,
individuals or
groups,
open parenthesis:
directly
or
indirectly
through directives,
orders,
financial,
military information,
and other types of support
close parenthesis,
against unarmed civilians
with the purpose of instigating
fear,
murder,
coercion,
repression,
subjugation,
occupation,
resulting in psychological
and physical injury
including
the deaths of
men,
women,
children.

Do you agree?
PEACE.

phoenix, from a distance

~Mahwash Shoaib (September 25, 2002)

at this height moonscape
brown-gray crust pockmarked
lines symmetrical stark apportion
op-art jewel-green and faded golden
in square patches circles
in afterthought erased
till gradually takes over the land.
by dry striations marked
ox-bow shaped arid riverbeds signifying
    coursed through these wrinkles once water
    written in it stories.

evidence of our neglect we find everywhere, ali:
locate in arizona baghdad
city of our disgust and desire
at the borders shall we be tourists

can be made green sand
line streets palm trees, blissful diners mists suffuse
color-schemed to age and belongingness the city
approval from the desert seeking, at its walls to block it only.
recalls the water but the desert
in the underground clear streams
embedded in the hills streaks.

is itself expansiveness this country
of formations red rocks and cliffs limestone, mesas dusty and mountains cacti-covered, land.
entered the earth the sun here
and in content flush left it.
the desert ways of seeing:
shade of patience, shade of silence in arms unravel
bustle in glare sunlit and moonlit hear
penalty of kohl-mountain but flash only permitted, remember
close our eyes we only for bear this light we cannot.

from others we take and take to them what belongs
and give back never
again and again as we will.
at a plateau we've arrived at—
fall sheer summits from here or ahead flat land.

of our denial the limits on bodies are spread
inevitability of
of comprehending to be committed the horrors
and of transports of millions the groans
in a sigh of wind condensed—
of this moment, the pain on skin of iron
be visited must not
burns both ways this rope.
glints in palm a raindrop, grain spinning in it
heavy this light only if we feel it all.
how battle can ever someone
so cruel this hope
this seed so precious
teeth i clench against.

equilibrium of bones (or, imagine us christiane amanpour)

~MAHWASH SHOAIB

september 16, 2001
we sleep without dream   we who fell surmised it was the shimmer of
blue was our destination,   we who fell   dominoes in the empire of
grief   our tears crystals torn from the hearts of stones   the spit gracing
your lips, the brick stroking the glass, your scepter elevated in anger   is
a revelation set deep within our bones   the hands serving you food at
the feet of commerce   carry the bowl half full of your piety   the
olives, the pomegranates, the mangoes   slippery beneath your soles
imagine the dark man standing in the sun   jean-clad legs half-sunk in a
pile of black garbage bags   the profile of a god   the woman lifting
straws on her bent back   in bright mirrored skirts, walking ample
toward her love   as dark eyes lock unto each other   we dream

march 29, 2002
chanda, we have found each other pale and pregnant with yearning you moved away every time I ran toward you but now when I stand still you hang stiller on the near horizon sulking like a baby heartbreakingly whole and encompassing, girthful, you are more than my eyes could ever hold the sky a splash of ink a child has run his fingers through you caught the burning orb in your hands and lay dormant for how you seem lit from within, this light might lend me comfort yet no cities are ever born in twenty-three years you have taught me the tabulation of patience a punctuated equilibrium of release and restraint water runs clear through my fingers and surahs hum over a white space empty of a body what can I say of this language of love

Little Mosque Poems

~Mohja Kahf

In my little mosque
there is no room for me
to pray. I am
turned away faithfully
five
times a day.
My little mosque:
so meager
in resources, yet
so eager
to turn away
a woman
or a stranger.
My little mosque
is penniless, behind on rent.
Yet it is rich in anger—
every Friday, coins of fear and hate
are generously spent.
My little mosque is poor yet
every week we mosque-goers donate

to buy another curtain
to partition off the women,
or to pave another parking space.
I go to the Mosque of the Righteous.
I have been going there all my life.
I have been the Cheerleader of the Righteous Team.
I have mocked the visiting teams cruelly.
I am the worst of those I complain about:
I am a former Miss Mosque Banality.
I would like to build
a little mosque
without a dome
or minaret.
I'd hang a sign
over the door:
Bad Muslims
welcome here.
Come in, listen
to some music,
sharpen
the soul's longing,
have a cigarette.
I went to the mosque
when no one was there
and startled two angels
coming out of a broom closet.
"Are they gone now?" one said.
They looked relieved.
My great big mosque
has a chandelier
big as a Christmas tree
and a jealously guarded
lock and key.
I wonder why
everyone in it
looks just like me.
My little mosque
has a bouncer at the door.

You have to look pious
to get in.
My little mosque
has a big sense of humor.
Not.
I went to the mosque
when no one was there.
The prayer space was soft and serene.
I heard a sound like lonely singing
or quiet sobbing. I heard a leafy rustling.
I looked around.
A little Qur'an
on a low shelf
was reciting itself.
My little mosque has a Persian carpet
depicting trees of paradise
in the men's section, which you enter
through a lovely classical arch.
The women's section features—
well, nothing.
Piety dictates that men enter
my little mosque through magnificent columns.
Piety dictates
that women enter
my little mosque
through the back alley,
just past the crack junkie here
and over these fallen garbage cans.
My little mosque used to be democratic
with a rotating imam
we chose from among us every month.
Now my little mosque has an appointed imam
with a classical training from abroad.
No one can dispute his superior knowledge.
We used to use our minds
to understand Qur'an.
My little mosque discourages
that sort of thing these days.

We have official salaried translators
for God.

I used to carry around a little mosque
in the chambers of my heart
but it is closed indefinitely pending
extensive structural repairs.
I miss having a mosque,
driving by and seeing cars lining the streets,
people double-parking, desperate
to catch the prayer in time.
I miss noticing, as they dodge across traffic
toward the mosque entrance between
buses and trucks,
their long chemises fluttering,
that trail of gorgeous fabrics Muslims leave,
gossamer, the colors of hot lava, fantastic shades
from the glorious places of the earth.
I miss the stiff, uncomfortable men
looking anywhere but at me when they meet me,
and the double-faced women
full of judgment, and their beautiful
children shining
with my children. I do.
I don't dream of a perfect mosque.
I just want roomfuls of people to kiss every week
with the kisses of Prayer and Serenity,
and a fat, multi-trunked tree
collecting us loosely for a minute under
its alive and quivering canopy.
Once God applied
for a janitor position at our mosque
but the board turned him down
because he wasn't a practicing
Muslim.
Once a woman entered
my little mosque
with a broken arm,
a broken heart,

and a very short skirt.
Everyone rushed over to her
to make sure
she was going to cover her legs.
Marshmallows are banned
from my little mosque
because they might
contain gelatin derived from pork enzymes,
but banality is not banned,
and yet verily,
banality is worse than marshmallows.
Music is banned
at my little mosque
because it is played on
the devil's stringed instruments,
although a little music
softens the soul
and lo, a hardened soul
is the devil's taut drumskin.
Once an ignorant Bedouin
got up and started to pee against a wall
in the Prophet's Mosque in Medina.
The pious protective Companions leapt
to beat him.
The Prophet bade them stop.
A man is entitled to finish a piss
even if he is an uncouth idiot,
and there are things
more important in a mosque than ritual purity.
My little mosque thinks
the story I just narrated
cannot possibly be true
and a poet like me cannot possibly
have studied Sahih al-Bukhari.
My little mosque
thinks a poem like this must be
written by the Devil
in cahoots with the Zionists,

NATO, and the current U.S. administration,
as part of the Worldwide Orientalist Plot
to Discredit Islam.
Don't they know
at my little mosque
that this is a poem
written in the mirror
by a lover?
My little mosque
is fearful to protect itself
from the bricks of bigots
through its window.
Doesn't my little mosque know
the way to protect its windows
is to open its doors?
I love my little mosque,
ego-ridden, cracked and flawed
as it is,
and I know
the bricks of bigots
are real.
I wish I could protect my little mosque
by hiding it behind my body.
My little mosque loves Arab men
with pure accents and beards.
Everyone else is welcome
as long as
they understand that Real Islam
has to come from an Arab man.
My little mosque loves Indian
and Pakistani men with Maududi in their pockets.
Everyone else is welcome because as we all know
there is no discrimination in Islam.
My little mosque loves women
who know that Islam liberated them
fourteen hundred years ago and so
they should live like seventh-century Arabian women
or at least dress

like pre-industrial pre-colonial women
although
men can adjust with the times.
My little mosque loves converts
especially white men and women
who give "Why I embraced Islam" lectures
to be trotted out as trophies
by the Muslim pom-pom squad
of Religious One-up-man-ship.
My little mosque faints at the sight
of pale Bosnian women suffering
across the sea.
Black women suffering
across the street
do not move
my little mosque much.
I would like to find a little mosque
where my Christian grandmother
and my Jewish great-uncle the rebbe
and my Buddhist cousin
and my Hindu neighbor
would be as welcome
as my staunchly Muslim mom and dad.
My little mosque has young men and women
who have nice cars, nice homes, expensive educations,
and think they are the righteous rageful
Victims of the World Persecution.
My little mosque offers courses on
the Basics of Islamic Cognitive Dissonance.
"There is no racism in Islam" means
we won't talk about it.
"Islam is unity" means
shuttup.
There's so much to learn.
Class is free and meets every week.
I don't dream of a perfect mosque, only
a few square inches of ground
that will welcome my forehead,

no questions asked.
My little mosque is as decrepit
as my little heart. Its narrowness
is the narrowness in me. Its windows
are boarded up like the part of me that prays.
I went to the mosque
when no one was there.
No One was sweeping up.
She said: This place is just a place.
Light is everywhere. Go, live in it.
The Mosque is under your feet,
wherever you walk each day.

Terror

~Faryal Khan (January 2003)

Who's the real terrorist?
Who's to say?
The country,
Full of ignorant people

You can't blame them
They're blinded by the media
Government let's them see
Only what they want them to see

But I can see too
The country run by a man
who talks about going to war
with NUCULAR weapons!

Children dying
Everyday
Who cares?
Not US

We can't see to find any weapons

But we're prepared to kill
Innocent civilians
and send our children to war

Oh wait—
We seem to have conveniently forgotten
Our weapons
Those ones

That bulldoze houses everyday,
Capture women and children
And shoot those boys
Those 13-year-old terrorists with rocks in their hands

But it's okay—
We can support such actions
Why?
Because "those" people are mad
Suicide bombers
Their actions are not justifiable
They're crazy, right?
Of course

Property taken
Boundaries made
Tanks
Gunshots

It's not that bad—
There's no reason to kill yourself
Can't you see?
We're the good guys
We know what's best
So let's run and play
This fatal game
But after all is said and done

Who's the real terrorist?

part three
JOURNALISM

Epigraph

~Nirmen al-Mufty (April 29, 2003, Iraq)

dearest al-warda,
so, i am still alive full of tears and pain
without any feeling.
just asking: was saddam so precious that iraq was the price??
baghdad is not the baghdad i knew
so i returned to kirkuk, my hometown.
a kurdish opened this internet cafe.
in the coming days we will keep in touch, inshaalah.

The Adventures of a Muslim Woman in Atlanta

~Nadirah Z. Sabir

(Post-9/11 selections from her *Atlanta Journal-Constitution* column, along with reader response)

Forward to September 11, 2001 Column

The early morning online crew had been working several hours, with TV monitors on mute, when someone noticed a plane was burning a hole in the side of one of the world trade towers. I ran down a flight of stairs to the art department to try to get a screen grab of what we were witnessing.

Down in photo, we looked up at one of the ever-present monitors just in time to see the second plane slowly plow into a second tower. With the first hit, I went into triage mode. The second hit sent me into shock. It would be weeks before I untangled my personal feelings from the need to act in my capacity as an online journalist.

We needed facts. We needed to slim down our page loads to accommodate the onslaught of readers looking for news.

I eagerly submerged myself in the task with the other editors. Only I wasn't like any other editor in this building. I am a Muslimah.

Hours later, co-workers from different areas of the building began to call: "Aren't you going to write something?... You have to write something, Nadirah."

At some point during that long night, I took a breath and typed out my feelings: "For American Muslims, a Familiar Disquiet," ran in the paper the day after 9/11, along with a torrent of coverage.

Journalism is basically a service-oriented profession. You're telling readers what they need to know, things that will ease their daily living, like when there's a car wreck up the road. Well, there was something coming fast. "For American Muslims" was more of a warning to Muslims and non-Muslims here in America who had no idea what they were in for in the aftermath of the terrorist attacks.

It was important to define some key areas of discourse before Muslims in America were shouted into silence.

For American Muslims, a Familiar Disquiet

I guess I won't be taking the train for a while. Some women will forego their headscarves if they have to go outside of their Muslim communities. America is on alert and on the defensive. So, too, are American Muslims. The children will lose a few friends at school and likely suffer a few taunts or even fights. Multicultural couples and families may feel the strain.

As Bush quotes a Bible verse and divides the world between "them and us" in his speech about a unified America, another generation of Muslims will make a choice: Walk the walk or go undercover. Either way, indigenous or immigrant, there is no escaping the fallout.

We don't yet know who is responsible for the attacks in Manhattan and Washington, other than the hijackers. So I am thoughtful with my comments. Others, however, are not.

Accordingly, many are feeling like easy targets right now. American Muslims sit high on that list: Arabs (whatever their religion), non-Arab Muslims, and anyone who could be mistaken for a member of the aforementioned groups—which is a whole bunch of people.

This isn't about sympathy. Save that for today's victims and for already shaky global diplomacy. This is about safety. Too many people use moments to rally as opportunities to act out. Though innuendo is high and wide, I haven't seen a single Middle East or Far East expert of Middle/Far Eastern origin publicly interviewed. But this is nothing new.

Muslim heads of state have condemned the heinous actions of today. Earlier, American Muslim groups spoke out. I suspect after the rubble is cleared from my hometown there will be more than a few *janazas* (funerals) held in New York. I'm still waiting to hear from some of my friends.

Others, who wear traditional Muslim clothing, are cautioned by Muslim groups to stay out of public areas for now. The Council on American-Islamic Relations is asking for additional security near *masajids*.

It's difficult to harness anger when the perpetrators aren't alive to face justice. It becomes easy to spread around the misery. State and Defense Department representatives are talking about bringing to account those who funded these attacks and entire countries who associate with people who associate with attackers.

A coalition of Islamic groups sent President Bush a letter today that read in part: "American Muslims, who unequivocally condemned today's terrorist attacks on our nation, call on you to alert fellow citizens to the fact that now is a time for all of us to stand together in the face of this heinous crime. It is not the time for speculative accusations and stereotypical generalizations that can only serve to harm the innocent and to endanger our society and its civil liberties."

In the first few days after the bombing in Oklahoma, more than 200 incidents of harassment, threats, and violence were reported. I recall one such incident resulted in a miscarriage. Congress passed anti-terrorist laws with Muslims in mind.

A year later came the bombings in Atlanta in Centennial Park and at a couple of health clinics that performed abortions. The prime suspect has become something of a folk hero in some quarters here in the South.

We were never invulnerable as a nation or a people. We simply have short, selective memories.

If we're going to talk about Muslims, we need to include Muslims in the discourse and decision-making. At the end of the day, no matter how many bombs we drop on countries in anger, or how many Muslims in America choose to blend in rather than battle insistent stereotypes, truth is, nobody's going anywhere.

We don't need subtly bigoted rhetoric to rally American Christians and Jews. We need a competent crack investigative team that will swiftly rout out those responsible and make all of that information public. We need an international tribunal for the culprits. And we need to bury our dead in peace.

Comment on Reader Responses

Plenty of mail followed that piece and others. Some was put into the op-ed section of the paper. About 30 percent of the mail I receive on any given day is hate mail. That rose to about 45 percent after 9/11. The threadbare gloves and the frayed masks were coming off all around me.

Reader Responses

Your article today moved me both to thought and to prayer. Though I am a Baptist and you are a Muslim, we both pray to the one God, the Father, The Almighty, the maker of all that is seen and unseen. We both pray to the God of Abraham, whom I believe loves us all as children.

I am praying for Muslim-Americans. As Americans you are the targets like all other Americans of the hate which is coming to us from abroad. As Muslims, you are the target of hate that may be arising from within our own country.

Although I am praying that the love and teachings of Jesus may be known throughout the world, I am also praying that followers of Islam will receive more press coverage at this time of crisis.

Though I probably know more about Islam than the average American, I am embarrassed to admit that if asked to name five followers of Islam, my list would probably include Osama bin Laden, the Ayatollah Khomeini, Saddam Hussein, and Mike Tyson.

If asked to name five tenets of your faith, I would probably be forced to include the concept of jahad [sic] as one of them. I am sure that this speaks very poorly for me, and I am equally certain that I am not too different from most non-Muslim-Americans.

Though I recognize that Islam does not have the equivalent of a pope, I am most hopeful that when groups of your religion's leaders condemn the events of last week and when leaders of Islamic countries do likewise, that such statements of goodwill and rationality will be prominently featured by the *Journal-Constitution* as well as other members of the news media.

My thoughts and prayers are with you and your family.

—George Duncan

Thank you for your article published in today's *Atlanta Journal*.

I have been reading many words on the Web (I cannot tolerate the televised media) and yours are among only a few reflecting right speech and mindful understanding of the lack of compassion in Bush and his administration.

We have very selected memories—forgetting our own "home grown" terrorists and our tendencies toward prejudice, the "they" all look alike.

I am a practicing Buddhist and many times have been told that "You do not look Buddhist."

My hope is that the rest of the global community will hold Bush in check. My hope is that my fellow citizens and American residents will not suffer at the hands of their neighbors, co-workers, and even family members because they use the Qur'an for guidance or their language "sounds like something Middle Eastern" or they look like a "Muslim."

We were and are a nation which has forgotten its own internal events of and tendencies toward hate. My hope is that we will realize why hate exists in the world and stop actively being part of the problem. Perhaps then the horrid acts of this past week will reconcile the world in right action not just in retaliation.

Thank you for your insights.
—Maria Gauthier, Williamsburg, VA

Regarding your September 16, 2001, column, American Muslims, Walk The Walk or Go Undercover:

I am a Christian man, husband, and father who lives in Roswell, GA. I served in the U.S. Army in Vietnam and I am now a Captain with Delta Air Lines. I am as patriotic as they come! In regards to your column I urge you to NOT forgo your head scarf, go underground, or do anything else to hide your great religion.

Neither Islam, nor true believers in Islam, condone the acts of evil that were perpetrated on our country. I do not believe the murderers who committed these evil acts represent Islam any more than murderers who bomb abortion clinics represent Christians.

I know it is easy for me to say, "walk the walk" as you put it in your column. But I hope you and your fellow true believers do just that! For my part, I will not tolerate any slanderous talk or actions directed at you or any other true believer in Islam.

Yours is a great religion. Your religion is NOT responsible for what occurred on September 11. Murderous criminal[s] are responsible and for their crimes they will be punished.

God Bless you and God Bless America.

Best regards and hope,
—Wesley F. McCann, Captain, Delta Air Lines

Thank you for your article regarding Atlanta's Islamic population.

I have friends who are of Arabic descent. I also have many Hispanic friends who are, what could be considered by some, to be "Arabic-looking." I have already heard that some of them have been harassed and insulted. I am very worried for them and even fear for their safety.

We are seeing that the victims of Tuesday's tragedies are not only those who had the extreme misfortune to be at "ground zero," but also the many Arab- and Muslim-Americans who are now the victims of misguided American anger.

A Muslim man said it best on the radio yesterday when he said "Hitler was a Christian, should, therefore, Jews hold ALL Christians responsible for the acts of this one individual?" It would be the equivalent of holding all white Americans responsible for the act of terrorism committed by Timothy McVeigh.

My thoughts and prayers go out to the victims of this terrible tragedy as well as their families and the families of those who are still missing. I would also like to send an apology to those Arab and Muslim members of our community who have been hurt by ignorant people who don't know any better. Please know that not all of us feel the way they do.

—B.D. Vega, Marietta, GA

Holding all American Muslims responsible for the 9/11 attack makes as much sense as holding all American Christians responsible for abortion clinic bombings. That said, it is unfortunate but unavoidable that innocent American Muslims will live under a cloud of suspicion for some time—especially while it is believed that active terrorist cells remain in the USA and threaten average American citizens. Survival takes precedent over good manners.

You wrongly imply that President Bush divides us between Muslim and Christian/Jew. He recognizes that some people are lovers of peace while others are lovers of war. America proved during the 20th century that we don't start wars but rather defend other countries against aggression.

Finally, we don't need an "international tribunal for the culprits." We can handle it just fine.

This cowardly and barbaric act was not perpetrated upon the "international" community but on American soil. This was an act of war supported by at least one country in the Middle East. We have the skill, will, resources, and the moral obligation to wipe these animals and their supporters from the face of the earth.

The rest of the world can walk with us or behind us, but would be most wise to stay out of our way.

—David Anderson

Forward to October 11, 2001 Column

A month later, two things seem very clear about my profession. It was an exciting time to be a journalist. And it was going to take some personal courage not to slip-slide into advocacy journalism to please authorities in a frightening time.

The questions loomed: Is starting a war in Afghanistan sanctioned under international law? Should we be taking military briefs verbatim? Where is the skepticism? Where is the breadth of democracy at work, the democracy we claim to believe in and want to share with the world?

For Muslims, it was imperative they understood they were going to have to exercise their legal rights or they would watch their rights atrophy under the weight of tribal hysteria—their own and that of some other fellow Americans.

Actions We Take Now Will Define Us for a Long Time to Come

It's been a month. Let's take a look at where we stand. Our military is in action, bombing and feeding Afghanistan. As New York, Washington, and the economy attempt to recover, the nation braces for bioterrorism and/or more suicide bombers. More death.

Congress and the press sit just outside the loop. Polls show the American public expresses complete, unquestioning confidence in our leaders. We don't want to think about the details of this engulfing ordeal. We just want it handled. And so our executive branch has managed to gain almost total latitude, creating a vacuum of front-line information, evidence, and discourse.

No questions. Only applause. Besides, we do have latitude. We have the entire Taliban regime and a margin of error of at least 6,000 civilians to kill before some of us can seriously think about checking our bloodlust. Afghanistan is a big, inconsequential target and a safe distance away. England's Tony Blair is a bit more forthcoming with pertinent data, but then he's much closer to the fallout zone.

The bombing of Afghanistan as a prelude to our long-lasting overseas agenda against Mideast terrorist groups isn't winning over too many Muslims overseas. Americans don't really care about that quite yet. We're still in the "they're all barbarians in need of a spanking, shave, and Macy's one-day sale" mode.

Being equally given to fantasies of superiority as are many Americans, some in the Muslim world and/or particularly the Arab world are actually surprised at our level of self-righteous bloodlust. Muslims are just as suspicious of statements by American and European leaders for calm and reason as Americans are of the moderating statements of Muslim leaders.

Many all over the world support our efforts to root out the terrorists who slammed into our lives. But that's about all they want. Most in South America, Europe, Asia, and Africa have been dealing with terrorism for many years. No one has been allowed the latitude by the world community to wage war over it. In doing so, we've taken a group of criminals trained by Americans to fight Russians then left to pillage Afghanistan and turned them into historical myth. Are they worthy?

Here in the States, most Muslims are completely-to-guardedly supportive. Many express the need to see criminals brought to justice, but they aren't interested in getting their religion and way of life sucked into the vortex of the rage that swirls openly—both ways. Too late.

Balance. Due diligence. Democracy. These are America's lessons.

Strangely, I can't think of a better place on earth for a Muslim to be right now than America—born, bred, or naturalized. This is not because it's particularly safe or pleasant at the moment. Rather, American Muslims can help offer a bit of balance and perspective—wanted or unwanted.

Civil rights attorneys are raising flags about people being detained secretly, without due process. Out of 600 detainees, 400 recently were released with no charges filed against them. Lawmakers are moving to protect long-term privacy rights while balancing the need of federal agencies to monitor suspects.

Muslims who are not direct targets of bias crimes are looking to head off longer-term, more generalized discrimination they've fought long and hard against. More than 800 bias incidents have been logged by the Council on American-Islamic Relations; right now they're averaging about 100 reports a week. The war is four days old and counting.

Local "militias," other hate groups, and their supporters are gearing up for the ever-coming "race war," I'm told. Before these groups actually lock and load, I would suggest they take the time to read up on what Arabs and Muslims look like. Here's a reminder: They look like a lot of people, including you.

Actually, this is a cakewalk compared to times past. Local authorities, agencies, and companies are showing little tolerance with bias incidents arising from the terrorist attacks. Acts of courage, kindness, and basic sanity abound.

Democracy is not some concrete thing we can package and sell overseas like a Happy Meal. It is an ever-evolving ideal that warps under pressure and prolonged heat.

We've got many miles to go until we reach the jagged, narrow ledge of hindsight. Till then, let's continue to show the breadth and depth of our democratic convictions. Because the rules we make for others in haste, gleefully in war, will be the rules we ourselves will have to live by, be defined by, long after the initial rush subsides and we want to forget.

Comment on Reader Responses

The response to the October 11 piece was moving and encouraging.

Reader Responses

Your comments hit right on the money for me. As Americans it is our duty to ma[k]e certain ou[r] Rights are not quietly stripped away under the Uproar of Patriotism. Keep up the good work.

Blessings,
—Felix Smittick

I've found such wisdom in your writings since the events of 9/11/01. Your voice is strong and oh so necessary at this time in our history.

Out here in the middle of the Pacific, we're a little more relaxed and protected from the currents swirling around the rest of the world. Nonetheless, we know that it is only a matter of time before we are sucked in to swim or drown with the rest of the "global village."

Education and understanding will be our best life-vests when that time comes. Thank you for helping us manufacture these vests while we yet have time.

Salaam, shalom, aloha,
—Stuart E. McKinley, Honolulu, HI

The war is more than four days old. It began in earnest one month ago.
—D. Kim Wimpey

Great piece sister. Only you could have written it.

May God bless you,
—Abdul Malik Mujahid

Greetings of peace.

I cannot help but write you in appreciation of your forthright and, I must say, courageous article, "Actions We Take Now... ." More important than the writing (which is certainly a treat, by the way) is your gutsy, honest message. I just wanted you to know it is appreciated.

Peace,

—Amer Haleem

Forward to October 24, 2001 Column

"Media, Misogyny Help Mangle Image of Muslim Women," was a piece written with Muslims and non-Muslims in mind. It is an exasperated rant from someone who grew up in both worlds and who can see the parallels, positive and negative, between Western societies and Muslim societies as they relate to women, men, and ego. The mistreatment of Afghan women was being used as an excuse to invade their country. Over and over the clips ran showing the execution of desperate and abused women cloaked in blue.

The entreaty to other women and, ultimately, to myself in "Media, Misogyny" was: Remember who you are.

Media, Misogyny Help Mangle Image of Muslim Women

The face of Muslim women has indeed been veiled, but not simply by the *burqa*. If it is a spreading conspiracy, Muslim men are not the only ones in collusion.

The Western media, whether through ignorance, personal politics, or selective reporting, have for years offered an exaggeratedly grim view of women in Islam. "For some reason, [media] latch on to a few examples of unjust behavior in the Islamic world, brand Islam as a backwards and 'fundamentalist' religion, especially in its treatment of women, and ignore that it was the first religion to accord women equal rights," Saimah Ashraf wrote at Stanford University in 1997.

In fact, the teachings of Islam fundamentally forbid oppression of women.

Muslim women in Afghanistan in the '30s, '40s, and '50s lived much freer lives than those same women who've endured the door-to-door slaughter of their male relatives and the ruin of their economy under the Taliban.

We here in the Americas are quick to pity these women. The

aberrant and abusive actions of some Muslims seem to fascinate us: genital mutilation, honor killings, acid throwing, polygamy abuses. These horrors exist, but they are sensational headlines that disguise the real story of women in Islam. That is, for every one "circumcised" woman, there are a million who aren't.

Every region has its challenges. "For example," wrote Ashraf, "many American women are discriminated against because they cover their heads; Pakistani women have political rights but are often exploited by men; Saudi women have no public role, yet they are 'protected' by Saudi men."

Western countries tell other countries they have to end abuse of women if they want full membership in the family of nations. Yet, every nine seconds an American woman is abused, typically by partners or dates.

Many of the problems we want Muslim societies to address have parallels right here in our own Western societies. We claim the right to free speech, yet when Muslims voice complaints about our foreign policy or about the vagaries of our culture, we can't deal with it; we close off communication… in times of relative peace, let alone today. Today critical thinking is simply anti-American, a manipulation.

Still, let's face it, some people are just plain mean and/or criminal. And an equal portion of those people consider themselves to be Muslims. Islamic and other laws against these crimes and abuses go unenforced, which in turn undermines the stability of communities.

Afghan women teachers, doctors, lawyers, and other civic leaders have tirelessly spoken out against gang rule, torture, murder/execution, rape, assault; they have set up underground schools for girls, refugee services including clinics and more.

Their call for help went largely ignored by both Muslim and non-Muslim nations alike. Meanwhile, a few organizations, including Muslim charities and other groups, have consistently advocated on their behalf.

Time and again it is proved that when a society so excludes women from discourse and decision-making, that society quickly slides backward into the caves of human antiquity.

Another, (and to me) more alarming source of misinformation about Muslim women comes from the example set by some Muslim men.

I've heard Muslim men who attend school, visit, or live in America try to seduce women or befriend men with the old:

"A Muslim woman wouldn't fit in here. I need someone more on my level."

"I'm only married Islamically. It doesn't really count."

"She'd understand. She has no choice. Polygamy is my right."

Polygamy is meant to be a protection for women in times of crisis, not a means to prostitute family life and values. Honor the womb that bore you, entreats a Qur'anic passage. It speaks not only to one's own mother, but to women in one's society and, ultimately, to all womankind.

Back in Muslim communities, these same men later explain dismissively to prospective mates: "Oh, I was married before but she wasn't a Muslim."

The prophet's first wife, Khadijah, was a successful businesswoman, older than her husband, who was not a schooled man. It is reported that he never hit her. He helped with household duties. He was neat and valued education. Today he is often quoted as saying: The ink from the pen of a scholar is more precious than the blood of a martyr.

Women scholars and human rights activists who are Muslim have always been among us—in good times and bad. They are the Arabic instructors in Senegal.

The princess and photographer in Saudi Arabia.

The master embroiderer in India.

The battered mother in Houston.

They run households. Lead civic charges.

They have run nations—Pakistan, Bangladesh, and Turkey.

They are the doctor and engineer who are no longer allowed to practice their professions in Afghanistan.

The successful businesswoman who married a man who would be a prophet.

These are real people. These are women of Islam. These and hundreds of millions more who are quite capable of telling their own stories.

We can be just as dismissive of their contributions as are some in the good ole boy Muslim networks that have sprouted over the centuries.

Comment on Reader Responses

In those early days after the attacks, when people were searching for perspective, the response to these pieces was overwhelmingly positive; some seemed relieved. I resisted writing simply in reaction to the latest outrages.

Reader Responses

I appreciated your editorial about the misrepresentation of Muslim women in America. I am an African-American, Christian woman, and I am disgusted that United States leaders and media are now using propaganda about the plight of Afghan women to gain support for "America's New War." (By the way, what was the old war?)

Afghan women were oppressed and mistreated before September 11, 2001. Where was the American attention then? It seems to me that political leaders and the media are using this horrible situation to elicit sympathy from the American citizenry, for political, not humanitarian reasons.

—Tiffany Dover

My sister,
Today I thanked God for you and your knowledge in action.... Knowledge is only power when it is used. Keep doing what you are doing.

Peace & Love,
—Cia from Austell

It is refreshing and informative to read your columns. I wish they could find a place in the print edition. They could help all of us to look beyond the generalizations and assumptions.

—Eric Hovdesven

As salaamu alaikum,
I felt compelled [to] write and thank you for that beautiful article "Media, misogyny help mangle image of Muslim women." I was really moved up[on] reading this article. Many times we do not agree, but I gotta give it to you my sister, you laid it out for them, they can like it or lump it and for that I thank you. I must say you don't bite your tongue.

May Allah protect us and continue to allow us to grown in this *deen* [religion].

Your sister in Islam,
—Fasaaha R. Booker

Good Evening[.] My name is Kimberley[.] I live in Orlando, FL. I saw your interview on CNN about two months after the 9/11 attacks on NYC. I enjoyed listening to your interview that night. I especially liked your comment on how, "Not every woman defines their femininity by heels and a miniskirt."

It was good to see an interview of [a] muslim woman who was not portrayed as uneducated, oppressed, suppressed, depressed, or whatever word is available at the moment.

I read most of your articles and they are very good and educational. Keep up the good work.

Thank You,
—Kimberley Lightbourne, Orlando, FL

Despite having read the AJC online on a daily basis for almost two years, I finally took the time during the last few weeks to include the "Living" section (believe it or not, I almost always skip the sports section).

I have been very impressed with your writing style, your logic process, and your respect for others. In a time when your peers in the other sections tend to be of the extremes, it is a pleasure to read the writings of someone who is not wearing blinders and looks at all aspects from all perspectives. And while I might not always agree with your conclusions, I can have higher respect for your point of view as you develop your position with logic and facts. Keep up the good work! P.S. I know this really doesn't matter, but I am a conservative, white male who almost always votes Republican.

Have a good day!
—Jeff Knapp, Marietta

I just wanted to drop you a note to let you know how much I enjoy reading you on ajc.com. I stumbled upon it several weeks ago and have read all that are posted. I am not a Muslim, so many of your columns have enlightened me to your religion. Thank you for "setting things straight" about many of the misconceptions that I had. Keep up the good work.
—Christy Clark, Alexandria, La.

Thank you very much for your piece, "Media, misogyny help mangle image of Muslim women." As an Afghan-American woman, I have felt these things while growing up in the U.S. and I'm glad to see you speak up. Thank you again.

Regards,
—Asiyah Sarwari

Thank you for this enlightening story about the misunderstanding of Muslim women and the Muslim faith. I have always believed all the horror stories to be the rule, rather than the exception. I am eager to learn and understand more.

Please continue to share your knowledge with the world.

—Judy Newman, Atlanta

Epilogue

I am rewarded with a diverse group of readers that include Muslims, Christians, Jews, agnostics, Republicans, military veterans, housewives, students, and readers who call up my column from around the world including India, Nigeria, Malaysia, and Germany.

These continue to be trying times in which everyone plays a part. All we can do is be true to our paths. I want to be able to look back on these years and know that I "trusted in the nectar of my own life."

Journal Entry from Tehran

~Anisa Mehdi

For Wellesley

July 8, 2001—This morning we drove about an hour and a half east of Tehran, along the foothills of the Alborz mountain range. Even in July the peaks echo with snow. The Alborz lie north of the city, cuddling it in a crescent-shaped hug. They split inner Iran from the refreshing resorts on the Caspian Sea. Around us the land is brown and dry, not flower-filled as in years past. Iran suffers from the drought that is parching Central Asia and Afghanistan.

Our destination that day was the village of Damovand, named after the highest peak in the Alborz Mountains. It felt to me like a small stucco town in Andalusia (formerly Muslim-ruled southern Spain), where I'd spent my junior year from Wellesley College. Damovand was built of clay and pride of place, filled with chaste children and self-important men. A dry riverbed cracks the town's center. Iran is struggling with the same drought conditions that have left Afghanistan parched and famine-prone.

We went to Damovand to meet Ayatollah Mahdi Hadavi Tehrani, who had been recommended as a candidate for a profile I was producing for ABC News *Nightline.* It was my second of three journeys to Iran. As executive producer for a PBS documentary on the diversity of the Muslim population around the world and as producer/writer for a concomitant series for *Nightline,* I had traveled to Malaysia, Turkey, Senegal, and Iran, identifying story lines about a living, thriving Islam in the modern world and finding the people to tell them. I'd been hired in 1999 by the Independent Production Fund to lead this film project. September 11, 2001, had yet to prove how timely our vision really was.

As we got close to the town, my guide and interpreter, Lily Sadeghi, pulled two filmy black sheets from her briefcase. These cloths, called chadors, cover a person from forehead to toe. They are often black, but not always. The chador, another Iranian explained to me, is a symbol of Iran and the Revolution of 1979, rather than a uniform of Islam. Indeed, women of Persia wore chadors even before Islam came to the land. Similarly, the pious women of next-door Iraq wear abayas. My own grandmother was one of them, living at the end of her days in a suburb of Baghdad, where my father had attended the High School of

Commerce, before moving on to the University of California at Berkeley courtesy of his government. He never went back. But I always yearned to know of his birth culture. This kind of work brought me close.

I was already dressed in a full-length black coatdress with a black scarf neatly tied over my hair. The chador/abaya covered this. Excessive? Maybe. But still, we donned the chadors for this meeting. As a reporter I've always applied the principle that I am out to seek information, not to make a point. And if, by wearing a chador, I show respect and help to earn the confidence of my source, I will do my best to wear it.

Although I don't think a person's religion should determine what church he covers, and it's not always true that a person of color can better report inner-city issues than a white reporter and so on, there is no doubt that my being Muslim was an advantage on this beat. Many Muslims worldwide have grave doubts about American reporters' objectivity on matters of Islam; they have great certainty about overall American ignorance about their faith. Getting access and developing trust takes time and investment on the part of reporters that they don't often have, given the time sensitivity of breaking news and deadlines.

In my case, trust was mine to lose. People I met loved it that an Arab-American, who was Muslim to boot, was on this beat. They didn't know such a person existed in what seems to be an all-too-obvious bias in American media against all things Arab and Muslim. Because we shared a common faith, a common experience of being the underdog, and because I was such a rare commodity in my sources' experience with western reporters, our work and the intentions of my team were regarded with many fewer degrees of skepticism. These factors also left me with an added responsibility to make sure the result really reflected the lives of the people we covered.

Being a woman was an advantage, too, in terms of reporting in "non-western" societies. In some "traditional" societies, women lead their lives separately from the men folk. I could have access to that world, where male reporters need not have applied. Also, I know enough about Islam not to be intimidated by rumors of its patriarchal bent; Muslim men have almost always afforded me the greatest of respect.

That's why I was so taken aback by the way Ms. Sadeghi and I were received by the Ayatollah's front man. Harsh, unkempt, and diminutive, the assistant measured up to all the existing stereotypes. He was dismissive and rude, snarling at us to cover escaped wisps of hair. He did not offer tea, which I had eagerly anticipated after the long ride from Tehran. Just one visit to Iran or any Arab nation (or Ireland, for that matter) will accustom one to sweet tea in small glasses within minutes of arrival to any home or professional encounter.

I wondered if the Ayatollah, too, would be such a man as my preconceived notions imagined: a stern and unyielding cleric, a la Khomeini. I was, in fact, a bit nervous as the meeting neared. Little did I know what was ahead.

Finally the assistant ordered us into a room with a desk and a few chairs. The Ayatollah was coming.

Mahdi Hadavi Tehrani is six feet tall if he's a foot, and his white turban gave him several extra inches. His multilayered robes were black over brown; his beard black and thick. But rather than frowning, foreign and fierce, he greeted us with a smile and a warm, no-handshake welcome. He was intent and purposeful and seemed intimately aware of his humanity and ours. "*Assalamu alaikum* (Peace be with you)," he greeted us in Arabic, then "It is nice to meet you, Mrs. Anisa Mehdi," in clear English. "Mrs. Sadeghi," he nodded to her. After motioning for us to sit he neatly fitted a tape cassette into the recorder on his desk.

The Ayatollah ordered tea from his hovering attendant, turned to me, and smiled. "My name is Mahdi, too."

It only took moments in that sparsely furnished room for my preconceived notions to dissolve. As we sat and gratefully sipped hot, sweet tea, Mahdi Hadavi Tehrani gently and utterly dashed all I thought I had ever known about clerical attitudes and authority in Iran. Articulate, informed, amiable, and imposing, he was meant for *Nightline*.

An Ayatollah is one who has achieved a specific high degree of religious scholarship, close to a Ph.D. Ayatollah Hadavi (that's how he's known) reached his in only ten years—about half the time it usually takes. Now he teaches Islamic law and jurisprudence at the internationally renowned Islamic Seminary in Qom, a city about three-hours' drive south of Tehran. His wife is a professor of Islamic philosophy at the women's seminary there. The family (with four children) summers in Damovand, at the foothills of the Alborz, where it's cooler, and he can enjoy some of his favorite sports, like swimming and hiking. This Ayatollah regularly practices yoga, which he explains is a way to strengthen and stretch the body and center the soul, similar to the results of the practice of ritual Islamic prayer.

Over the course of the next several months Ayatollah Hadavi and I remained in regular e-mail contact, working out his willingness and availability for the extensive on-camera interview and documentary videotaping to come.

Taping for the PBS program and *Nightline* series were to take place simultaneously. That's called "cost-effective." We were scheduled to shoot in Malaysia, Turkey, Egypt, Nigeria, the USA, and Iran for the two-hour PBS documentary and to interview selected individuals for *Nightline* from Iran, Malaysia, and Turkey. The purpose of the PBS film was to demonstrate diversity among the world's 1.2 billion Muslims and explore what appears to be a revival in enthusiasm for Islam across the globe. We were also intent upon illustrating the kinship between Islam, Christianity, and Judaism. On September 11, 2001, that mission became all the more important.

While prejudicial views of Muslims solidified in the minds of many Americans on that fateful day, many also recognized the dire need to know more about Islam. Motivation went beyond "Know thy enemy." For many the search was, and is, response to a profound desire to understand more and so to sculpt a safer, wiser future for our ever-shrinking planet. Knowledge is the best chisel for that process.

To a varying degree of accuracy, media played an immediate role in educating Americans about Islam and Muslims. The hard-forged efforts of our documentary project were suddenly undercut, "scooped" as we say in the business, by a flock of instant experts on the subject. The prevailing question for my team became: "What sets us apart?" The answer emanated from our original mission: depth, diversity, and kinship. In the wake of September 11, PBS's flagship documentary series, *Frontline*, found that mission appealing and invited us to be part of its 2001–2002 season.

We interviewed and videotaped individual Muslims from these select countries. Their stories, we hoped, would reflect some of the variety, passions, and problems present in the Muslim world writ large. With the Ayatollah, the opportunity was to smash a stereotype and present a three-dimensional human being, whose title has a very bad rap in the West.

On the banks of the Bosporous, we met women struggling for the right to wear their headscarves to university and in Turkish government jobs. Naciye Elagoz and Guzzeyeh Bingol dressed smartly in long coatdresses, with large patterned scarves picking up the hues of the coats pinned neatly at their chins. Not a hair errant. The fiercely secular Turkish state discourages this form of Islamic religious expression, to the point of banning headscarves from public facilities and public office. Both Naciye (NA-jay) and Guzzeyeh (gu-ZAY-ah) were science students at Istanbul University, but they are now officially forbidden to attend. The way they cover is viewed as a part of a political movement bent on turning Turkey into another Iran. Our subjects argued that this was their personal choice and reflected piety, not sedition. On a warm July day in an outdoor café in the embrace of the Blue Mosque, I asked Naciye Elagoz about the perceived threat she presented. She smiled, although her brown oval eyes were sad and confused, "I am not dangerous," she insisted. Nevertheless, tens of thousands of Turkish women are barred from university because their hair is covered. This story made a striking contrast to the abounding stories of enforced covering by the Taliban in Afghanistan.

In Malaysia we profiled an activist who is using the Qur'an, the Holy Book of Islam, to advance women's rights. Zainah Anwar and the organization "Sisters in Islam" challenge what they say are centuries old patriarchal interpretations of the text. In brilliant, Fletcher School of Diplomacy English, Anwar extolled a 21st-century reading of the Qur'an. Rethinking the Qur'an, from a gender-free bias, she found, sheds light anew on the rights, advantages, and opportunities mandated for women in the 7th century in this text that Muslims believe is the word of God (Allah), as revealed to the prophet Muhammad. Patriarchy may still exist in parts of Malaysia, Central Asia, Africa, and South America—just as it is found in our own society. Some women keenly feel the negative impact of sexist tyranny: no reprieve from the responsibilities of the home, arranged marriages, patronizing attitudes, and limited access to money and financial independence. These are cultural norms, Anwar emphasizes. They are not standards rooted in the principles of Islam, any more than beating wives or children is rooted in the principles of Christianity. "It's hard for us as believers to accept that God is unjust," she says with passion and logic, "and that God is unjust to half the human race just based on the fact that we were born women." Anwar and many other Muslims believe that these male-dominated systems will evolve, as they have only recently in western societies, to achieve more equitable standards for all people.

In country after country we found people engaged in daily life, working, studying, raising children, struggling, suffering, satisfied; people with passions that either met or debunked notions of how Muslims live and, indeed, what it means to be Muslim in the 21st century. One thing was consistent: From village to village, sympathy came pouring forth for the loss of life in the September 11 tragedy. So, too, came cautions about the U.S.'s oft-imprudent reach around the world. In Kano, northern Nigeria, Dr. Datti Ahmad explained why some people in the third world lauded Osama Bin Laden. "I can understand their feelings," he said, his white robes a striking contrast to his jet-black skin. "They feel here is one man who has given the U.S. a run for their money. The one country that is killing Muslims all over the world... Here is one who is giving them a run for their money so they love him."

In the aftermath of September 11, news media inspected Islamic "militancy" with an electron microscope. When *Frontline* invited us to join its season, in fact, we were asked to expand our focus from diversity and kinship, to reiterate the fundamentalist nature of Islam that so many other reports highlighted. We hadn't interviewed militants for two primary reasons: (1) everyone else was looking at militancy and we wanted to look at everything else, and (2) post-September 11, most "militants" were wise enough not to go on camera. In the end, our section on the emergence of a variety of *sharia* law, newly imposed in northern Nigeria, sufficed to represent a harsher, less-forgiving element of Islam and in particular, the difficulties that might result for women. This element clashed nicely with the Malaysian sequence in the documentary.

Three and a half years in the making, the finished film premiered on May 9, 2001. We called it, simply, "Muslims." It reflects some of the principles of Islam that I observe. It includes some "truths" others hold to be self-evident, with which I disagree. Overall, "Muslims" seeks to provide another lens through which people may reflect on the human religious experience, with its nuance and culturally charged confusion. Perceived and actual male supremacy within Islam is one of those confused issues: I believe it is rooted, rather than in religion, in the weaknesses of human nature that are prevalent across the globe in any age. My recent journeys confirm that as surely as human nature is not going to change, the discussion of patriarchal systems must not concentrate solely on women's rights and grievances. Men too need to be engaged in rethinking their roles and assumptions, their biases and what they base them on. And women need to assist in that process—as Zainah Anwar is doing in Kuala Lumpur. "The word of God, the Qur'an, the text of the Qur'an is divine revelation," she observes. "That is unchangeable. But human beings' understanding of the word of God—this is not divine."

Hearing Anwar speak gives me goose bumps. Her chorus resonates with what I learned about Islam from my father. A favorite verse was, "O Humankind! We have created you from a male and a female, and made you into nations and tribes that you may know one another. Surely the best among you is the one best in conduct. Allah is knowing, aware" (Qur'an chapter 49, verse 13). Dad used to always point out that it wasn't a man or woman who was best; it wasn't a Muslim or a Jew or a Christian who was best; it was the person who conducted him or herself the best in the eyes of God and humanity. He always affirmed the flexibility of Islam, the reasonable approach of the Prophet to matters of life, an emphasis on moderation and modesty—not abstinence and abayas.

That suppleness of mind and view is a great asset as a reporter. Instead of hardening on a thesis, I'm happy to let some of my ideas fly out the window, like who Ayatollahs may be; I welcome the reality I find in the field and embrace the personal lessons that come during the process of producing and reporting. The personal lessons stick like new skin, living with me long past the time when I remember how to spell the names of my sources, making an impact on life at home—which was constantly affected by the flow and flurry of this project.

Throughout the process I've been a wife and mother. The lure of field production is strong, but it exacts a penalty in private life. Three weeks at a time away from home is my maximum because, as far as I'm concerned, my eleven- and nine-year-old daughters need their mother present. This principle was reaffirmed regularly as I explored the values and priorities of Muslim family life for the documentary. My own desire to be home with my two daughters, to see to their education and excellence, was reinvigorated and validated. My stand on dressing appropriately and not intentionally attracting the attention of the opposite sex also finds support in Islam. (No belly shirts and hip huggers for my girls!) At the same time, a mother's role in a Muslim family is not restricted to the home. She should use her talents professionally, and what she earns is her own. I see it's essential that I do this work because of the unique background I bring to it. I am also a role model, as my mother, a teacher, was and is to me.

It is important for my children to be aware of this struggle for fairness, accuracy, and respect. Reporters can reinforce respect for our common diversity, or they can promote fear and distrust. We can play a mighty role in helping stabilize our world and building understanding among its inhabitants, or we can perpetuate indifference. Communication is now accomplished at the touch of a keypad, and journalists easily travel to far off places to see how others live. There is every opportunity for continued, penetrating, and humanizing coverage of other cultures, religions, and people of faith. I am certain that this kind of reporting is essential if we are ever to defuse present dangers and resolve today's tensions with grace.

Yesterday

~Barbara Nimri Aziz (September 12, 2001)

Every Tuesday morning I leave home 200 kilometers from New York City to make my way out of the hills where I live and to drive to the radio station in Manhattan where I work to broadcast my two weekly programs. Listening into my car radio at 9 a.m., 60 kilometers from the city, I heard the reports of the catastrophic event in the city. I pulled off the road weeping uncontrollably. That lasted a few moments. Shaking, I decided nevertheless to continue toward the city even though radio bulletins announced that all bridges and tunnels into Manhattan were closed. Using my cell phone, I called into my radio station; all lines were cut. (The station is just half a kilometer from the World Trade Center where building #7 houses the phone exchange, including ours.) I did not expect the office to be in danger. Tuning into the station on my car radio, I heard the voices of my colleagues doing a fine job. I was sorry I could not get into the city to be with them, helping our stunned public through this, with them through the shock, doing what journalists must do at such a time.

I drove on, and at thirty kilometers from Manhattan, climbing to a crest on the six-lane highway from which one can see beyond the treetops far off the stunning skyline of Manhattan. It is always breathtaking to see the metropolis from that point and identify its architectural highlights. It was a clear morning, but yesterday, reaching that point, I could no longer see the distinctive two towers at the bottom of Manhattan Island. What I saw was an enormous cloud of smoke sitting over the area. I began to weep again, driving on still. I finally stopped at the home of friends fifteen more kilometers down the highway and joined them watching television. The various news channels repeatedly replayed the crash of the plane into this enormous building, then the crumbling of the towers. Attempts to phone into the station and various offices and homes in NY city were futile. Cell phones were not functioning. Finally I got through to my sister, then to two of my scheduled guests, Sami al-Arian in Tampa, and Fadwa el-Guindi at the UN. (Of course the program would be postponed.)

As I watched the spectacular (a spectacle indeed, so crushing—you have all seen them) TV shots of the crash and the tumbling buildings, I felt sickened. We viewed the cinema-like scenario on TV over and over, and I knew that inside that inferno and fuming rubble were thousands of lives being incinerated. Like all of you, I wanted it to be just a film, just a film.

Weekly, I pass through the World Trade Center, usually exiting the subway that ends there, strolling through the busy mezzanine (now a mass tomb) and out to the street to walk to the station. Those two towers are—were—so massive; I have always been aware of their immensity. They spread over many large blocks across the city pavement and tower above the area, dwarfing everything around, even the 19-story building where I work.

Today, Wednesday, our own radio station shut down along with other communications centers in lower Manhattan whose phone lines are connected to the main transmission center in the complex. Whether my colleagues were evacuated or our transmitter stopped, I did not know.

My thoughts quickly shift from the dead and dying (there will be time for them) to the future implications of this catastrophe—first for Arabs and Muslim-Americans should it be proved that the criminals were from Arab/Muslim origin, and then for all of us in this country. Why? Not because of more terror attacks here, but because of the expansion of intelligence activity within the country that is inevitable. After earlier, less horrific incidents, Congress hastily passed anti-terrorism laws that severely cut back on our civil rights. Most citizens were unaware of these changes at the time, since the immediate target of the laws was local Muslims and Arabs. But such laws apply to all, here and abroad, and they greatly expand the power of our intelligence agencies and cut back citizens' civil liberties.

I have spoken to few people in the past 30 hrs. When I do, I find myself arguing with them even though we are all grieving and in solidarity. We all know so little, really. We (the public) are all afraid. We are all speculating and grieving inside, and afraid for our future (yes, the future of this disneyland of democracy and stuff we strive to possess, stuff that we take so for granted, for ourselves). I think many of us are very angry, feeling very vulnerable, and this is why I think I am arguing with whomever I speak to. As soon as I can, I end these discussions and turn to be alone, with my ear on one radio station or another, listless, not knowing what to think. Linked with all this is my anger at the much lauded surveillance intelligence systems that are supposed to protect this country—not me but my American investments and toys.

Surely this tragedy is a huge intelligence and military blunder by our own government. We (and the world) pay heavily for such protections through funding surveillance and weaponry machinery and by relinquishing our rights. With all its bravado and secret budget, our intelligence people could not prevent this! And now, in that failure, they will lash out at many many suspects, here and abroad.

It is amazing, as I hear news of suspects being identified, how swiftly the authorities have now zeroed in on the possibilities and how much information they have gathered about the criminals who flew those planes. But it's after the fact. How swift they are now.

While I personally am "safe," I wonder if my personal and professional mission is safe. For thirteen years, against many obstacles and with considerable risk and investments as a journalist, I have lobbied against sanctions and devoted myself and all my skills to fighting stereotypes and educating the U.S. public about our Arab culture, people, and Islam to help people understand our dreams, our accomplishments, and our rights. This hard work could be all wiped out, just as our community work and education efforts were wiped out by the Gulf War in 1991.

It is still possible that emerging facts focusing on Arab/Muslim perpetrators of these awful crimes turn out to be wrong. It may not matter. Because in the end, whoever did this horrible crime, our government has to change its policy toward the world's peoples and has to reverse its own acts, which devastate the lives of millions if not billions across the world.

I try to be optimistic by thinking that underneath, behind the militant posturing and threats, the leadership of this nation will reflect and will reconsider their own barbarous military policies across the world, and will change.

Will our experience of fleeing threat in the streets, of feeling uncertain about our future, of searching for the dead and watching so many die, finally connect us to so many others around the world for whom these are daily fears and events and feelings?

Are You O.K.?

~Barbara Nimri Aziz (March 20, 2003)

Ron called me in Amman from the U.S. not long after I had arrived in from Baghdad. "Are you OK?"

It had been a fourteen-hour journey across the desert and an unexpectedly lonely one. I needed to sleep.

Jordan had closed its border to fleeing Iraqis a week earlier. Magdy, a Palestinian dealer who lived in Baghdad, was in a panic and initially planned to join me in a convoy. He was to bring his son and girlfriend. Abu Amar's family and I were to share a car. In the last hours of the last days, I managed to obtain an entry permit to Jordan for the family of four Iraqis. Under pressure from desperate friends, I remembered ex-minister Sayed. His nephew was a high official in the Jordanian Home Office. Before that, I had phoned Dara in Amman; she too had connections. But, she admitted, she had failed to secure passage for any of her friends in the preceding days. By nightfall, Sayed's nephew came through. Jordanian authorities, he told me, were not happy about Umar, who at 22 posed a threat if he decided to join an Iraqi revolutionary group in Jordan. Still they sent us a fax permitting Umar, his father, and two younger children, Sara and Ali, to enter. The permit was awaiting us at the border. Um Umar had refused to leave. She would stay behind in Baghdad with their two youngest children… and 22 million other Iraqis.

We would travel together and stay together, all the way. I went to Abu Umar's house with the car to collect him and three children. When I arrived, while Um Umar served me tea, she said, "We are going to stay here—together." She seemed content, not unhappy. I could see, however, that the children were forlorn. They didn't know what they wanted to do, and they were perplexed by their parents' uncertainty.

So I left—alone. Magdy and his party postponed. Separated from his wife, he had been certain she would allow him to escape with their five-year-old boy, young Saad. But she proved reluctant to give the boy up and it would take him another 24 hours to convince her.

On the highway west, there were almost no other travelers. Any my driver, Faisel, and I saw were fleeing toward Syria and would disappear into the night once they reached the fork that would take them northeast.

Leaving Baghdad, we noted long lines of cars and pickups at petrol pumps. Besides stocking up on bottled water, Iraqis were filling cans with gas. They remembered the last war. We too needed gas—for the drive across the desert. Two pumps where we stopped had sold out. We drove on, with enough fuel for only 100 miles. At Falluja our tank was almost empty. No gas at the single pump there. I was annoyed at Faisel for leaving Baghdad without a full tank. But it was no use complaining. We had barely a gallon of gas, he said sullenly. Even if we turned back, we could not reach Baghdad. The border was anther 350 miles. He purchased an empty 5 gallon plastic tank and a length of plastic hosing and pulled back on the empty highway. It was 2 A.M. The desert night had turned very cold. A huge trailer truck passed us and rolled on. Faisel sat in the car with me. Only after another 20 minutes, we saw the lights of a vehicle approaching from behind us. Faisel jumped onto the road and waved the empty tank. It passed with a roar into the black night; then we saw its red break light. It backed up and stopped in front of us. The driver was going to Syria, closer than the Jordan border. He could spare a few gallons. He tried to cheer up Faisel and helped him drain five gallons from his tank, then pour it into our Chevrolet van.

We drove on and did the same thing a hundred and forty miles later, finally limping into the Trebil customs depot. There were no other travelers leaving Iraq. No one was entering. It was 4:30 A.M. The Iraqi customs officers were unusually quiet, yet insisted on all the procedures.

At the edge of the no-man's land between the two border crossings, an Iraqi woman and two teen daughters sat on the stone curb of the customs house. They had been refused entry to Jordan and were waiting for a lift east, back to Baghdad.

"Are you OK?" repeated Ron on the line from New Jersey. His voice was shaking. I had slept for half a day and woke to learn that, 14 hours behind me, Magdy had arrived with his little boy and his girlfriend. He had to pay triple what I did for my taxi. They too were delayed by gas shortages. Their driver had given a lift to an Iraqi engineer wanting to escape, and who eventually jumped ship some 50 kilometers before the Jordan border. A few other journalists had just made it to the frontier.

Phone contact to Iraq was now impossible. Ron's voice came through from New Jersey over the international line. The question seemed so simple. It was hard for me to focus.

"Am I OK?" having left behind a nation, terrorized by the threat of war for months, not knowing who their enemy would be.

"Am I OK?" having failed to talk at least one family into fleeing, using the coveted entry permits I had obtained for them, still in the envelope at the border.

"Am I OK?" hearing my friend Nisreen ask me for forgiveness for any slight or hurt or misdeed she may have committed against me. She wanted to face death with all her sins cleansed. For the past two days she had been phoning friends all over Baghdad, cleansing herself like this, often praying. Her 19-year-old son, a boy she needed to protect her, was weeping beside her. He hardly understood.

"Am I OK?" leaving a country whose freedom from sanctions I had fought for over the last decade—words I had struggled to transmit to Americans readers and listeners.

"Am I OK?" a journalist without a cell phone. I knew as soon as the invasion began that phone lines into and out of Iraq would be cut. What could I have done there without a phone to transmit my observations? And what could I have observed, under curfew, without being able to reach even my Iraqi friends on whom I relied for comfort and trust as well as information. In the last hours in their panic, Iraqi security had imposed more restrictions on foreigners. I was a person who depended on my agility and flexibility to move within the city. Without that, I could do nothing. Then, when the American tanks arrived in Baghdad, it would surely be even more difficult to move around. Schools were already shut. Families I knew were too frightened to host a foreigner. And each had their hands full with their indecision and their immediate needs. I would be of no help to anyone. I could not even volunteer to help at a hospital.

At least I knew a few freelance journalists who had cell phones. Then there were the many Arab journalists with Abu Dabi TV, LBC, Al-Jazeera, and Al-Arabiyya. They would tell the other side of the war about to ignite.

part four
RELIGIOUS DISCOURSES

Muslim Women's Rights in the Global Village: Challenges and Opportunities

~Azizah al-Hibri

Introduction

In this age of information technology that shrank our world into a global village, it is fair to ask how this recent development has impacted Muslim women's rights across the world. Having just traveled through nine Muslim countries, ranging from Pakistan and Bangladesh to the Gulf States, Egypt, Syria, and Lebanon, I would answer that it is leading, slowly but surely, to reassessment and change.

Attempts to accelerate the pace of this change, however, without full understanding of its complex topology, and the deep-rooted commitment by most Muslim women to spiritual and cultural authenticity, could halt or even reverse this process at great cost to women particularly and Muslim societies as a whole. Hence the challenges and opportunities.

Pious Muslim women are generally bewildered by the laws and judicial systems of their societies, which are supposed to be Islamic. It is well understood that the hallmark of Islam is justice. Yet Muslim societies have been dispensing injustices to women in the name of Islam. Some women seeking divorce in Islamic courts have been trapped within the system for years. On the other hand, divorce and remarriage have been rendered much easier for men. Also, various *Shari'ah* (Islamic law) protections for women in case of an unhappy marriage, divorce, or custody have been ignored even by the women's own families. While Western feminists have been focusing on such issues as the veil and the perceived gender discrimination in the laws of inheritance, Muslim women I spoke to did not regard these issues as important. They were more interested in reexamining family law and in the proper application of all Islamic laws, including the laws of inheritance as they stand. In short, Muslim women want more understanding of and adherence to Islamic principles. They appear to believe that existing laws and practices are not conducive to a happy home life or a just society. Surprisingly, Muslim women have the support of many Muslim male jurists who share their concerns.

Several factors have forced Muslims to reassess the status quo. The colonization experience, wars, Western education, and Western modes of communication have been primary among these factors. Colonization exposed the soft underbelly of the indigenous systems of governance while at the same time challenging and marginalizing the Muslim individual's religious beliefs and cultural values. Wars dislodged established social structures, especially those relating to the family. Finally, through the twin lenses of Western education and modes of communication such as satellite television and the Internet, Muslim men and women are experiencing instantaneously, though vicariously, the post-colonial Western worldview and Western ways of life. Generally, they like a good part of what they see, such as democratic governance, freedom of speech, independent women, and comfortable, technologically advanced societies. There are other things, however, they decidedly do not like, such as sexual permissiveness, the accelerating divorce rate, growing violence in society, especially among the youth, and the treatment of the elderly.

Consequently, many Muslims, male and female, are struggling today with the following questions: How do they introduce progress into their societies while at the same time protecting their deep-seated spiritual beliefs and cultural identities, two valuable foundations that colonialism tried unsuccessfully to destroy? How can they benefit from the Western experience, including its recognition of the legitimate rights of women, without inadvertently destroying their highly valued familial ties? In this context, the experience of those North American Muslims who have successfully integrated their religious beliefs and ethnic heritage with the American and Canadian ways of life becomes very valuable. It is a living proof of the fact that Islam is not merely an "Oriental" religion but a world religion which is capable of meeting the needs of Muslims in all historical eras and all geographical locations.

The Role of North American Muslims

For this reason, beginning a discussion about Muslim women's rights in the Global Village by offering a North American Muslim perspective is neither irrelevant nor insignificant. In fact, my audiences in the various Muslim countries were very interested in my perspective. Once they recognized my serious spiritual commitment and jurisprudential knowledge of the topic, they wanted further information about women's rights in Islam. There is, however, one drawback when a North American Muslim speaks. While non-American Muslim women and men may like my jurisprudential views on women's rights and welcome them, some may view them as exclusively suitable to the circumstances of North American Muslim women. On the other hand, others may be encouraged by them, perhaps as ushering in a new way of organizing their society that may conflict with some outmoded aspects of their culture but not with their religious beliefs. Such views would offer a fulcrum for change in the Muslim world.

For the sake of this second group, and for the sake of American and Canadian Muslims who have asked me repeatedly about Muslim women's rights, I shall focus in this article on those women's issues that are most important for the Muslim community. In drawing my conclusions, I shall rely mainly on basic and traditional Islamic sources to show that problematic jurisprudence was often the result of a misunderstanding or misapplication of the Qur'anic text resulting from cultural distortions or patriarchal bias. In preparation for this discussion, we need first to lay the foundation for understanding Islamic jurisprudence and its relation to culture.

The Relation of Religion to Culture

The distinction between (and relationship of) culture and religion is critical for understanding Islamic jurisprudence. Most importantly, the Qur'an is the revealed Word of God, whereas culture is human fabrication. So, while a Muslim is bound by every letter, word, and phrase in the Qur'an, she is not bound similarly by her cultural values. For example, a Muslim may reject a particular cultural custom or value, yet remain part of that culture. She cannot, however, reject even a single word in the Qur'an and continue calling herself a Muslim. It is that simple and clear for Muslims. Consequently, cultural assumptions and values that masquerade as religious ones are insidious insofar as they mislead Muslims into believing that they have divine origins, thus denying Muslims the right to assess them critically, or even reject them. Some of the major misleading cultural assumptions relate to issues of democracy and women's rights. The two issues incidentally are not unrelated.

Cultural assumptions and customs have often been introduced legitimately into the Islamic legal system. The Qur'an celebrates ethnic, racial, and other forms of diversity; and the *hadith* (reported words of the Prophet) emphasizes the equality of all human beings. For this reason, jurists have encouraged various cultures to retain their cultural identity by including their customs in their legal systems. The only condition for such inclusion was that these customs be consistent with the basic tenets of Islam itself. In case of inconsistency, the cultural customs must be rejected. This approach permitted a variety of Islamic civilizations to blossom, each with its own cultural heritage but all sharing the same basic religious law. Unfortunately, however, some customs that conflicted with Islamic tenets increasingly found their way into the laws of various Muslim countries. Even today, many countries that claim to be following Islamic law often use religion to justify repugnant laws that are really based on custom. Because such justifications are offered in Muslim societies whose religious education has mostly likely suffered in the last century, Muslims are often unable to discern the cultural roots of objectionable laws and their conflict with Islam. As a result, devout Muslims hesitate to criticize any part of the law. In other words, confusion as to the religious character of some laws has effectively resulted in silencing important critical voices and keeping society bound by repugnant customs mistaken for religious injunctions.

It is furthermore important to understand that Islamic laws as they relate to *mu'amalat* (dealings among people) often reflect differences of jurisprudential opinion among major Muslim scholars. These differences have many roots. Allowing custom into the legal system is only one of them. Another root derives from the right to freedom of conscience, which is guaranteed in the Qur'an itself. For this reason, it is established in traditional Islamic jurisprudence that scholars have the right to engage in their own *ijtihad* (jurisprudential interpretation) to develop laws that are best suited to their jurisdiction and era. That *ijtihad* is then reflected in the legal system of the country.

Unfortunately, however, several factors have combined throughout history to narrow the scope of *ijtihad* and limit freedom of thought. As a result, many schools of thought disappeared and no new ones replaced them. Furthermore, scholars continued to adhere to established schools of thought even when these were no longer best suited to their societies. Only recently, for example, did Morocco revise its personal status code to eliminate a provision allowing the father to force his *bikr* (virgin) daughter into marriage. The provision derived from the Maliki tradition and represented an obsolete cultural interpretation of the parental relationship, yet it remained as part of the law for a very long time. A closer look at the Maliki interpretation would have revealed its inconsistency with the *hadith* that requires the consent (or permission) of a *bikr* for the validity of her marriage. Such inconsistencies were often overlooked by earlier jurists who were caught up in their own cultural perspectives. As these perspectives become outmoded, it becomes important to expose and eliminate them.

It is not possible, however, to critically assess Islamic law without a proper Islamic education. Politics, unfortunately, has played a major role in denying the average Muslim a good religious education. This denial, in part a colonialist legacy, helped political regimes confuse the masses about what is in the Qur'an or what the Qur'an actually says. Such confusion did critical damage in areas of Islamic law relating to issues of governance and democracy. Recognizing their responsibility toward God and Muslims, jurists made repeated attempts to clarify Islamic law on these matters, as they struggled to keep political influence out of the mosque. But authoritarian rulers quashed these efforts and punished those leaders who stood in their way. Islamic history is littered with stories of the torture or jailing of various highly distinguished jurists whose crime was that of refusing to echo the views of the political ruler and shroud them with religious legitimacy. This state of affairs continues until this day, a fact which does not bode well for freedom of thought or belief in these countries. How can Muslim women begin discussing their rights when Muslim men and women cannot even speak freely?

Basic Introduction to Islam

To understand Islamic law, one must start with the basic principles of Islam. The primary source of all Islamic law is the Qur'an. It is supplemented by the *hadith*. Other important sources are those of *ijma'* (consensus) and *ijtihad* which is based on rules of logic as well as on religious text. It is important to note that Islam has no clergy, nor does it have an ecclesiastic structure. Each individual has direct access to the Qur'an and *hadith* and is in principle entitled to engage in *ijtihad*, so long as she has the requisite knowledge. Thus not only countries but also individuals are entitled to their own jurisprudential choices.

This fundamental right of Muslims to freedom of jurisprudential choice and to unmediated access to the Qur'an and *hadith*, combined with Islam's respect for local custom, makes it clear that North American Muslims are not bound by the cultural preferences of Muslims in other countries nor by their jurisprudential choices. We live in and are part of North American cultures that also celebrate diversity. We are free to retain from our ethnic heritage these elements that continue to be viable and useful in our new society. But we are fully bound by our religious beliefs. We cannot be selective among them. We are entitled, however, to interpret Divine Will in ways that are best suited for our own jurisdiction and era. Of course, such interpretations do not apply to the *thawabit* of Islam, i.e. to matters that are fixed, clear, and fundamental, such as the unicity of God.

The fact that our governments espouse democratic principles and do not stifle our freedom of expression facilitates our efforts. North American Muslims are free to engage vigorously in the time-honored tradition of *ijtihad* in order to authentically define their own jurisprudence. Unlike their brothers and sisters abroad, they do not have to be concerned about either political censorship or retribution.

In the matter of Muslim women's rights, North American Muslim women are not bound by the patriarchal assumptions of other cultures. These assumptions have been rejected for the most part in our societies. We are only bound by the Qur'an, as illuminated by reliable *hadith* and what it says about women and their rights. Furthermore, in discovering what the Qur'an says, we are not bound by the patriarchal aspects of interpretations offered by earlier jurists. These aspects reveal themselves as patriarchal when the jurist incorporates into his logic patriarchal assumptions not present in the Qur'anic verse itself, such as the assumption that women are emotional and irrational.

In the United States and Canada, many of our Muslim women are capable professionals whose mere existence presents a counterexample to these patriarchal assumptions. Many Muslim women in other countries have made similar gains, but are being hindered in their progress by patriarchal forces in the name of Islam. They are also being hindered from rebutting patriarchal claims by an authoritarian structure of governance. For example, every Afghani man and woman I spoke to during my travels is fully aware that getting an education is the duty of each Muslim male and female. Yet the Taliban forces have managed to impose a minimalist interpretation and a patriarchal educational policy through sheer force.

Because of the various obstacles facing Muslim women abroad, they tend to be quite supportive of the serious efforts by North American Muslim women to rid Islamic law of patriarchal cultural influences. In the rest of this article, I shall present my views on Islamic law as it relates to various issues of importance to women. These views are all based on the Qur'an itself; they also rely in part on the *hadith* and on traditional juristic sources.

The Qur'anic View of Women

Basic Equality

As an American Muslim woman unburdened by patriarchal assumptions, I have a distinct advantage over earlier interpreters when I study the Qur'an: I can read it with fresh, liberated eyes. Reading the Qur'an, I discover that it has only one creation story. The Qur'an states repeatedly, for emphasis, that both the male and the female were created from the same *nafs*. Consequently, there is no hierarchy, even a temporal one, in gender creation. In the Qur'an, the fall of Adam is not blamed on Eve. Rather, both were tempted by Satan and sinned in the pursuit of power and eternal life. Furthermore, God forgave humanity after the fall. There is no continuing burden of the original sin. Men and women are responsible toward God for their own mortal choices. They are both judged by the same standards; they also have the same rights, duties, and obligations in matters of *ibadat* (worship). There are some differences between them in the realm of *mu'amalat* (dealings), which regulates civil matters. These will be addressed later. In short, a Muslim woman is as complete a spiritual being as the male. She is as entitled as he is to read and interpret the Qur'an and to live a full pious life.

Legal and Financial Rights

In the realm of *mu'amalat*, the Muslim woman is an independent legal entity, not lost through marriage. A Muslim woman retains her own name after marriage. She also retains her financial independence. She can own property in her own right whether she is married or single, and no one, not even her husband, may access her funds or properties, or demand any form of financial support from her. Any money or property of her own that the wife gives her husband, even if she is richer than he, is regarded as a loan unless she expressly specifies otherwise. Islamic law, however, differentiates between the financial rights and obligations of the two genders. The male, while also financially independent, has additional financial responsibilities. He must support the women in his family regardless of their financial condition, unless there is a financially able male relative who is closer to them. For example, a father is responsible for the support of his daughter, regardless of her age, but if the woman marries, that responsibility is transferred to her husband. The logic of these differences in obligations may lie in the fact that the Qur'an is simply providing women with added security in a difficult patriarchal world. Put into today's legal language, the Qur'an engages in affirmative action with respect to women.

Right to Sadaq

The Qur'an also gives the woman additional opportunities to accumulate wealth. For example, upon marriage she has the right to expect a gift from her husband, which could range from teaching her a few verses from the Qur'an (if she does not know them already) to a few silver coins to an immense fortune, depending on the parties' mutual agreement. This is referred to as the *sadaq* or *mahr* of the woman, sometimes erroneously described as "bride price." The *sadaq* signifies the willingness of the man to undertake the responsibilities of marriage. The woman has the option of asking for the full amount of the *sadaq* (or designated property) in advance, or of deferring part of it to become due at a specified later time, or upon such event as death or divorce. In the case of death, *sadaq* becomes a senior debt of the deceased husband's estate to be satisfied ahead of all other debts. Therefore, the *sadaq* is at times more valuable than the wife's inheritance from her husband when the estate is overburdened by debt.

In the case of divorce, the *sadaq* offers the woman a clearly defined property or amount of money she could rely upon after the divorce, without need for further negotiations. Whereas some rich women tend to settle for a symbolic *sadaq*, many women view it as their security net in case of death or divorce. Some women may prefer to take the full amount of the *sadaq* at the outset. In that event, these women are free to invest the amount of the *sadaq* in any venture they choose. They may start a business with it or even give it to charity. The husband may not touch it or any profit resulting from it.

Of course, patriarchal reality in Muslim countries is quite different from the Islamic one. Today, many fathers negotiate the amount or type of *sadaq* on behalf of their daughters. In some cultures, it is a sign of prestige for the family to settle for a symbolic *sadaq* regardless of the financial interest of the daughter. In these cases, many fathers do not adequately protect their daughters' interests. In other cultures where a substantial *sadaq* may be at stake, the father may appropriate the *sadaq* from his daughter to cover wedding expenses (which are customarily his responsibility). If he does not, the husband may "borrow" it from the wife after marriage. More commonly, some cultures pressure the wife to "waive" the deferred part of her *sadaq* altogether as a gesture of good will toward the husband. In all these cultures, the woman has become highly vulnerable financially and has lost a good measure of her God-given independence.

Right to Work

There are other ways, however, in which the Muslim woman can accumulate wealth. For example, she can work. The Qur'an states that men and women have a right to their earnings. Khadijah, the first wife of the Prophet, was a business woman and continues to serve to this day as a lofty ideal for Muslim women. Again, until recently, patriarchal laws prohibited women from entering the work field under the guise of protecting women's morality or because of women's perceived physical limitations. New economic realities have set in, however, and now many personal status codes in Muslim countries no longer prohibit women from working.

Right to Inheritance

Another source of wealth available to the Muslim woman is her inheritance. Islam guarantees for the woman a share in her relatives' inheritance specified on the basis of her degree of kinship to the deceased. The false view in the West is that Islam gives a female a share in the inheritance equal to half that given to a male. The Qur'an does specify that a *sister* inherits half of the amount her *brother* inherits, but also specifies that other females of different degrees of kinship may inherit more than other males.

Nevertheless, given the Qur'anic specification, it appears that the male sibling inherits double the amount inherited by his sister, but there is one important difference between her inheritance and his. The amount inherited by the sister is a *net* amount added to her wealth. The amount inherited by the brother is a *gross* amount from which he will have to deduct the expenses of supporting the various women, elderly men, and children in his family, one of whom may be the sister herself. As mentioned earlier, even if the sister is wealthy, she is not required to support herself. Her closest male relative has that obligation, which she may waive only if she so chooses. Consequently, the net increase in the wealth of the brother is often less than that of his sister.

These facts illustrate what Muslim scholars have known all along, namely, that inheritance laws in Islam are quite complicated and cannot be reduced to a single slogan. Patriarchy, however, has simplified the inheritance picture drastically. Many Muslim women receive no share of their inheritance at all. Some are forced by their own families to turn their inheritance over to their brothers. Worse yet, many brothers take the inheritance and disappear from the lives of their sisters who have no closer male relative obligated to support them or capable of doing so. Historically, Muslim courts prosecuted such behavior and compelled the brother to support the sister. Today, many injustices go unnoticed, and the balance of rights and obligations in the Muslim family has been severely upset.

The Qur'anic View of Gender Relationships

Basic Principles

The Qur'an states clearly and repeatedly that human beings were all created from the same *nafs*. Furthermore, it states that God created for us humans from our own *nafs* mates with whom we could find tranquility. Elsewhere, the Qur'an describes the marital relationship as one characterized by tranquility, mercy, and affection. In fact, the husband and wife are each other's "garments," that is they protect each other's privacy and cover each other's shortcomings. This view has important consequences in various areas of gender relations which will be briefly addressed below.

Nevertheless, it is often argued that the superiority of men over women was asserted in the Qur'an itself. The main verse used in this argument is the one which refers to men as "*qawwamun*" over women. The word "*qawwamun*" is a complicated old word, rich with meanings. One translation of the meaning of this verse states: "Men are the protectors and maintainers of women, because God has given the one more (strength) than the other, and because they support them from their means."

The term "*qawwamun*" in the Qur'anic verse was translated above as "*protectors and maintainers*," but traditional patriarchal interpreters (and the average Muslim man) understood the word "*qawwamun*" to refer to the superiority of men over women (mostly by virtue of their physical strength, as suggested by the above translation). Ancient Arabic dictionaries, however, include among the meanings of "*qawwamun*" those of guiding and advising. These meanings are more consistent with the general Qur'anic view of gender relations than the ones preferred by male jurists.

Properly translated, the verse recognizes a male's *qiwamah* over a woman *only if* he (1) is supporting her financially, *and* (2) has been favored by God in certain matters he is advising the woman about (and about which he knows more at that time). Otherwise, the male cannot assert his *qiwamah*, whether it is advisory or otherwise. Yet that one verse has become the hallmark of patriarchal bias, since it has been interpreted to mean that all men are superior to all women at all times. As some scholars explained, men are always in a more favorable position vis-a-vis women because of their physical strength. Furthermore, by restricting the woman to the home, society insured that women will almost always need to be supported and advised by some male. This point of view has encouraged oppressive males to move away from the Islamic ideal of marital relationships.

Housework

Because of the Qur'anic view of marital relationships, scholars viewed the marriage contract as a contract for companionship and not as a service contract. As a result, they stated that the woman is not required to clean, cook, or serve in her house. If she does these things, then she is viewed as a volunteer. Otherwise, the husband is obligated to bring her prepared food and take care of the house.

Despite these facts, in many Islamic cultures today the home is viewed as the wife's realm, and she is viewed as responsible for taking care of it and for raising the children. In fact, the Moroccan personal status code states explicitly that one of the wife's duties is the duty to "supervise" the household and manage it. In many families, this means that the wife is required by law to do the housework since she cannot afford house-help. This is contrary to the juristic views mentioned above.

Motherhood

The Qur'an views pregnancy as an arduous experience. Perhaps partially for this reason, Muslim jurists do not obligate the mother to nurse her baby, except as a last resort. Children are raised by both parents who consult each other on important matters. This fact is of course not surprising in light of the Qur'anic view of ideal marital relations. Furthermore, when the Prophet was asked by a Muslim as to whom should the latter honor most, the Prophet answered, "Your mother." The questioner then asked, "Whom should I honor most next?" The Prophet repeated the same answer. Three times did the Prophet repeat, "You mother," and only on the fourth time did he say, "Your father." He also stated that paradise is under the feet of mothers.

Despite this surprisingly modernistic view of maternal obligations, in today's Muslim societies Muslim women are obligated by social pressure if not by law to nurse their children and be the primary caretakers. Not only is this obligation contrary to tradition, but it also often affects the human development of mothers, especially with respect to education and career. Yet many men continue to emphasize the fact that mother's milk has special health benefits and that her care in the early years is crucial to the child's emotional well being. Assuming that the thesis is correct, it is not clear that either the nurse or the caregiver has to be the mother. A wet nurse would impart similar benefits. Wet nurses are readily available in many countries, but are rarely used these days because of social pressures. Yet the Prophet himself was nursed by a wet nurse. Furthermore, well-to-do families of Mecca had a tradition of sending their children to live for several years in the desert in order to teach them better Arabic and expose them to cleaner air. As a child, the Prophet himself was sent away from the city of Mecca into the desert to live with his wet nurse. He never criticized that practice. Actually, he had warm memories of the woman who raised him. These facts open the door to many scenarios of child rearing that can accommodate the special needs of both the mother and the child without unduly burdening either.

Clearly then the problem in Muslim societies is not Islam but the existing cultures. Many of these cultures continue to subscribe to *jahiliyyah* (pre-Islamic) values prohibited by Islam. The continued adherence to cultural values rejected by the Qur'an is best exemplified in the area of ethnic and racial differences as these relate to marriage.

Marriage and Ethnic Differences

Not only does the Qur'an teach that all humans were created from the same *nafs*, but it also teaches that human ethnic and racial differences were purposely created by God so that we would [have an impetus to] get to know each other (enjoy each other's company). The Qur'an adds, however, that the closest to God in God's sight are those who are most pious. In other words, diversity is a divine blessing, which we should celebrate rather than fear or loathe. Furthermore, God judges us solely in terms of our piety, not the color of our skin.

Still some schools of thought continue to require that a prospective husband be of the same ethnic background and social status as the prospective wife, that his profession, financial status, and lineage be suitable to hers or else the father may prevent or void the marriage.

The Structure of the Family

Some personal status codes in Muslim countries designate the husband as the head of the household, require the wife to obey him, or both. It used to be in Egypt that if the wife left her marital home, the police could return her to "the house of obedience" by order of the court. While the forced return to the house is now gone, the concept of obedience remains the centerpiece of the code. For example, if the wife "disobeys," she may be denied maintenance. That is a serious matter for financially vulnerable individuals.

Conclusion

In short, patriarchal bias inherited by Muslims from their cultures survived the clear injunctions of the Qur'an to the contrary. It prevented interpreters from seeing the simple truths of the Qur'an and seriously delayed the advent of the ideal Muslim family and society. Of course, these biases do not surprise our Creator. The Qur'an in fact takes into account the depth of the entrenchment of certain cultural beliefs and customs by adopting a philosophy of gradualism with respect to social change. Therefore, to understand the Qur'an properly, we need to understand its underlying philosophy of gradual change.

The Qur'anic Philosophy of Change

Basic Rationale

The Qur'anic philosophy of gradualism is predicated upon the fact that fundamental changes in human consciousness do not usually occur overnight. Instead, they require a period of individual or even social gestation. For this reason, the Qur'an uses a gradual approach to change entrenched customs, beliefs, and practices, except in fundamental matters, such as the belief in the unicity of God and the prophethood of Muhammad (SAW). Obviously, absent these fundamental beliefs, the Qur'anic message would not carry its proper divine weight.

The Qur'an flatly prohibits behavior which conflicts with fundamental moral principles. For example, it prohibits murder, and more specifically, female infanticide. The gradualist philosophy of change was applied to lesser though quite important matters. The best known example relates to the prohibition against drinking wine in a society which was used to drinking; it was imposed in stages. A less-known example comes from the area of constitutional law.

The Qur'an specified in a few verses only the fundamental constitutional characteristics of an Islamic state, such as *bay'a* (voting) and *shurah* (deliberation). It left it up to the Islamic societies themselves to flesh out this basic constitutional structure in accordance with their varying levels of social consciousness and political and constitutional maturity. The disparate results are evident across the Muslim world.

But the Qur'an did not recognize only societal variations in levels of consciousness and development, it also recognized individual differences. For this reason, its philosophy of gradual change applied to individuals as well. This is most evident in the area of ethics.

The Qur'an describes various actions and words as "good" and others as "better." This approach recognizes that not all humans are capable of the same understanding or behavior. For example, in the area of criminal law, some Muslims may insist on the rule of "an eye for an eye" in determining the punishment of a criminal. The Qur'an does indeed introduce this standard of justice. But, it continues to say repeatedly, that it is better to forgive, and asks: How could we mortals expect forgiveness in the afterlife, when we are so unforgiving in this life? In other words, one could insist on one's right to punish a perpetrator of a crime, but it is better to transcend this mode of thinking, if one can, and forgive. Clearly then, there are various levels of being a good Muslim; some of which are better than others. The better ones tend to require higher consciousness, deeper moral insights, and greater tolerance of human frailty.

In addressing the patriarchal oppression of women and other groups, the Qur'an utilizes the gradualist approach to change in both the societal and individual arenas.

Addressing the Oppression of Women

The Qur'an and the Prophet repeatedly mention slaves and women, exhorting Muslims to treat them well. In his last speech, *Khutbat al-Wadaa'*, the Prophet himself analogized the status of women to that of powerless slaves, beseeching the male audience to treat them kindly. Unfortunately, given their patriarchal blinders, many Muslims perceived such prescriptive statements as sanctioning the underlying social conditions themselves. This fallacious reasoning was uncritically validated by existing social prejudices and resulted in centuries of misinterpretation and oppression. More importantly, it misunderstood and thus misconstrued the basic Qur'anic philosophy of gradualism by perpetrating the *status quo* instead of trying to raise consciousness. So it took over a thousand years in some Muslim societies to prohibit slavery. We should not wait another thousand years to recognize the rights of women in Islam.

It is important to note, however, that while some Muslim societies and individuals misunderstood the full force of the Qur'anic message, others with a higher level of consciousness did not. For example, while in the past some Muslims kept slaves, arguing that slavery must be acceptable since it was referred to in the Qur'an, others understood the ideal of Islam and freed their slaves to gain favor in God's eyes. It is also for this reason that, while some Muslims continue to engage in polygamy, many pious male scholars have refused to marry more than one woman for fear of violating God's express Qur'anic warning that polygamous men *will be* guilty of injustice.

Having raised the issue of polygamy, I must now address it and discuss the Qur'anic verse referring to it. It is a question of major concern for many Muslim women, even in North America. I shall then turn to another issue of concern to our community, namely that of wife abuse.

Polygamy and Its Cultural Entrenchment

The Qur'an was revealed to a culture steeped in polygamy. In *Jahiliyyah*, men married more than a hundred women at a time. It was therefore unrealistic, given human nature, to prohibit polygamous behavior abruptly. The Islamic approach to this situation as in other matters was to limit the practice severely, designate avenues for ending it, and provide a prescription/description of the ideal state of affairs that excludes the practice.

The Qur'anic statement on polygamy is more complex than some scholars are willing to admit. For example, the permission to marry up to four wives is premised upon the possibility that orphan women may be oppressed. The significance of this condition has been overlooked by many scholars. Yet it clearly links the permission to marry more than one woman to a specific situation and an obsolete practice which were both in existence at the time of the Prophet. The Qur'an states that if men feared being unjust toward orphans, then these men may marry up to four wives so long as they treated them equitably and fairly. Yet the Qur'an states in the same chapter that it is not possible to be equitable and fair in these situations. Although it is not possible to understand this verse about polygamy in all its complexity without understanding fully the social practice it was revealed to avoid, one thing is nevertheless clear: The Qur'an expressly states that polygamy results in injustice. Consequently, it is not an optimal way of arranging marital relations. For this reason, some pious men abandoned polygamy in the hope of reaching a higher state of marital and human relations, namely the one described in the Qur'an. Others opted for the minimal standard, despite its questionable application to contexts broader than those referred to in the revelation.

Violence Against Women and Its Cultural Entrenchment

Another example of Qur'anic gradualism appears in the verse most often quoted to justify violence against women. It states that: "[a]s to those women on whose part you fear disloyalty and ill conduct, admonish them (first), (next) refuse to share their beds, (and last) beat them (lightly)." So let us examine this verse next, as well as the circumstances of its revelation.

The *Jahiliyyah* society was a rough desert society, plagued by tribal wars. Many *Jahiliyyah* men beat their wives. They carried this practice into Islam and were so violent that the women complained to the Prophet (SAW) about the situation. Acting on his own, the Prophet (SAW) prohibited the practice by allowing the wife the right to *qisas* (retribution). That very evening, the men complained loudly. They came to the Prophet and revisited the issue, arguing that his ruling allowed their wives to gain the upper hand.

At that point, the Prophet sought and received a revelation which reflected the Qur'anic philosophy of gradualism. The verse appeared to contradict the Prophet. The Prophet himself stated when he received the revelation that "Muhammad wanted, but God did not want (to order a flat ban on "hitting" one's wife)." As we shall see later, however, the revelation simply changed the approach prescribed by the Prophet for eradicating wife abuse. It did not authorize wife abuse. It only introduced a transitory stage for change, while preserving the Qur'anic view of ideal marital relations.

It is a well-known jurisprudential rule in Islam that "verses in the Qur'an explain each other," i.e., that the Qur'an is an integral whole and thus the full and proper meaning of any verse cannot be understood in isolation from other verses in the rest of the Qur'an. Relying on this fundamental jurisprudential principle and the principle which asserts the thorough internal consistency of the Qur'an, I now turn to a popular verse in the Qur'an that Early Muslim women at times inserted in their marriage contracts. The verse enjoins spouses to "live together in kindness or leave each other charitably" (Qur'an 2:231). Based on this and other verses in the Qur'an, Muslim jurists asserted the principle of prohibition of harm among spouses (*la dharar wala dhirar*). This principle still underlies many provisions in the modern personal status codes in Muslim countries. Additionally, a Muslim woman has the right to take her husband to court or divorce him for abusing her.

The Prophet himself repeatedly denounced spousal abuse. On one occasion, he asked "How can one of you hit his wife like an animal, then he may embrace her?" On another, he asked: "How can one of you whip his wife like a slave, and he is likely to sleep with her at the end of the day?"

The Prophet (SAW) also echoed various Qur'anic descriptions of ideal marital relations; he told the men, "The best among you, are those who are best toward their wives." He added, "and I am the best among you in that respect." This statement is significant given the emphasis

Muslims place on emulating the Prophet. He never raised his voice at home, got angry, or asked another to serve him. He cut meat, took care of children, and sewed his shoes. Yet many Muslim men today forget these important prophetic statements and examples and limit their emulation of the Prophet to the style of his dress or his grooming habits.

How do we reconcile all these facts, Qur'anic and prophetic, with the single Qur'anic verse that permits husbands to "hit" their wives? How do we reconcile the verse with the Prophet's continued insistence that husbands abstain from beating their wives? We do that by developing our insights further to gain a deeper understanding of Qur'anic meaning. This is not a quick process. In this case, I shall take a few steps along this road to illustrate my point.

The Philosophy of Gradualism and Violence Against Women

This is how the philosophy of gradualism was used in the context of wife abuse. First, the Qur'an imposed on the husband various limitations before he was permitted to resort to "hitting." He was required first to communicate with his wife. The man must advise his wife about what he thinks she did wrong. This step gives the wife the chance to respond and explain. If the misunderstanding is not resolved by communication, and the husband remains angry, he can separate himself physically from his wife for a while.

Many jurists viewed these steps as directed against the wife, first to "admonish" her, then to make her "suffer from sexual abandonment." Clearly, they miss the fundamental point. These prescribed stages are steps in anger management for an aggressive patriarchal male who is likely to use force as a first resort.

Second, the Qur'an totally excludes righteous women from the scope of "hitting." It limits the possibility of "hitting" one's wife to extreme cases in which *nushuz* is feared by the husband. According to major jurists, *nushuz* is a word that in the context of the verse appears to refer to disloyalty toward the husband, dislike, disobedience, or discord. This is a questionable interpretation, because the Prophet himself appears to have interpreted the word "*nushuz*" differently in his *Khutbat al-Wadaa'*. According to various reports, the Prophet stated in that address, "You [men] have rights against women, and they have rights against you. It is your right that they do not bring someone you dislike into your bed, or that they commit clear adultery (*fahishah mubayyina*). If they do, then God has permitted you to desert them in bed, and [then] hit them lightly. If they stop, you are obliged to maintain them." Unfortunately, some jurists have interpreted the word *fahishah mubayyana* broadly to include disobeying one's husband in less significant matters. Others, however, have maintained that it is simply adultery. We now turn to discuss this matter further, before answering the last question in this discussion, namely: "What is hitting?"

Many jurists living in patriarchal cultures broadened the definition of *fahishah mubayyana* significantly. By broadening this definition, they broadened the scope of instances in which the husband may resort to "hitting." This is against the letter and spirit of the Qur'an which states that husbands should live with their wives in kindness or leave them charitably. Nevertheless, even if we were to accept the broader definition of *fahishah mubayyina*, the man still cannot "hit" his wife as a first resort; on this fact major scholars agree. He is required to take several steps before resorting to "hitting." If all these steps fail, then the husband may fall back on his original approach of "hitting" his wife.

The Qur'anic Concept of "Hitting"

But what does "hitting" mean in this case? Many scholars have pondered over the Qur'anic permission to "hit" one's wife and its attendant circumstances. Given their deep belief in Islamic justice, they realized that they must look deeper into the Qur'an for a better understanding of this verse. So they have interpreted this passage, as they should, in light of the basic principles governing marital relations as articulated by the Qur'an and the Prophet. This approach forced them to modify their common understanding of the act of marital "hitting." As a result, these jurists issued a series of limitations redefining the act of "hitting" itself. For example, the man may not hit his wife on the face. Furthermore, any "hitting" which is injurious or leaves a mark on the woman's body is actionable as a criminal offense. Furthermore, if the husband reaches that unfortunate stage of "hitting," he may hit the wife only with something as gentle as a *miswak* (a soft small fibrous twig used as a toothbrush in the Arab Peninsula). Finally, given the Qur'anic ideal of marital relations, scholars concluded that a woman abused physically or verbally is entitled to divorce from her husband. They lowered the bar significantly on what counts as abuse. This position was developed in ancient Arabia, over fourteen hundred years ago when the world viewed beating one's wife as a right. Today, we can transcend the earlier stages of human interaction and insist on the achievable Islamic marital ideal of tranquility, affection, and mercy.

The Story of Job

An important Qur'anic precedent on the issue of domestic violence is found in the story of Job. When Job was being tested, his wife lost her faith and blasphemed. As a result, he took an oath to strike her as punishment. A dilemma was thus created: A Prophet should not engage in such violent and unworthy behavior. In addition, a Prophet may not violate his oath. The divine solution to this dilemma is expressed in a Qur'anic verse. It instructs the Prophet to satisfy his oath to discipline his wife by "striking" her with a handful of grass (or basil). The intent of this instruction was to satisfy the promise without harming the wife. In this way, Prophet Job resolved his dilemma. The Qur'anic resolution of Job's dilemma offers Muslim men a way to vent their frustrations which is consistent with *all* of the Qur'anic verses as well as the Prophetic tradition.

To summarize, the Qur'anic approach to the problem of wife abuse is two-pronged: First, it provides a harmonious view of marital relationships based on tranquility, affection, and mercy. These relations are in turn based on a view of humanity that is characterized by mutual respect, equality, and dignity. Second, it develops a graduated approach to the problem of wife abuse, which is aimed at curbing the aggressive instincts of the patriarchal male and re-channeling his anger into more productive, or less destructive, outlets. In doing so, the Qur'an takes into account the very nature of human beings and the need for "a gestation period" for them to achieve a higher stage of development and communication.

It is worth noting at this point that some jurists have already concluded in light of the totality of the Qur'anic revelation that it is better for a man not to reach the last stage of "hitting" at all. If conflict persists, another Qur'anic verse prescribes mediation. If that also fails, then the parties should leave each other "charitably."

Conclusion

In the United States and Canada, there is a sincere attempt to overcome many deeply rooted prejudices and harmful behavioral patterns, including wife abuse which has been criminalized. American and Canadian Muslims who are part of these societies have a historical opportunity to live up to the highest standards of Islam, to be the best Muslims they can be. Given our level of social consciousness and development, we have no excuse to continue abiding by standards more suitable to those of *Jahiliyyah* or other highly patriarchal cultures. That time is gone hopefully forever. Furthermore, we have a duty toward the rest of the Muslim *ummah* (community) to lead by example. If we do that successfully, other Muslims in other countries, male and female, may be moved by our insights into a faster "gestation period" to reach the Qur'anic ideal of marital relations.

Muslim Women Rule and Other Little-Known Facts

~Mohja Kahf

Muslim Women Rule

At least four Muslim-majority countries with democratic systems have elected women to the top leadership position over the last few decades. Turkey had Tansu Ciller, Pakistan, Benazir Bhutto; in Bangladesh, one woman (Khaleda Zia) succeeded another (Shaikha Haseena) as prime minister, and Indonesia, the most populous Muslim country in the world, is currently headed by a woman, Megawati Sukarnoputri. I'm not saying each of these was an excellent leader. I'm just pointing out that Muslim countries have been led by women, good, bad, and indifferent. Nor is this just a twentieth century phenomenon. Further back in history, you will find Muslim queens who ruled in Yemen, India, and the Hausa kingdom in Africa. Have I created any cognitive dissonance yet? How about if I ask: How many times has a woman been president of the U.S.? Prime minister of France, Germany, Russia, Italy? Head of the United Nations? Try none. Our U.S. Congress has the same percentage of women as there are in the parliament of—guess what country—Iran. Actually, that may not be true anymore—after their last election, Iran may have more.

Music Lovers and Others

Not that rulers are the only Muslim women worth mentioning. Sakina, a great-granddaughter of Islam's leading figure Muhammad, was a music lover and bon-vivante who hosted concerts and judged poetry slams at her home and partied so heartily that once her roof caved in from the combined weight of her talented guests. She married five times. By contrast, Rabia al-Adawiya was a solitude-loving ascetic who taught the art of divine love in ninth-century Iraq. Wallada was an urbane poet in eleventh-century Moorish Spain who died at eighty, a happily single woman surrounded by friends.

Muslim Women Own

According to traditional Islamic law, women's property belongs to them independently of husbands or any male family members. English women did not get that right until the Married Women's Property Act of 1884. Court documents show that this right was not buried, but was in fact exercised by Muslim women throughout history. For example, women in fourteenth-century Egypt built mosques and endowed schools and hospitals. Today, wealthy women in Saudi Arabia and other Gulf states continue this tradition by endowing charities and trusts. It is common to walk into a mosque in the United Arab Emirates, Kuwait, and other Gulf countries where wealth is widespread and to see a plaque or hear a story identifying the benefactors of the mosque as women.

Marriage: Free and Contractual

Islamic marriage is contractual and women can put stipulations in their marriage contract to further protect their rights. Pre-nups are standard practice. Women cannot be forced into marriage according to traditional Islamic law. This law is often "maneuvered around" in traditional social systems, overruled by other powerful forces besides religion.

Domestic Violence Banned

Islam does not encourage or even allow husbands to beat their wives. Yes, there is a verse in the Qur'an that seems to suggest so, but to misread it that way perverts the entire fabric of Islamic law and the spirit of marriage set forth elsewhere in the Qur'an. No Islamic commentator, male or female, ancient or modern, considers the verse as permitting abuse. Of course, this never stopped a wife-beater. Domestic violence is as much a problem in the Muslim community as it is in other communities.

Polygamy Discouraged

Polygamy, which was unrestrained in pre-Islamic Arabia (and by the way also among the Biblical patriarchs, who belonged to the same ancient Near Eastern heritage), was curtailed by the Qur'an. Even so, in some places women use polygamy to their advantage, creating autonomous female spaces, while in other cases, men dominate the way polygamy is practiced. Alas, far fewer Muslims have polygamy in their lives than many fine Hollywood productions would have us believe.

Gender Equality

Women and men are considered equal souls. The Qur'an's version of Eve does not have her corrupting Adam; they get the idea simultaneously and eat the fruit together. Ethical and spiritual egalitarianism is paramount in Islam. Does this even need to be said at this late date? At least, that's how it's supposed to work. On the ground, workaday Islam often turns out to be about as patriarchal as its brother Abrahamic religions, Christianity and Judaism. Religion is not the only show in town. None of the above laws, values, or concepts are necessarily the determining factor in Muslim women's lives. Religion is not the root of every feeling and practice among Muslims. Many Muslims are secular. Among those who consider themselves religious, a wide range of interpretations of Islam holds. Just as there is a spectrum of Protestant positions on gender, just as Catholics and Jews hold a range of views, the Islamic world contains multitudes, from off-the-chart fanatic Taliban on one end to very progressive Muslims on the other, with numerous kinds of reform-minded as well as traditional Muslims in between. The 1980s and 90s saw the emergence of organizations of gay and lesbian Muslims, adding to the mix.

Factors Besides Religion: Local Cultural Practice

Sometimes a local practice enhances women's rights and sometimes it works against them. Honor killings are an example of a local custom that violates traditional Islamic law and hurts women. Matrilocal marriage is a local practice in Malaysia and parts of Africa that increases women's autonomy.

Economics

Some of the underdevelopment that restricts the lives of Muslim women and their families has its roots in the global economic system. Class status, personal and family wealth or poverty, and whether one lives in a rich country or a poor one, are other economic issues that influence women's array of choices.

Politics

A woman's life can be hobbled by the same political conditions that hobble men's lives. For example, what's the point in saying, "Women don't vote in Saudi Arabia"—when men don't either?

No Such Thing as a "Muslim Woman"

This variety is why there really is no such creature as "a Muslim woman"—it's an overly general category. There are Afghani Muslim women from impoverished refugee camps, aristocratic Iranian Muslim women Shakespearean scholars, American Muslim women soccer moms, Klingon Muslim women aboard the Starship Enterprise, and so on. I myself am a Klingon.

Pseudo-Feminists Abroad

I love it when people who are not feminists and do not remotely support women's rights in our own country, where we don't even have an ERA, suddenly turn into the loudest women's rights advocates when they look with smug superiority at the Muslim world. Hello, the U.S. supported the Taliban coming into power; only a few alert people worried back then about allying with a regime that was bad for women. I guess women's rights turn into human rights concerns only when it's convenient for generating wartime public opinion.

Brass Tacks & Blue Jeans

Of course, there really is sexism among Muslims. We can start working on it together as soon as we sweep away the stereotypes about sexism among Muslims. Stereotypes cloud the air between us, make Muslims defensive, and obscure the real issues. Energy spent clearing away stereotypes over and over could be better spent getting down to brass tacks, working to clear away the problems of Muslim sexism depending on where in the world it occurs. These real problems include, for example, the poverty of economic and health resources for many third world Muslim women, the sex trade against women in southeast Asia and elsewhere, the double burden of brutal foreign occupation and homegrown patriarchy for Palestinian women, marital laws in the Gulf states that are biased against women marrying foreign nationals causing a high rate of older single women who want an honorable alternative to their single state, obscenely perverted rape laws in Pakistan, and the "glass dome" and misogynistic attitudes keeping women from leadership positions in American Muslim mosques and organizations.

These problems are not inherently more unyielding than problems related to sexism in any other group of people. Our own American misogyny (date rape, weak laws against domestic violence, glass ceilings, 79 cents for every man's dollar) just look more familiar to us, less harsh somehow, more workable. We think we can fix our own sexism with homegrown ingenuity, but we often assume that Muslim women's problems must be solved for them from abroad, all their veils replaced with blue jeans for them to be truly liberated, all different marriage practices brought into conformity with our own. Muslim women and men have a wealth of their own cultural resources to use in the struggle for women's human rights. Feminism is alive and well among Muslims and has been for some time, even when U.S. foreign policy interests don't bring a spotlight on it. It is the continued struggle of Muslim feminists (both men and women), aided by friends of any background who are willing to educate themselves beyond stereotypes, which will liberate them. Not the condescending attitude that they must be "rescued" from their heritage by cheerfully ignorant proponents of American cultural imperialism or militaristic U.S. policymakers sprouting overnight feminist principles.

Interview with Dawn *Newspaper of Pakistan Regarding the Role of Religion and Status of Women in Pakistan, Jan 2003*

~Riffat Hassan

Dr. Riffat Hassan's article in Dawn, *Pakistan's leading English-language newspaper, about interpreting the Qur'an received so many e-mails that the paper's editors conducted this interview to get Hassan's response to readers' queries. In the article, Hassan had criticized both Dr. Farhat Hashmi, a conservative who preaches a return to the veil, and Asma Jehargir, a human rights advocate, whose program for change Hassan finds too secular for Pakistan.*

Q: Many readers felt that your article reduced the real essence of your message to a mere criticism of Dr. Farhat Hashmi and Asma Jehangir. What is your response?

A: I'm not claiming that what I wrote had to be taken as a final word. I focused on these people whom I thought were in a pivotal position, and people are entitled to know what these positions are. Now, of course, [my articles were] written from my point of view and [are] subjective. But [they were] an invitation to these and other people to engage in this debate. I would like that debate to be in the public arena because it is not a personal conversation. It deals with matters which relate to the public.

Q: Why has your writing not produced a similar response from the subjects of your criticism as it did from your readers?

A: It's true in a way that there is no direct response from the other side. The large number of e-mails I received after the articles' publication showed that they were obviously written by people close to Dr. Farhat Hashmi. My critique can be called one-sided if the people I've focused on are not given the same opportunity to respond. As I've said repeatedly, it's an open invitation to dialogue. Now, it is up to Dr. Hashmi and Ms. Jehangir to step forward to answer some questions.

Q: Why is the Muslim world wary of starting an issue-related debate?

A: Partly, it has to do with intellectual decadence. We have just lost that tradition of intellectual critique we had in the first 300 years of Islam's growth. Look at Muslim Spain: That was the precursor of European renaissance.

An intellectual critique is basically about asking questions, analysing the data, and making room for discussion and dissent. Going back to the Aligarh Movement and modern renaissance of 1850 to 1950, not only in the subcontinent but also in Egypt and Turkey, we saw the reopening of all the old questions and reevaluating them. As recently as the freedom movement in the subcontinent, we had different points of view without the passing of fatwas on dissenting opinions. We had the atmosphere of debate as recently as 1930 when Iqbal died, moving on to the progressive ideas of Maulana Fazlul Rehman, the architect of the Muslim Family Laws in Pakistan. He was later hounded out of the country. The last five decades in Pakistan have seen a period of darkness.

Q: Do you think that the women's movement in Pakistan has become stagnant in the post-Zia era?

A: What Zia-ul-Haq did was so extreme that it provoked a reaction in the form of a women's movement. The Women's Action Forum was a reaction to the discriminatory laws against women. I think the role these women played at that time was heroic and historic. But then the scenario changed dramatically. Western donor agencies started funding non-religious organizations, like the Human Rights Commission of Pakistan (HRCP). The West was playing on both sides, funding the Islamic extremists as well as the non-religious.

I feel many of the women organizations don't have the vision in terms of what their goals are. Instead of being pro-active they are reactive and working in small slots. They don't see the whole canvas.

If you accept my analysis of the existence of two extremes, you will also accept that the middle is occupied by the silent majority. This is where the moderates are, this is where the progressive people are, and the place from where the answers are going to come eventually. Right now, this silent majority is in a state of paralysis and dormancy. My movement would like to focus on rousing it from this state.

Q: Was your article a reaction to the Dr. Hashmis and Asma Jehangirs of this society or was it pro-active?

A: I would not like to use the word reaction. But in some ways it was a response. A large part of my article is pro-active, which is entirely based on myself. Before talking about the other two women, I lay myself bare and talk about myself as a person so that a reader can have a fair chance to understand my perspective.

Q: In the light of numerous exegeses of the Qur'an, how can you validate your interpretation as correct?

A: My position on the Qur'an is that it is a sacred text, revealed through the agency of the archangel Gabriel to the Prophet (PBUH). So he is the recipient of the revelation. The source of the Qur'an is God. What we have received through the Prophet (PBUH) is the text. Now, that text is made up of words. Every Arabic word has a root and every root has multiple meanings. Theoretically it means that everything in the Qur'an is capable of being interpreted in many ways. It is inherent in the nature of the language because it is a Semitic language and such languages work like that.

Given this fact, the question is, how does a person do an exegesis of the Qur'an? It involves a methodology called hermeneutics, which is a science of interpretation of Scriptures. When I started doing the interpretation, I felt that the existing hermeneutics, developed by scholars, was not quite applicable to Islam because our beliefs are different. I developed my own hermeneutics and criteria. In order to know the meaning of a word, we have to see what it meant in 7th-century Hijaz, not what it means today. Then, I applied the method of philosophical consistency to interpret the different meanings of the same word used more than once in the Qur'an.

But the most important principle I developed is the "ethical criterion." That is, if you believe God is just, which to me is His essence, and the Qur'an is His word, it must reflect His justice as well. The Qur'anic text cannot be used as a means to perpetuate injustice, nor can the Qur'anic text justify injustice in any way. If a certain verse of the Qur'an is being interpreted to justify, for example, the Hadh crimes, then it is in contravention to the idea that God is just. Therefore, this interpretation can't be accepted no matter who is doing it. Besides, I have never ever stated that my interpretations are the absolute truth, are final, and have to be accepted.

Q: Keeping in view your progressive stance on Islam, the irritation of the extremists is understandable, but why are the feminists of Pakistan so critical of you?

A: Now let me just focus on Asma Jehangir. I divide Asma's work into two or three different categories. There's Asma who is a human rights activist, who has taken cases, gone to courts, and fought for women. For that I have a lot of respect for her. Our differences are ideological. I differ with Asma and other champions of human rights when they take a position that human rights and Islam are incompatible. Words like secularism, fundamentalism, and feminism change their meaning from region to region. For instance, secular in India means anti-communalist, while in Pakistan and the rest of the Muslim world it means anti-religious.

There are many paradigms, many models possible for human rights. You can make a model of human rights on secular grounds, you can make it on humanistic grounds, you can make it on Marxist grounds, and so on. They are all possible and within the realm of legitimacy. I am not saying that it is only by staying within Islam that the human rights paradigm can be created.

Theoretically, these people are not wrong. My contention with them arises when they exclude Islam in a country that is 99.9 percent Muslim. You've lost it when you begin your discourse by taking out Islam from the discourse.

The second point is that extremism feeds extremism. The more these people steer clear of Islam the more people will be drawn to it, resulting in *deeni madrassahs* and al-Huda centers. These extremisms are feeding each other. I have analyzed these feminists very closely and come to one conclusion: that they hate Islam. Any mention of Islam is anathema to them. So it is not that Dr. Hassan is against them, it is they who are hostile toward me. It is my point of view that represents the majority, not theirs. I work within the mainstream, whereas some of these organizations are funded to take an anti-Islamic stance.

Q: In your opinion, why are more people drawn toward Dr. Farhat Hashmi and not you?

A: It's a question of understanding Farhat Hashmi's strategy, where she started, and which groups did she target. She's always had the support of powerfully rich people. Why did they support her? My theory is, they wanted to use her to stem the feminist movement because, since the time of Zia-ul-Haq, it was the only movement in the country. I am also quite sure that she has the full support of the Jamaat-I-Islami. So she started by targeting rich women. Soon she had their financial support as well.

Dr. Hashmi now has the means to construct al-Huda academies everywhere, and they are now targeting students. Dr. Hashmi is going to the youth for its support. In a remote place in Bhurbhan, not even a single school exists for girls. Dr. Hashmi has established the al-Huda for girls there. They are all wearing *hijab*. Had there been a proper educational institution that might not have happened. Dr. Hashmi and her group have an excellent marketing strategy. Wherever they see [a] gap, they fill it with their ideology.

Q: Why can't your progressive ideology, which you say represents the silent majority, fill that gap?

A: I have certain disadvantages in a sense that I don't live in Pakistan. I'm an academic. I don't have anybody backing me. My life is so much formulated and dominated in its core by Iqbal who said that when you want to start a movement you have to start with few, like-minded people.

What I'm trying to advocate is a vision of Islam as a moderate and rational religion. Such a thought can only be understood by educated and aware people. If I had the opportunity and a permanent base in Pakistan, I would like to go from one college to another, starting with the progressive institutions, to talk about a progressive Islam. I'm sure the impact would be phenomenal. We just don't have the same amount of money.

Q: If the extremists can have the elite's sponsorship, why can't the progressives have it?

A: The right-wing have the support of bigoted but very, very intense people. The support is so intense that they are willing to put their money and life on it. The liberal progressive groups have wonderful discussions in their living rooms, arrange good seminars, but don't want to do anything beyond that. There is a lot of awareness in them but not the intensity to act.

Q: How can the right-wing be countered?

A: Taking the example of Allama Iqbal, the first thing he did to rouse the people was to articulate their sentiments. So articulation is required to make them realize their oppression. Like Iqbal's Shikwa and Jawab-i-Shikwa', we need to convey hard-hitting messages to intellectually challenge the majority. Iqbal tapped the disadvantaged people and appealed to their sense of deprivation, but at the same time his message was addressed to the rich and intellectually advanced people. In the present context too the same kind of direct involvement is needed. People should be made to realize that each day of inactivity is making them lose ground.

I am envisaging a movement of the urban educated people. And that movement can only become successful if we have more than one strategy. We need a core of dedicated people.

I tell you, if we had 50 such people in Pakistan we could have a revolution. Those people need not agree on details, because liberals always have dissenting views on details. But they should at least converge on one vision. Let us agree that there are certain things which are wrong. Violence is wrong. Injustice is wrong. Oppression is wrong. No matter which religion you follow or whatever your school of thought is, these things can never be justified.

Q: Just as you believe that education is every Muslim's fundamental right, no matter which exegesis is being followed, a majority of the Muslims feel the same way about the hijab. *Most of the letters we received challenged your interpretation of the* hijab. *How can you defend your interpretation of the Qur'anic verses to mean otherwise?*

A: The word *hijab* means curtain. The law of *hijab* laid down in Surah Nur applies equally to men and women: "Lower your gaze and guard your modesty." The Qur'an puts a lot of emphasis on dignity, elevating the position of human beings, calling them the children of Adam and putting them above the rest of Allah's creations.

In Surah Nur, the Qur'an has instructed that if human beings don't want to be treated and seen as sex objects, they should not act like them. It is not restricted to dress code; it includes the way you talk, walk, and how you conduct yourself in public space. The message is to be mindful of your human dignity. Of course, there is more elaboration in the context of women, but it is not gender specific. Neither is it related to age.

I'd like to refer to a verse in Surah Ehzab which incites a lot of discussion: "Prophet tell your wives and the believing women that when they step out of their homes they should wear the *jilbah* (which was a cloak not covering the face) so that they are seen as chaste women and not molested."

Now the point is that was a society in which women were molested. That was a society in which female infanticide was practiced, a society where women were bought and sold and could be inherited. So when a woman in such a society stepped outside, it was assumed that she was prey to all. The Qur'an did not order the women not to step out of home. It was not restrictive but enabling of protective legislation: "You should wear a garment so that when people see you they are able to recognize you and leave you alone." Nowadays, what you wear is not a guarantee of morality. The reason for which *jilbah* was prescribed no longer exists, which does not mean that the law of modesty does not exist. That is still the primary law, only the expression is no longer mandatory.

Q: It is believed that the Qur'anic injunctions are for all times. Do you think with the change in time the Qur'anic injunctions have also changed their meaning?

A: This question can only be treated if we pose another question which is more relevant and that is about the Qur'an itself. What is the Qur'an? How can a person see and approach it? The Qur'an is not an encyclopedia. It is not a book of history. Neither is it a book of law. It's a bit of everything. There are some ethical principles in it instructing you to act. And then there are basic values, starting from the principle of Tauheed and one God. God is the universal Creator, everybody is created equally, importance of reason, importance of education and social justice. These are some of the ethics of the Qur'an with which you can build a framework. Those ethical values are for all times and are universal principles.

A major part of the Qur'an refers to the conflicts of that time: the Prophet's (PBUH) struggle with the Meccans, his struggle in Medina, his struggle with the Jews, and other historical phases which are basically references and are not principles. They have to be read in a certain way and are meant for our instruction.

I'll give you another example from the Qur'an where it is written, "take not the unbelievers for your friends." Today, that has been turned into a principle. It is not a principle and was revealed in a certain context. How can such a principle be for all times? In several verses Allah has referred to the Ahlul Kitab and given them a lot of importance. People who pick Qur'anic verses out of context have twisted the verse. In any case, Jews and Christians are not unbelievers.

A lot of times the Qur'anic text is superimposed. For example, the Qur'an talks about *kafereen* and *munafiqeen*. If you read the translation you will find the words have been translated as Jews and Christians. That is what I'm trying to say here. It is not in the original text but has been superimposed.

In every age the Qur'an has to be reread and recontextualised.

Q: Many readers wrote in about your daughter Meher's decision to work in films as un-Islamic. As an Islamic scholar, do you not think that your daughter's decision to appear in a film is un-Islamic?

A: It is not. Mehr has not worn an indecent dress. But when she is on a set, she is performing a role. I don't think there is anything un-Islamic about it.

Q: But in the context of Islam, how can you justify acting in films?

A: Islam is not against creativity. In fact, it promotes creativity in every sense. Allah has put a lot of emphasis on aesthetics. One of His names is Jamal. Islam is not against beauty. It can be in anything like fine arts and performing arts. What it is against is exhibitionism. Mehr has also worked in the United States. She is very selective about her roles and would not accept any with nudity in it. Mehr is an extremely conservative person, but at the same time she is very professional. I honestly don't think there is anything wrong in what she is doing.

part five
FICTION

Witness

~Farrah Qidwai

The night before we couldn't sleep from the bustling noise of the upper west side Astor Hotel and its patrons. Ali and I lay in bed and listened while the lives of those around us unfolded plumply like the petals of a flower. Babies cried, couples made love, fought, and made love again. But the next morning, it was so quiet as if those voices never existed. I woke up earlier than Ali but did not get out of bed right away. Instead I entangled my limbs with his and tried to memorize the pattern of his breathing. I would have stayed that way too if I hadn't remembered the Duane Reade plastic bag waiting for me in the bathroom. Anxiety pressed sharply down on my chest. Exhaling, I gently undid the knots our bodies had formed and slid out of bed.

In the bathroom, water dripped from the faucet of the sink while I sat on the cold closed lid of the toilet seat. My heart felt heavy from the loneliness of that sound. I breathed deeply and used my fingernails to slice through the cardboard box I found in the bag. Through the closed door, I heard Ali yawn. I knew his mannerisms so well I could imagine him clearly in the next room. While still in bed, he turned on the television and flipped through its channels. On the floor, his suitcase was packed and ready for his flight home to California later that afternoon. Airport tags from his summer travels still hung triumphantly from the suitcase handles like graduation tassels. I had spent the entire day before avoiding that bag, denying the eventual departure it signified. Time and I were not on speaking terms; I was convinced that Ali and I had been cheated during his brief visit to New York. He spent a few weeks with me after returning from a long trip to Cairo and Istanbul. I spent the entire summer without him in chilly San Francisco. With each wintry gust of wind, the streaming clouds in the sky tricked me into believing time was passing quickly when in fact it was not.

Can't think about that right now, I told myself while I spread my legs and peed onto a plastic stick. I waited there for a few minutes, holding my life in one hand, and the pregnancy test in the other, waiting for a strip of color to appear. Although I wore no watch, the seconds ticked away incessantly. I looked at myself in the mirrored wall across from me and imagined wrinkles appearing, my dark brown hair turning wiry and white. I closed my eyes and pictured a calendar with the days of my last menstrual period circled in red. My period was two weeks late. I opened my eyes and whispered a prayer, preparing to receive the final judgment when I heard Ali shouting in the next room.

"Oh my God, baby, come here!" From the urgency in his voice, I thought there was a fire in the room. I dropped the pregnancy indicator and ran into the bedroom.

Ali sat on the bed wrapped up in a white sheet watching the television. My heart was beating loudly like an angry knock at the door. "What's wrong?' I asked breathlessly. He pointed to the TV. The twin towers were burning. In slow motion, CNN played footage over and over again of an airplane flying directly into the World Trade Center. I was shaking as I sat on the bed next to Ali; my bladder felt like it might give out at any moment. Ali held my hand as we silently watched both towers engulfed in flames. Horrified, our eyes soaked in the images without blinking. I didn't understand a word coming out of the reporter's mouth; the looped images revealed their narrative with each beat of my heart. *Buildings burning. Beat. Bodies falling. Beat. My neighborhood reduced to soot and rubble. Beat. My neighborhood. Beat. My neighborhood. Beat.* My world was reduced to the Hollywood-like images on the television screen, and I forgot the suitcase on the floor, the airline ticket on the nightstand, the pregnancy test, now ruined, lying in the toilet.

"Hai Allah!" I cried out, and then thought, *Please God, let it not be a Muslim who's responsible for this.*

The cell phone calls began shortly afterwards. My mother first, crying so hysterically that for a second I thought something had happened at home. The reality of the attack still hadn't sunk in. My mother couldn't say anything after I reassured her I was fine and just sobbed spasmodically, relief releasing more tears from the well of her heart. My father said something in Urdu and took the phone from her; I wondered if a moment of tenderness could have possibly been exchanged between the two of them. Crisis has a way of making allies out of the staunchest enemies. My father cleared his throat excessively so I wouldn't hear the tears choking his words. My parents had just moved me into my graduate student apartment on William Street a month before. They couldn't understand why I wanted to move to New York in the first place; they had lived poorly as Pakistani immigrants in the city years before. I was too independent, they thought, but they gave up arguing with me. Now their worst fears were confirmed. They knew I was only a few blocks from the World Trade Center. I imagined that the familiarity of the images they saw on television just made them feel more hopeless. Fifteen hundred miles away, they watched ocean waves of smoke tearing down Fulton Street, past the electronic shop at which we bought my cheap answering machine, past the deli we had eaten at when I first moved here, past the entrance to the subway I took everyday to school.

"Behta, mere jaan, where are you?"

My father's names for me echoed in my head, *my child, my life*. I felt like crying. I couldn't tell my Muslim parents that their baby was in a hotel room with a man. I couldn't tell them that their baby might be carrying a baby of her own. My mouth was dry; words felt lodged in my throat. I started to cough violently, choking on my own regret.

"I'm in my apartment, Dad." Ali looked up at me with his eyebrows furrowed. *What?*, he mouthed, silently. Anyone else would have reassured their family that they were as far away as possible from the attack. I shrugged my shoulders under the weight of my own lie. In my parents' strained voices, their fear of losing me was palpable. I couldn't tell them the truth. I was still their little girl, their baby.

"You're in your apartment? Is it smoky? Can you breathe in there?" my father asked. I rubbed my temples with my fingers and felt my veins throbbing. My pulse beat wildly like a telegraph, but I couldn't decipher the message transmitted. I closed my eyes and tried to imagine my apartment at that moment. Was it filled with smoke? Was it covered with debris like the other buildings shown on CNN? I wondered if my home remained unscathed in the midst of the war zone lower Manhattan had suddenly become. I turned to the television for help. It didn't seem like a strange thing to do; consensus on how to feel and who to blame was already reached and being televised in bright graphics. At the bottom of the screen, beneath the blanketed buildings, a rolling message indicated that Mayor Giulliani was evacuating lower Manhattan. I took that as my cue.

"My apartment's fine, Dad. I'm fine. Don't worry. But they're evacuating us soon. I'm gonna go get a hotel room, okay? I'll call you when I get there. I gotta go."

My mother came back on the phone.

"Leila behti, I love you so much. Please be careful," she said, her words punctuated by fear. I could picture her beautiful face covered with tears, one hand clutching at the skin of her throat.

"I will Mom," I said, really listening to her for the first time.

We said *Khuda Hafiz* and then hung up. My armpits were damp with sweat. The cell immediately rang again; it was Ali's family. He rubbed his face as he talked with them. A slight stubble had blossomed beautifully along his jaw line, sharply contrasting with the light complexion of his skin. He told his mother he loved her three times before hanging up.

I called my school next and found out that my apartment building was fine—uninhabitable for a while, but not damaged.

"Can I go back tomorrow?" I asked, my voice surprisingly small.

"Are you kidding?" the receptionist huffed, "You'll be homeless for a week, at least."

Homeless.

I felt like I might throw up. For the rest of the day, the phone continued to ring as loved ones called both of us from all parts of the country. For each of my relatives, I repeated the same lie I told my parents. Growing up in a conservative Muslim household in America, I had extensive practice lying to my family. I could never have survived high school without this skill. But this was too much. I felt like I was falsifying historical documents, lying under oath. Whenever someone recited a prayer for my safety over the phone, I felt my stomach lurch. Each family member told me the same advice: "Don't go anywhere; it isn't safe for Muslims." *But I'm homeless now*, I thought. Which home was I to stay in?

Still, Ali and I didn't leave the hotel room the whole day. We opened the door only once for Abdul, the young Moroccan man from downstairs who brought up our room service. Abdul had noticed the Allah pendant I wore on a necklace the day we checked in. He had greeted me then excitedly with, "Asalaamalaikum!" His hands fluttered happily like butterfly wings as he asked us about our families. He told us about his family still in Rabat, the young wife and baby he dreamed each night of going back to. I looked at Ali then. His father had died a few years after arriving in America, when Ali was just ten years old. His mother was left to raise two children in a country in which she didn't speak the language. I thought about my own parents, whose love had unraveled under the pressure of poverty. Migration had amputated all of our families. I understood Abdul's warmth; the loneliness of this country makes immigrants and their children grasp at anything that reminds them of home. We long for small things here; a friendly face, a familiar smell, the correct pronunciation of your name. In the short visit in the hotel lobby, Pakistan, Iran, Morocco didn't seem so far away.

But when Abdul knocked on the door and brought up the well-done burgers Ali and I ordered, he was less enthusiastic. He hardly smiled. His eyes, which were light brown colored like milky tea, had dark saucers encircling them. The uniform he wore, impeccably pressed the day before, looked as if he had been sleeping in it. He handed me the food without greeting me, looking over his shoulder a few times. When I said, "Thank you, Abdul," he flinched; a brief wave of consternation dilated his eyes like a camera flash. I glanced down to the nametag on his chest that now said, "AL." I nodded sagely and remembered my mother's warning when I spoke to her earlier: "Don't tell anyone you're Muslim."

Abdul left without a word; I watched his retreating figure in the hallway before I closed the door.

Ali and I watched television all day in bed, reliving the horror of the attack every fifteen seconds as footage of the buildings burning was replayed. On MSNBC, a "Mideast expert" said that the attack was the work of "heathens, carpet baggers, a real bunch of wackos." Hearing this, I remembered watching as a child a cartoon featuring Arabs with big noses and menacing swords. An entire civilization was reduced to the grotesque and obscure. After the dark skinned villain was tarred and feathered, I remember shamefully searching my face in the mirror for any traces of his features.

CNN kept showing the same reel of footage of Palestinian kids dancing up and down, cheering for the destruction known for the first time in America. The reporter was disgusted and kept repeating how "sick" those people were. I didn't know what to believe. Starving children will cheer for anything if a cameraman gives them candy. And if those children really were cheering, how could I blame them? The death and destruction made real for most Americans through their television sets was a fact of life in the Muslim world. The connection of those deaths to the United States is only too clear: Palestinian children killed by Israeli soldiers shooting American bullets. But that carnage never gets shown on television. I guess those kids' lives don't have enough value for news stations and corporate sponsors to care. The children on the screen were so skinny. I fearfully hugged Ali close; one of the little "enemies" on the television looked a lot like a childhood photo Ali had once showed me. I carried that photo around with me, showing everyone that that's what my children would look like one day.

I groaned and leaned back in the bed, rocking my stomach softly. I barely touched my burger; the meat tasted raw and bloody. The bed was a mess: The sheets were half lying on the floor, the pillow was damp from where I left my towel earlier that morning. The linen strewn about reminded me of the hospital room my father stayed in when he had a heart attack. We had sat on the edge of his bed politely then, uncomfortable with the false family intimacy his illness had brought on. But here in the hotel room, our bed seemed like the only home Ali and I had. I slept through most of the day, sporadically but deeply, the way I fall asleep on airplanes after I've taken Dramamine. I dreamt about blood and babies. I woke up every time gasping for air. Ali sat up in bed next to me with one hand in my hair. Each time I stirred in my sleep, he would lean over and kiss my forehead, rub my back. He occasionally cursed the television, usually when some teenager asked with tears streaming down her face, "Why do they hate our freedom so much?" Ali shouted at the television, listing off statistics of different world atrocities "our freedom" was responsible for. But even this sounded half-hearted as he too grew exhausted.

We awoke the next morning to the hotel telephone ringing. In my half awake state, I was afraid that it was my parents, that they had somehow found me in this room even though it was reserved under Ali's name. I put one hand to steady the wild beating in my chest and used the other to pick up the receiver.

"Hello?" I asked scratchily, welcoming the disguise morning put in my voice.

"Good morning ma'am," an unfamiliar male voice said, "this is the front desk downstairs. Will you be checking out today?" I looked at the clock and silently groaned. It was only seven o'clock. I had wanted to stay in Ali's arms as long as I could.

"Ah, y-yes, my boyfriend has a flight to catch today. We'll be checking out." Ali lay at my side sleeping like a little boy, his face resting on his two sandwiched hands. I wanted to lean over and kiss the beautiful half moons of his closed eyelids, delicately fringed by long black eyelashes. I wanted to stay like this forever.

"The airports are still closed today ma'am." The deep voice of the receptionist jarred me out of my quiet reverie. "No one is traveling today. Will you still be staying on at the hotel?" Hope began to fill my rubbery heart, the flesh warped with stretch marks from so many sudden inflations and deflations.

"Can I call you back and let you know?"

I hung up the phone and climbed on top of Ali. I nestled my face into his neck and whispered into his ear.

"Ali, baby, wake up. The airports are closed today. We have to spend another day in the hotel." He smiled with his eyes still closed. I rolled out of bed and went into the bathroom.

On the countertop sat the cardboard box which had held my pregnancy test. I tried my best to avoid its presence in the bathroom, reaching the long way to grab at the toothpaste and toothbrush behind it. *Maybe I'm not pregnant.* When I had spoken to my sister Alia the day before, she and I went over the dates of my period together. I could hear her pencil scratching against paper while she took notes on a pad that most likely advertised birth control pills. In her calm, doctor-like manner, she assured me that I probably wasn't pregnant.

"Don't worry, Leila," she said, and for a second her voice was soft the way she spoke to her ob-gyn patients at UC San Francisco. "But don't do that shit again. I swear, you have always been so fucking irresponsible." I had nodded my head at the time as if she could see me through the phone line. She was always right about these things; it was stupid of me to have unprotected sex. But Ali had felt so good to me that night, I didn't let go of him when he wanted to go get a condom. *What are you doing?,* he asked with his eyes as his body rode mine. I just held onto him tighter until we both came. I couldn't explain why I did it. I think I wanted a part of him to stay inside of me forever, even after his bags were packed and gone.

I threw the pregnancy test box in the trash and took a shower.

Ali came into the bathroom and spoke to me over the steam of the water.

"We're checked in for another day. I changed my flight to tomorrow. But this means we have very little money left." I finished rinsing my hair and turned the shower off. As the water level in the tub slowly fell, I felt the blood in my body being drained. I had maxed out my credit card so we could stay in the hotel for the last few nights of his visit. Ali was nearly broke after all the traveling of his summer. I didn't have a job yet in New York. And I was homeless. I sat down in the empty tub and brought my knees close to my chest. Water streamed into my eyes from my hair. I didn't care; I was already crying.

"It will be okay, baby, we only have to worry about today," Ali said, wrapping a towel around me. I shook my head and resisted his embrace.

"*You* only have to worry about today. What am I gonna do the rest of the time I'm here?" I put one hand protectively on my stomach and started to panic.

Ali was quiet for a moment before he responded. "Baby, I think you should call your parents and ask if you can come home until your apartment opens up," he said, flinching a little as if he anticipated a negative response.

I had never before asked my parents this. I left Minnesota when I was eighteen and never went back. I was tired of cutting my hands from the shards of my broken family. I loved both of my parents, of course, but could not stay at home with the two of them. Every childhood memory of their fights was relived as I pictured my parents now avoiding each other politely like strangers in their own home. I didn't want to go home and hear my mother recount my father's exploits with his mistress. And what if I was pregnant? Would my mother be able to tell? I pictured what my baby might look like. Would it have Ali's eyes? I had just started graduate school; Ali was only in his second year of medical school. How could we have a family right now? I squeezed my eyes shut to stop them from overflowing with tears. My head ached from the congestion of thoughts. I hugged my body close as I realized I couldn't abort this baby, not our baby, not after everything that had just happened.

"What if I'm pregnant?" I whispered, hoping that no one, not even God would hear. Ali held me by my shoulders and looked me gently in the eye.

"We'll get another pregnancy test and deal with that when we know for sure. But for now, we have to worry about your safety and getting you home." His forehead gently creased into wrinkles. Ali had always looked so young to me, but at that moment he looked much older.

"Come on, get ready and let's enjoy our last day together," he said, helping me out of the tub.

We left the hotel and were surprised by a strong splash of sunlight. The smell in the air was acrid now; the chemical cloud had permeated all of Manhattan overnight. The street was mostly empty. We could clearly hear birds chirping in the trees above the quiet. It sounded so strange to me. *Birds can still chirp after all this?* Ali and I walked to a grocery store, silently looking at the fliers of missing people plastered over lampposts and telephone booths which had appeared overnight. The photos were bright and vibrant compared to the drab concrete and steel they were posted on. "So much life," I said sadly and thought about my belly.

When we reached the Food Emporium, our stomachs were growling loudly. In the chaos of the day before, we had only eaten one meal. Like kids, we pressed our hands against the glass that covered the hot items at the deli. We picked out a rotisserie chicken along with roasted garlic potatoes and macaroni and cheese. While Ali grabbed a couple of rolls, I picked out a few pieces of fruit that weren't bruised and a container of apple juice. Our voices echoed loudly in the nearly empty store.

At the checkout counter, a middle-aged man silently rung us up, wearing a nametag that had an American flag sticker next to the name "Bob." He had thick stubble on his double chin and watery eyes that reminded me of an undercooked fried egg. He glanced at us occasionally as he rang up our items, sneering stronger each time. When Ali gave the man his credit card to pay, American Bob studied the name on the plastic carefully.

"Ali Hussein, huh?" he grunted. "What kind of name is that?"

Ali pushed me back slightly before answering: "Persian." American Bob didn't respond. When the credit card receipt printed, he ripped it out and slammed it on the counter. Ali grabbed a pen that hung from a silver metal string and signed carefully. American Bob shoved the bag filled with food into Ali's chest.

"You know, in this country," he snarled, "we face people in the eye and don't kill 'em like a bunch of cowards." I felt the muscles in Ali's arms tensing, but I rushed him out of the store before he could educate American Bob on just how American we were.

"Can you believe that fucking guy? 'Face people in the eye.' Huh.

What does he have to say about napalm? Or the atomic bomb?" Ali asked when we left the store, pushing my hand away when I went to grab it. But I didn't respond; I wanted Ali to keep his voice down as we walked to Central Park. I felt very afraid for our safety after the American Bob incident; my father was attacked by some vengeful white men after the Oklahoma City bombing and that wasn't even committed by Muslims. I didn't want to imagine what acts of violence would be committed in the name of patriotism now.

At the park, we found a somewhat grassy spot and sat down for our brunch. My eyes started to water from the air. Ali pulled a drumstick off the chicken, buttered up a roll, and spooned out potatoes and macaroni for me onto a plastic plate. I peeled an orange and fed him from my fingers. A couple walked by with matching tracksuits and dreadlocks, listening to music bubble out of a tiny radio. I tensed my shoulders, anticipating a sneer or something worse. But they gave us a genuine, albeit tired, smile as they passed us. A Hi-Tek song came on the radio and a woman's voice soared as she sang, "Today I made up my mind, to get away, everyday I sit and pray, everyday." I looked up into the sky, expecting to see an airplane slice through a cloud and complete this movie scene. But there were no airplanes in the sky; no airplanes that flew that day.

Ali and I spent the rest of the afternoon and early evening in the park, mostly talking and people watching. Saturated sunlight lingered beautifully on his skin before it receded into night. Both of us were reluctant to return to the hotel room and start our "last evening" together. I thought about buying another pregnancy test at a drugstore, but decided to wait. I didn't want to find out right before Ali left. I wanted to enjoy our few remaining hours together. On the way home, we stopped to pick up dinner at a tiny restaurant with a giant American flag draped on the wall. Flags like that appeared overnight in different businesses throughout the city, especially in foreign-owned ones. While Ali ordered our food from the Chinese waiter, the two of them shared a laugh over a misunderstanding. In the flickering light of the fluorescent bulb, the two men laughing on different sides of the counter would have made a great photograph.

That night I could not sleep as I tried to remember every detail of the way his body felt next to mine, the way his heart beat with my own.

We checked out of the hotel the next morning. Ali had a flight to catch from Philly and my parents had arranged for me to stay with Masood Uncle, an old family friend in Queens, until I could get back into my apartment. Before we left I begged Ali to shave off his goatee. The facial hair was relatively new, something that came out of his trip and the solidarity he felt with other Persians, Turks, and Arabs during his visit. The purpose of his trip had been to feel that bond with people who looked just like him, something he never knew growing up lonely in the states. He was extremely light skinned, but with the goatee he looked very Middle Eastern. I knew how important the facial hair was to him. Growing up dark-skinned in Minnesota, I also knew how much courage it takes to look different. But I didn't want him to take any chances. I looked into Ali's handsome face and felt terrified for his safety. He was so obviously Muslim looking. How could he not run into trouble at an international airport right now?

"Without the goatee, you can almost pass for white," I pleaded with him.

But he firmly turned down my request. "I guess I picked the wrong time to stop passing."

We took the subway to the bus depot, transferring once at 42nd Street. Luckily, Ali's flight was from Philly, not New York. He didn't have to worry about LaGuardia or JFK. The bus terminals were packed with people desperate to flee New York City. A few men and women gave Ali very nasty looks. But most people looked wide-eyed and scared as they held onto their belongings. Every twenty minutes, someone would yell, "BOMBSCARE!" and we'd all run terrified to the door. People were pushing and shoving; when I reached to help an elderly woman who had fallen in the pandemonium, a police officer yelled at me to keep moving. Out on 41st Street, we felt safe momentarily away from the potential bomb in the building. But we had all been conditioned by television the nights before to expect images of planes flying into burning buildings; the open sky terrified us.

An elderly white woman gripped my shoulder and shouted, "Oh lord, help us!" She wore a checkered scarf around her hair that looked almost Palestinian. Her plea would have made sense in the West Bank, but not here. I held onto Ali's hand so tightly the rings on my fingers were cutting off my circulation. As we were rushed out by the police, I felt terrified and hoped we would all make it safely outside.

I prayed loudly, "Bismillah Ar-Rahman Ar-Raheem Al-hamdu lillahi

Rabb il-'alamin."

In the midst of the panic, an older redheaded woman heard me and sneered.

"Bitch," she said, as she continued to push and shove her way to safety.

The rising blush on my face surprised me as much as her insult. Instead of anger, shame seeped through me like urine in a bed wetted by a child. I felt self-conscious and scared in the depot until Ali got on his bus. Then all of my fear and anxiety transferred to him.

"Don't go," I begged Ali, right before he stepped on his bus. I was afraid I might not ever see him again. He hugged me close, put one hand through my hair as I sobbed into his chest.

"I have to, baby," he said softly. I looked up at him, my eyes lost in an ocean of tears. At that moment, the conductor of the bus yelled for the final call. Ali took me into his arms and hugged me tightly.

"Leila, please, ask your parents to buy you a plane ticket home after you stay with your uncle. I'm so worried about you." I nodded my head but didn't answer; I was too busy breathing him in. I wanted to remember his smell forever.

He pushed a few strands of hair out of my face. "I love you," he whispered in my ear. He backed away slowly while my big eyes puckered, clutching at this last image of him. Alone, I slumped against a dirty cement pillar and sobbed. An elderly black woman came up and hugged me. Her skin felt soft and velvety like worn paper that's been left in the wash. She smelled of a perfume my mother occasionally wore. "It's gonna be all right, honey, you'll see. Just believe in God, okay?"

I thanked her, left the bus depot, and took the 7 train to Queens.

I had no memory of Masood Uncle or my parents' other friends from when they lived in Jackson Heights in Queens. Mostly I remembered the old apartment building we all lived in, the hum of the dirty air conditioner as it perched uneasily in the box of the window frame. Twenty years after we moved away, I now clutched the address and phone number of Masood Uncle written in blue ink on a scrap of paper. The writing was blurred from the sweat of my nervous palm. On the train I felt sick from the pepperoni pizza I had eaten for lunch at the bus depot. I worried nervously that the greasy smell of pork still clung to me and would betray my sins when I arrived at my Pakistani home away from home. The car of the train smelled like body odor; I checked my own armpits to make sure it wasn't me. But in the intimacy of the train, we all took on each other's smells like grief. The odor was so thick I felt like gagging. I was relieved when the conductor announced, "74th Street and Roosevelt." In the crowded stairway, I felt safe and inconspicuous for the first time since the attack, surrounded by brown faces.

When I got out of the station, I walked under the elevated train tracks covering Roosevelt Avenue like a steel burqa and waited at the corner for my uncle to pick me up. Queens smelled like it usually did, as the aromas of different foods from around the world mingled with exhaust and garbage. A pigeon shit on my shoulder. Disgusted, I wiped it off with a tissue from my pocket. I crossed the street and stood at the opposite corner looking for his car. An older woman with her head covered sat on a dirty crate begging for money near the stairwell coming out of the subway station. She was at least seventy-five years old and spoke Russian.

I had taken Russian in high school, so I could understand her when she said, "Please help me, I am hungry." I plunked two quarters into her empty McDonald's coffee cup and smiled sadly at her. She looked so small, so brittle. I turned to see a construction worker leaning against a payphone watching us. He was muscular and tall, wearing a dirty t-shirt with the American flag on it and dirty blue jeans. He was squinting his eyes as if the sun was shining into them, two piercing blue beads. The local train rumbled menacingly above our heads.

Two cars on the street started honking and I wondered if it might be my uncle. I walked onto 74th Street and looked for a tan Honda civic over the crowds. Slightly annoyed, I thought, *Why did Uncle want to pick me up here?*

All of a sudden a man's shouts erupted from the crowd. I turned to see the construction worker still standing next to the old Russian woman.

"You bitch! Nobody help this fucking cunt!" he shouted. I tried to see who he was yelling at, but I could only see the old woman. I didn't even consider that he was yelling at her. I searched for the victim of his venom but could not find her. He was walking in tight circles furiously, occasionally turning his head to spit. His face was a red explosion of fury. The old woman stood a few feet from him; terror and bewilderment mingled on her face in fluid waves. A crowd was slowly starting to gather around them.

"Get out of here, you bitch." He gestured with his arm like a showman to emphasize his point. The old woman flinched. She pulled her headcovering closer to her face protectively. "Why don't you go home? Huh? Answer me, you Arab bitch!" He stared down at the little old woman. She opened her toothless mouth a few times, but could not speak. It was clear that she couldn't understand this man, who was shouting in English because he mistook her for a Muslim. The old woman whimpered and tried to hide a little under the platform stairwell. She held her hands up protectively to cover her face. This display of weakness only frustrated him further. He scratched furiously at the dirty blond stubble on his chin. "Uh-uh, no way, you are getting the fuck out of here. Right now. You understand? Go back to your fucking teepee in the desert you fucking A-rab!" He roughly grabbed her by the arm and threw her hard into the newspaper stand on the corner. I winced when I saw how awkwardly she landed on her leg. I stepped forward instinctively to help her, but the construction worker gave me a look like I was next. Fear coursed in icy rivulets down my back. My heart beat wildly. A ring of people, as diverse as any corner in New York City, silently watched this attack. Unwilling to help, a bond of complicity overcame their differences. I stared imploringly at first, then in frustration at the men in the crowd who did nothing to stop this attack. The old woman cowered, screaming in Russian for help. But the construction worker's deep voice overpowered hers. "I am an American, bitch," he said, pointing to his chest. "And I am telling you right now that we don't want your kind here anymore."

He turned away, and for a moment I thought he was finished. The crowd stood watching, holding their collective breath. The old woman took this as her cue to escape. She grabbed for the dirty white crate she had sat on earlier. Suddenly, a burst of pigeons took off in flight like fireworks. The ground started to shake and for a second, I thought, *We're all gonna die*. But it was just the 7 train passing overhead.

The first punch didn't look real. The blood that trickled from her nose was too red, like stage blood. But with the second and the third punch, I realized this could only be real life. Since the attack, no white people had shown any great kindness to me, but I still could not believe the beating I was witnessing. Vomit lurched up in my throat, but I swallowed it down. I was frozen in my cowardice. I could only keep thinking, *I'm next, I'm next*. The beating didn't even last a minute, but the horror of the act made time stand still. Finally one of the men in the audience pulled him off of her and said weakly, "That's enough." I felt faint. I tried to move through the crowd to get to the old woman but the corner was congested as people began to disperse. A few moments passed before I heard a car horn honking repeatedly. A Pakistani man waved from a tan Honda civic. I rushed to the car, hoping this was my uncle. I had already opened the door, when I asked, "Masood Uncle?" He nodded, "Yes, Leila behti, come on." When I got in the car, he waited for me to buckle my seatbelt, but I turned to him and said, "Uncle, we gotta get the hell out of here." I turned my head to watch the old woman, but she and the construction worker were already gone, swallowed by the shifting crowds.

* * *

At Masood Uncle's apartment, Afshaa Auntie waited with Omar, their five-year-old son. Auntie opened the door for us while Uncle carried in my bag. We had no introductions; she immediately took me into her arms, and even though I didn't mean to, I started crying. Auntie didn't let go. Finally, I pulled myself out of her embrace and sheepishly smiled; I worried that I smelled bad and that she would notice. Their apartment was a small one bedroom; Omar slept in a children's bed next to his parents. A doubt appeared for a second in my mind, *Where am I going to sleep?* But I pushed it out of my head as soon as I could. Auntie asked if I was hungry, and even though I had just eaten a little while ago, I felt famished. She had prepared a huge meal of chicken korma, matter keema, and gosht. The food smelled delicious. Fresh rotis sat steaming at the center of the table. In between bites, I mumbled, "The food is wonderful Auntie, thank you. You shouldn't have gone to so much trouble." She waved off my thank you with a hand that held roti. Omar, eager to help out, grabbed a can of Sprite and gave it to me. "What do you say, Omar?" his mother asked sternly. "Would you like some Sprite, Leila Baji?" he asked sweetly. I looked at my reflection in the mirror on their wall and saw streaks of dirt on my cheeks. I wondered why Auntie would insist on formalities at a time like this. I smiled at Omar and thanked him.

Over dinner, I described the pandemonium I had seen at the bus depot and train station to Uncle and Auntie, who were both too shocked at first to say anything other than "toba toba." Omar watched us silently, fear pooling in his huge eyes. "Sorry," I said, gesturing toward the little boy and looking helplessly at Auntie. "What can we do?" Afshaa Auntie asked, looking exhausted. "He already saw everything on the TV."

After dinner, Omar pulled me by the arm into the corner of the bedroom that was "his." "Leila Baji, Leila Baji," he said excitedly, the words slurring into one another from the excess saliva in his mouth. "Do you like Batman?" he asked me.

"Yes," I lied.

"Batman is more stronger than Superman. Batman is most toughest in world." He spoke English with a thick Pakistani accent even though he was born and raised in New York. Until then, I hadn't realized just how isolated the South Asian part of Jackson Heights really was.

"Batman is the toughest in the world," I corrected Omar's English gently.

"Yes, Batman is most toughest in the world. Only he can kill the bad guys," he lisped. I rubbed his soft face with my hand. He was just a baby really.

"What bad guys?" I asked.

"The bad guys who blew up the buildings." I pulled Omar onto my lap and hugged him, wondering when some kid at school would accuse him of being one of those bad guys.

Afshaa Auntie put on a Hindi movie, "Mohabatein." She asked if I had seen it before. "Yeah," I said weakly, trying to disguise the fact that I had hated the three-hour Bollywood musical version of "The Dead Poet's Society."

"You want to see it again?" she asked me, her arched eyebrows arching even more with excitement.

"No, that's okay Auntie," I said. "It's three hours long."

Auntie smiled and nodded her head from side to side. "No, no, it's okay. We can watch it. Don't worry about us." She popped the cassette into the VCR and sat on the floor humming the theme song. I didn't argue with her.

"Come sit on the couch, Auntie," I said.

"No, that's your bed. You rest there." I fell asleep before Shahrukh Khan, the hero of the movie, made his first appearance.

That night the rains fell.

Thunder seeped into my dreams. As I slept I dreamt the same

nightmare over and over again. I would wake up, my mouth dry and parched, only to fall asleep back into the same dream. In my nightmare, the sound of thunder turned into gunshots. I dreamt that Ali was being held up by a mob whose faces were covered in masks. I stood in the corner screaming, holding a crying baby that was ours. When the mob started to attack Ali with the butt of their rifles, I rushed over to help him. They held me off until they stopped, until Ali was no longer moving. Kneeling down, I reached over to lift his bleeding face and saw that it was not Ali, but my father.

My cell phone rang and woke me up. It was Ali, calling me to let me know he arrived safely and was at home in his mother's house in California. I was so relieved to hear from him, but I rushed through our conversation. Uncle and Auntie were sleeping in the next room; I didn't want them to hear me talking on the telephone to a man.

The next morning, I heard Uncle get ready for work, but I pretended to still be asleep. I didn't know him well and was embarrassed to have him see me sleeping. I pulled down my t-shirt to make sure my stomach wasn't showing at all. After Uncle left, I took a long hot shower and massaged my shoulders under the water. In the bathroom, I cursed myself for not buying another pregnancy test. But where would I have taken it? I couldn't discard the wrapper at my Auntie's house. *I'll take it at home,* I told myself, but then remembered I was homeless.

After my shower, I sat down to a breakfast of roti and spicy omelets with Auntie. I wore the same clothes and hoped Auntie wouldn't notice. But the rest of my clothes were boyfriend appropriate, not Auntie proof. The apartment was empty except for us. The schools had opened up again and Omar had already left on a bus an hour ago. CNN was on the television even though neither of us watched it.

"What do you need to do today?" Auntie asked, breaking a piece of omelet with her roti. I looked over into the living room at the blankets I had folded on the couch.

"I think I should go to Minnesota and stay with my parents." I blurted, feeling relieved as soon as I said it. "I'm going to see if I can get a train ticket out of here for a while."

Auntie protested softly, "Behta, you know you can stay with us as long as you like." I smiled and squeezed Auntie's hand. It's amazing how kind strangers can be.

"Thanks Auntie, but I think I should go and be with my family." She smiled but didn't respond. I noticed a gap in between her front teeth. In the dim morning light that filtered in lazily through the small windows, she looked beautiful to me.

When I arrived at Penn Station, I was amazed by how long the lines were; it was easy to get lost among the slithering serpentine trails. In the midst of chaos, bureaucracy prevailed. There was a line just to get into the official line. I spent the entire day in this endless snake waiting to get to the Amtrak counter. Penn Station was crowded and noisy, but occasionally above the constant hum of human traffic, a scream was heard, "God please save us!" People in line in front of me sat on the ground, propped their heads against their packed bags. Some cried. Others chatted calmly, as if they were in line for concert tickets. I spoke to a man from Ghana who was a harp player traveling with a band. He plucked strings while I told him about my homeless situation.

"In Ghana, we believe that when we witness a tragedy," he said, plucking another chord, "our spirits flee because they fear death. Only your family can call your spirit back and this they do by taking care of you. The spirit will return if you take care of the body and the best way to do that is to take care of the stomach!" He laughed at the end of his story and then picked up his harp and moved along the line.

My stomach was grumbling. The harp player's mention of food reminded me of how hungry I was. I reached into my bag and took out the wrapped bun-kabob with ketchup my Auntie had thoughtfully packed for me. The strong smell aroused some suspicion. For the first time since childhood, the smell of Indian food brought out a sense of shame, palpable and thick like menstrual blood. I remembered childhood taunts about Indian food smelling like farts when I was a girl growing up in Minnesota, the only brown child in a snowstorm of white faces. I quickly swallowed the kabobs to diffuse any evidence that I was "foreign."

When I finally got to the ticket counter, the blond woman politely informed me that Amtrak was sold out until November. "Try the airlines," she said, trying to be helpful though both of us knew how scary that thought was.

I felt hopeless. Auntie and Uncle were perfectly hospitable, but I couldn't stay there that long, taking up space in their cramped one bedroom apartment. I went outside to think more clearly. Traffic viscously moved along. I called my father on my cell phone, thankful that I had thought to bring my charger with me when I left my apartment. "Dad?" I said, when he picked up the phone. "Hi Behta, how are you?" He sounded so nearby I wanted to cry. I took a deep breath. "Dad," I asked, fighting back tears, "Can I come home?"

My father took care of everything online from his office. Ready to brave the terror at LaGuardia, I agreed to a flight for the next day.

That night at dinner, Uncle told me about an old Pakistani friend of his who had gotten assaulted earlier that morning. "Where does he live?" I asked. "Virginia," he said. I looked down at my plate and said nothing. Virginia was a long way from New York; hatred travels at the speed of light. We ate our rotis and chicken in silence. While I helped Auntie with the dishes, she told me she was taking Omar to school tomorrow. "He had a little problem with the kids in the bus," she explained, a little embarrassed. I smiled sympathetically at her and mentioned that it was better for Omar this way. We watched another Hindi movie that night, "Kaho Na Pyar Hai," with Bollywood's hottest star, Hrithik Roshan. I hadn't seen the film before. Omar was so happy, he kept jumping around the room, karate kicking the sofa ends.

"Leila Baji, Leila Baji," he said in between kicks. "Who you think is the most strongest, Hrithik Roshan or Jackie Shroff?" I had to search through the database of my mind to remember which actor Jackie Shroff was. The latter was probably twenty years older than the new Bollywood heartthrob.

"Hrithik Roshan, I think," I said.

"Thas' right," Omar said, jump kicking an affirmative yes. "He is the most strongest man. He's like batman, but most strongest. He beat Jackie Shroff in 'Mission Kashmir.' Hrithik Roshan can save the world, even from the bad guys." I wanted to believe him; I wanted to believe that Bollywood dreams could come true. But on this side of the screen, Hrithik Roshan, with his brown skin and slight stubble, would probably get mistaken for one of the bad guys. I pulled Omar to my lap and kissed the top of his head. We watched the rest of the movie in silence. That night, Omar dragged a mattress to the living room floor and slept beside me, holding onto a Batman doll the whole night. I welcomed the protection.

I was anxious getting up the next day. The alarm jarred me out of a dreamless sleep at six in the morning. I got ready in the bathroom quickly, disappointed again with the refusal of my period to arrive.

Auntie packed another bun-kabob for me. She had tears in her eyes when she hugged me goodbye. I did too; I had a feeling I would never see them again, this family who saved me during a time of war. She and Omar looked so small in the weak morning light.

Uncle had promised to take me to the airport. He was gruff as we left the apartment,, ripping the bag from my hand, rushing through the front door of the building. In the car, he breathed deeply before turning the ignition. The circles under his eyes looked darker; he seemed to have aged overnight. He turned the car onto the street and abruptly dropped me off at the next corner. "I don't have enough petrol. You can take a cab from here." I reached into my pockets, found two dollars and a few cents. But I said, "Okay, thank you," anyway.

Kindness ran empty like the gas tank.

I got out and slammed the door. "Khuda Hafiz," I said through the glass, but he took off too fast to notice. I walked to the corner store to take out $40 from the ATM there. I crossed my fingers while I waited for the cash to dispense, hoping I didn't have a negative balance. With the smooth bills in my pocket, I hailed a cab from the corner.

A taxi pulled up right away. "Yes miss, where to, miss?" The driver was South Asian and in his thirties. His identification read Mohammed Bilal.

"LaGuardia Airport, please." I said.

"Yes miss, okay miss." I cringed a little when he called me "miss." I was at least 10 years younger than him. I should have been calling him "bhai," the respectful term for older men in our community. But in the space of that taxicab, commerce overtook culture.

"You are from India, miss?" he asked.

"No, Pakistan." I answered with a small smile.

"Same thing, miss. India, Pakistan, we are no different, miss. In this country, they only see skin color, miss."

"You're right," I said. "Where are you from?"

"Miss, I am from India." We drove in silence for a few minutes. I watched as trees bled into one another on the passing streets.

"Are you Muslim?" I asked. His back stiffened in his seat.

"No, miss. I am not Muslim, miss." He said this tersely, and then was quiet for a moment. Despite his Muslim name, I didn't question him further; I figured that a lot of people were lying about religion for their safety.

Mohammed ran a red light on Roosevelt Avenue. I looked at my watch. I was six hours early for my flight. "I'm not in a rush, you know," I said through the plastic partition. "You don't have to run any red lights for me." He shook his head and looked at me through the rearview mirror. He had a mustache like my father's.

"Miss, I running red lights so the peoples won't throw stones at my taxi."

"People are throwing stones at your cab because you're Muslim?" I asked, unable to simply hold the information in my lap.

"I told you miss, I am not Muslim. To all the Indian/Pakistani drivers, they throwing stones at us, miss." Neither of us spoke then; I worried that I had offended him by calling him Muslim. But wasn't it obvious to him that I was Muslim too? He continued to run every red light until we got onto the freeway.

"In this country, miss, the people are very angry at foreigners now, miss. But we are scared too. When buildings fall down, many desis die too. But miss, we all human, right?"

"Yes," I agreed from the backseat, wanting to say something more meaningful. But my body hurt too much from sleeping on the couch to say anything profound. My back was damp, sticking slightly to the cheap cracked vinyl of the seat. I massaged my shoulders and neck. The rest of the ride, we spoke politely about my schooling and the value of education.

When we got to the airport, he turned around and smiled broadly at me. "Miss, you are good girl, miss. Parents must be very proud of you, miss."

"I hope so," I smiled back, but weakly like watered down tea. What would this countryman of mine say if he found out I might be pregnant and unmarried?

"Yes, you are good girl, miss. Don't forget that, miss. Don't let anybody tell you anything else. We all humans, miss." I fought back tears as I paid him, truly believing his words. As I got out, I wanted to say something to him, a prayer for his safety, this cab driver who was Muslim but not, who must run red lights to ensure his safety on the road.

"I hope everything will be okay," I said finally. He stood for a few moments holding my bag from the trunk, not saying anything.

"Insha'allah, miss, Insha'allah." We both smiled at this prayer. I looked up into the sky and noticed wisps of clouds floating poetically like the Arabic he just uttered. I read its prayer and answered back, "Insha'allah."

Villa Orient

~Maniza Naqvi

Though still under construction, the expansion of the Villa Orient in Sarajevo, I am told, is almost near completion. It worries me, this, *almost* and *near*, but not quite there. Never there. But that's the way it is around here. The last unwanted wall in the architect's plan is currently being demolished, the one between the old hotel with its eight rooms and the new portion with thirteen additional rooms which include a restaurant, a conference room, a gift shop, and a reception lobby.

The owner expects an increase in international travelers who will be able to pay in hard currency and help finance the loan repayment for this expansion. I have a feeling he may have been a few years too late. The war is now over. The journalists are gone. The Networks with their famous women chief correspondents are gone. There are other more pressing locations now. A network's job is never done, though this war may be, for now.

Throughout the day, construction workers drill, hammer, batter, pound, and shatter to bring portions of the old structure down. And all this happens just on the other side of my hotel room wall where on a weekend I stubbornly continue to remain in bed, determined to make the most of a Saturday morning. For a regular like me in the old part, in room 003, sleep is a must, deep into the morning on a Saturday like this one to battle jetlag and field fatigue. And to feel that time is mine to spare or to waste. The bright sun outside, against which I have drawn the diaphanous red rayon curtains, still manages to bathe the room and me in a pink light.

It sounds dreadful out there. The sounds that make me sick: sounds of war, as though just beyond this wall there were a war zone. Of course there isn't. Perhaps this is what it sounded like here in those years of siege. Perhaps this is what it sounded like to those trapped inside buildings in Jenin as the bulldozers fell upon their houses in March 2002. This is what it sounded like in Kabul in April 1978 under the heavy bombing as I lay shaking on a cold floor under a dining table. This is what it must've sounded like in Towers One and Two. Or on October 7, 2001 over Kabul? Or in Baghdad in January 1991, or in Belgrade in 1998? Or here in Sarajevo in 1994?

And now I can fall asleep to these make-believe sounds of war. I find myself standing amongst smoldering fires in burnt out ripped up houses surrounded by bodies, torn up and bleeding and all the men dead… only some of us left and I as the oldest woman there… leading the call to prayer besides the rubble of what used to be a mosque. And I who never has now know all the words, I who can't carry a tune suddenly can and I do. There I am, smoke rising from smoldering fires all around, women and children lining up behind me… the leader of the prayers, the imam, the muezzin, Hya alsalah, Hya alsalah Hya alfala, hya alfalah… and I awake to the sounds of the azaan at the nearby Ferhedija Mosque.

I wake up in alarm, grief struck and frightened, but then the sound reaches into my bones and relief rushes through my veins. I try to calm down. Was it the past I dreamt of? Or something still to come? The news now is of Iraq and only of madness. The constant ratatat of the jackhammers is deafening and I wonder if the others in the hotel are reminded of the siege, or war, or this or that, a car accident, an operation gone bad, a beating, a rape, a hideous act of violence? Or the shock of losing a friend, as he feels justified enough, back in the States one clear summer night, when all reason too has collapsed into a hysteria of pinning responsibility into a singular identity and a singular motivation after September 11, 2001: "Perhaps a suicide belt for you, this year?" For I am a Muslim, and he is funny. And all is fair game for we have been friends for more than a decade. Forgive them for they know not what they do, what they say. How can they not?

Construction sounds very much like destruction. When does the noise of a jackhammer sound like a jackhammer and not a metaphor? When is this just the sound of construction? To me, since I was not here when the surrounding hills were the frontlines, the hills are just hills, nothing else. Or perhaps, because I can only imagine the war, the hills are nothing but, while everyone else has moved on, climbed that mountain so to speak, and are able to see just hills.

Having arrived in the evening, I did not discover until precisely 8 A.M. the next day on Saturday when the first power tool was switched on that I would not require the travel size alarm clock for the duration of my stay. And that the reminder of war would be constant for the rest of my stay. The expansion had to go on, management explained, and they would be only too happy to help me move to the hotel Europa if the noise was an inconvenience. The owner, who treats me like a welcome friend, even offered to send me to Dubrovnik for the weekend. I chose instead to stay. As it turns out I am the only guest staying in the hotel—stubbornly refusing to go elsewhere, staying on despite the chaos and the mind-rattling ratatatat all day long. I like the Villa Orient. I feel at home here. Like I do in New York. Everyone running it seems to be from someplace else, internally displaced refugees. I like to think that the people who run it, mostly a staff of women from Magli, Zenica, and Travnik, and an older gentleman who's lost everything in Banja Luka, have grown to like me too. I catch a glimpse of the owner from time to time when he stops in to check the accounts or the construction next door. I feel at home here because they make me feel at home here. And coming back here has become, because of their warmth, a kind of homecoming. Or I like to think so, though we hardly have language in common. Just gestures and smiles.

But Villa Orient is expanding. It is everything that I would want in an inn. Squatting on the edge of the Stari Grad, the old town, at 6 Oprkanj Street, really a short winding alley way wedged into its bustling street of cevabcici-kebab houses, it is nestled amongst the sound of azans from the surrounding old mosques, the Ferjadia mosque and the Gazi Husrev-Bey mosque. The new rooms and even some in the old section on the second floor look out onto the clay baked tiled roofs of the old city and the green blue copper cone topped minaret of the Ferhadija, whose dome is framed on either side by two elegant Cyprus trees. I noticed that a few houses closer in have patches of their still unrepaired, bombed-out rooftops covered by those red Polypropylene sheets stamped with the UNHCR sign which flap in the breeze. An eyesore.

Perhaps the owner of the Villa Orient could assist and support the uplift of the neighborhood? It would, I would think, be in his own self interest to improve the view for the guests and that would mean more business for his hotel. Yet the UNHCR sheets are a reminder of the war and could serve as a bit of sightseeing perhaps for the war-tourists. It's a dilemma, how to balance a memorial to those who die in violence with moving on gracefully? Finding this balance seems to be the new order of things everywhere anyway. Two of the new rooms, the presidential suites, have views of the National Library, which too is under restoration, and of the surrounding hills which are covered in newly restored houses with red-tiled roofs and with the smattering of white tombstoned cemeteries. From a distance, these look like a profusion of flowers, though perennially in bloom.

The women who work at Villa Orient are all uniformly kind to me and I cannot tell from their sentiments or expressions as to which aggrieved group each of them belong. Only in the conversations with one or two of them whom I have gotten to know better do I find out who is a Serb with a boyfriend, who killed during the war, who lost everything in Banja Luka, or who wants nothing to do with thinking about the war and just wants to get on with life. And another who—and this astonishes me because I have not been in one—who wishes it were still war, because then the people were equal and the rich and poor shared the same pot of food, the same loaf of bread, and the same fire against which to warm themselves. And usually in all this, it is precisely the one I have guessed belonged to a certain group, say, Muslims, that turns out to be the Serb. Impossible to tell these people apart.

The women tell me that the owner of the hotel, a lean and trim, shy looking man, has taken a large loan for its expansion, and it's a wise decision in my opinion. The Villa Orient sits on an ideal location. Anyone coming to Sarajevo would want to stay here. The hotel is in the heart of the old city where throngs of people stroll at a leisurely pace in groups or in couples, enjoying each other's company and observing others throughout the day, or sit sipping coffee along the sideways. It is in close walking distance to all the sites: the old mosques, the churches and the cathedrals, orthodox and catholic, and of course the synagogue. There is an art gallery next to the orthodox church on Tito Marsala, the street with the tram car. Further down is the old 16th century hamam which has been converted into a cultural center, the Bosniak Institute, by a wealthy philanthropist recently returned from Switzerland who had left after WWII. He has already built his final resting place in the restored building's courtyard. I see in his generosity a desire to preserve and nurture the culture he loves. He has also ensured his own longing to return and be loved by the beloved. Bells ring and azaans call out throughout the day above the sound of music at outdoor cafes. And a bit further down, all the Bosnian food places and handicraft shops filled with Bosnian rugs and copper pots and do-dads are located here in the cobbled walk thoroughfares. The traffic on most alleyways here is pedestrian, while cars and the tram move along the boundaries of the old city.

Yes, Villa Orient has an ideal location. The expansion is in keeping with the architecture of the old city, and the owner, I am told, will blend the modern with the traditional for its interior décor. Across the street is a cobbled alleyway where two pool tables are constantly in use in smoke-filled coffee and beer-only bars. There are many small shops and cafés along this alley, which opens out onto the cobbled plaza in whose center is the water fountain called Bascarsija. Here hundreds of pigeons waddle and flutter while passersby feed them for good luck or perhaps for atonement and blessings.

At the hotel, the boiler room is directly above the room in which I stay and throughout the day or night it creates a soft comforting gurgling sound that permeates my room, like the cooing of pigeons or when it is raining and cold outside or snowing and I am snuggled in my bed, its sounds like a soft snoring. It's times like these, burrowed thus under heavy blankets when I am newly arrived from a long journey, that I get the sensation of sinking back or being inside myself or perhaps inside the womb, the room breathing around me as though I'm a child waiting to be born. Outside I can hear the muffled voices of the staff deep in conversation at the reception or calling out to each other, the periodic ring of the telephones or the sounds of the azaan, and everything seems to extenuate and intensify my sense of well being and security. The journey from the States to Sarajevo had been particularly difficult the last few times. I am searched and questioned for almost two and a half hours before being allowed to board the flight. I fit many different profiles and then all this travel to these countries where there are Muslim populations makes me a definite must for questioning before I can board a plane. I have therefore arrived here this time tired, sad, and self conscious. Usually, when I come here after a long journey, I sleep deep and long. This room has become my excelsior that transports me to a deep undisturbed slumber. But this time there is all the banging and the destruction of the expansion.

But the expansion is a smart idea of a keen businessman. There are many foreigners who come here and the eight rooms were simply not enough to meet the growing demand. Even 21 are not enough, but that is the maximum number he can afford at the moment. All the aid agencies and the military agencies of all the countries of the world send people to this city, and so many want to stay in a place which will afford them a flavor of the culture, a sense of authenticity, a chance to rub shoulders with the people, do a little handicraft shopping, partake in a little of the local fare. Such activities make bureaucrats feel as though they are immersing themselves amongst the people. This allows them to see what lies in the heart of Europe. *Hijabs*, blond hair, blue eyes, ski-fit bodies, cutting-edge trendy clothes, church bells mingling with the azaan. Wine, beer, chai, kebabs, steaks, grilled calamari from the coast and baklava. It all fits so well. Yes, Villa Orient is perfectly placed. Human rights lawyers, forensic DNA experts, NATO officials, army colonels, relief agencies, and the IMF and World Bank all mingle at breakfast and depart for the day from here to their local offices to mingle elsewhere with each other over scheduled meetings for the day, reuniting in the evening at the pool tables and at the numerous cafés. Here, on weekends, in the shade of the minarets and under the sun, no doubt, many of us can boast of having read Proust, revisited Madame Bovary, and completed a round two of all the works of Chekov and Tolstoy in all their entirety. We are here, legends in our own minds, to save and rescue, but we are alone. A perfect convergence of noblesse and novel. And there are many such convergence points: dance clubs, bars, pool rooms, an art gallery or two, and boutiques, and outdoor markets for flowers, vegetables, and fruit. Villa Orient is perfectly placed.

One afternoon, I visited a gallery in the center of the old city, next to the Military House, the Dom Armiya. I had stepped in to see an exhibit of quilts. The quilts were made by refugee women in a camp in Austria who were then relocated to Gorazde after the war. The colors of the quilts were vibrant and yet muted in tones of reds, oranges, yellows, grays, blacks, burgundies. The quilts in their constructions reminded me of Rothko paintings: colors put together, that one would not ordinarily think of matching with each other but obviously belonging with each other, creating harmony, enhancing each other's depth and vibrancy, melting into each other, somehow making it inconceivable to think of one without the other. No doubt there are women in Afghanistan doing similar projects to be displayed, perhaps, in the Whitney someday. I wondered how much is their own sense of color and design and how much is the sensibility of a fashion trend somewhere else for which appropriate materials and thread are handed out. My cynicism, I am aware, threatens me.

But just as I mused upon this, the empty gallery was transformed by a rehearsal in progress for a recital by a string quartet. The musicians, all very young, perhaps in their mid-teens, let me stay to listen. A violinist had just begun warming up, framed against a large window, through which I could see the Catholic Cathedral in the distance, the Orthodox church on the right, and the minaret of Gazi Huzrav Bey mosque behind it. And during the practice of the quartet, the sound of the azaan mingled with the sound of the music. A young, rambunctious string quartet; the gray haired conductor stopping and starting them; occasionally the sound of a jackhammer outside reverberating through the music; the glimpse of a military uniform outside the window, So there it is: the colors of the quilts, their intricate stitches creating patterns; my cynicism; the music of the string quartet; the sound of the jack hammer; the military uniform; the churches; the mosque; a sudden rain shower, a sudden snow fall, or splendid sunshine; all of these and at their confluence an essential mystery occurring. In places like this, in moments like this, I find my faith and I locate myself.

Walking around the construction site of the hotel, on a site visit, as it were, I note and am happy to report that it is indeed almost completed: paint in place; tiling done; cables for electricity and pipes for gas and water all laid. They just need to be connected. And of course, all these need to be concealed behind or beneath fittings. Duct tape needs to be removed, banisters need to be put in, internet connected, and perhaps a treadmill or two in a small room in the basement; even one would do. The water fountain in the main lobby area needs to be tiled and hooked up. Really, the whole thing is more or less ready, just needs the finishing touches: the fittings, the connections, the carpeting, curtains, blinds, beds, linen, lamps, telephones, paintings, towels, all the furnishings. Then surely in a few weeks from now, it should be, if everything goes according to plan, open for business. If everything goes according to plan, the Villa Orient will do thriving business. No, it won't be long now until it's up and running, hustling and bustling, and open for business. All traces of destruction erased. Why, who knows, once it's all up and running, perhaps it will be so booked up, there won't even be a room for me.

Circumference

~Humera Afridi

The woman has trained herself to wake up to precise images: aquamarine sea, limestone villas, sand the color of caramel custard. For a week now, she has awakened to this collage of all the beaches she has known.

Each morning the dream fills the barren plain that has been her mind since he left exactly one week earlier; each morning the dream dissipates more quickly. She uncurls herself from her ajrak duvet. The yellow of pomegranate rinds and the warm reds of madder that had thrilled her when she bought the block-print comforter from a handicraft store are invisible now. She reaches for the remote and turns on her radio. She has no television; she is still new here.

Less than a mile from where she lives there is a world destroyed, mangled, spitting fumes of burnt steel, flesh and plastic. *The price of hubris*, the radio announcer posits based on a comment made by a right-wing televangelist. The woman slides her feet out of bed but keeps her head on her pillow and listens. Today has been declared a national day of prayer and mourning. The barricade north of Houston Street has been lifted. She is free to roam beyond the circumference of the five square blocks where she has been zoned for the last four days since the attack. Anxiety prickles at her, anxiety about this strange new freedom.

She has three tea bags left—she has been conserving her rations as there have been no deliveries below 14th Street—and she steeps one now in a white mug and slips on her jeans and prepares to venture beyond the frontier. She will buy her first newspaper; she will buy sugar. She searches for her I.D. card, removes the stud from her nose.

Her lover—though after this last time, could he really be called that?—said, *We should leave it at the level of skin. No telephone calls, no e-mail.* This woman who moved alone to the city three weeks ago cannot get her lover's words out of her head. She mutters them, remembering the breadth of him against her, wishing she'd said them first. She slings her surgical mask around her neck, rummages in her closet for a dupatta. She is not devout nor one to carry the baggage of tradition, yet she gropes about for a scarf to cover her hair.

She thinks of her husband. He will call soon from the home they had shared until three weeks ago. She will miss the call. On the fourth day after this world has been sabotaged, she knows that the other man, the one with whom she has this arrangement, this mutual exercising of lust, will not telephone. Each time, in the days following his visit, the sensation of his presence dissipates, but now she does not let him out of her head. To do so would mean creating space for the horror outside.

Three people on her street—all Caucasian. Smoke belches and curdles from the site, subsumes the neighborhood in an acrid haze. She positions her mask over her face and walks north. Two people pass her and glare. Is she imagining it? On the first afternoon, a woman outside the deli said, *These fucking Arabs! I don't understand them.* Then, looking at her closely, said, *You're not Arab, are you? I mean, you're not Palestinian?*

At Houston Street she shows her I.D. to a South Asian police officer, forces a pinched smile. People cluster on either side of the blockade. As she crosses the street it feels as though she has left a country behind. Four men shove past her; one of them mutters something loud and incoherent.

Earnestness is not what the city is about and she wears her sin too close to her skin. She flags a cab, *11th Street and 1st Avenue, please*. She does not say Madina Masjid. The driver peers at her through the rearview mirror. He is brown and complicit. It is Friday, the day of communal prayer.

The woman feels she is driving through a palimpsest. A new city, an altered reality, has layered the streets which she has not been permitted to walk on for the past few days. The few people out of doors cluster around posters of the missing, reading their lives, learning the maps of their bodies, the birthmarks and tattoos that render them unique. She wonders about the people alive, the ones putting up the posters, going from wall to wall with tape, watching the sky for rain.

The car stops at a red light. She cannot believe that the man who fucked her seven days ago hasn't bothered to e-mail, to call. She cannot believe she is thinking of him still and that she has thought more about him than at any other time, in any other year. She cannot believe she is becoming this sort of woman, the sort of woman who baffles her.

A voice rasps through the window: *I'm going to fucking kill Osama. I want you to know I'm going to get him.*

Okay, okay, very good, the driver says like he's soothing a colicky baby.

The man at the window looks at her, says: *I'm telling this cabbie here I'm going to kill Osama*. He has a scruffy orange beard, a thin pasty face.

The light turns, the tires screech, the driver swears under his breath in Punjabi.

Once out of the cab, she wraps her hair in her dupatta. There are three photographers and two white journalists in denim skirts and bright stockings. There are no Muslim women in sight. But it is Friday, she thinks, they must be inside. She approaches a man in a mustard kurta-pyjama, asks for the women's entrance. He looks over the length of her body, tilts his head. *Why? Do you want to pray?* She disregards him and walks into the squat building. There is office carpeting, sheet rock walls; it smells like someone's cooking. There are only men. One says, *Yes?* as if she's a foreigner. It is evident to them she is not a mosque-goer; she lacks the protocol.

Where are the women, please?

No women here, he says abruptly and opens the door to let her out.

Standing in front of this mosque, she feels stripped to the bone: shameless, adulteress, wine-drinker. Her jeans seem to say this to the men as do her boots and the fact that she is here alone on a day when the women are secure at home.

You are here, she thinks, in this city, among things and people, vehicles and street vendors, but you cannot say a word. The sins of this life seem as flat as copper pennies ground under heeled boots, worthless as vanity, lost in dirt. There is a sudden newness to the street, there is a sudden stark separation of the soul from the world that sifts around and through the body. You are here, she thinks. When you awake tomorrow, and the day after and the day after that, this is where you will be.

Theater

~Humera Afridi

In less than the time that it will take her to step out of her studio apartment, walk east to her new favorite café, and retrace the short street blocks back to her place and the welcome of dogs, the western part of a city on television will be eviscerated. But she does not know this yet. She continues to watch the screen, her body limp and sprawled on the bed, her head angled up toward the source of the streaming images: the television mounted on the wall. She is not accustomed to watching television for hours on end. How death-like for the body to lie, feigning sleep or paralysis as the mind imbibes the sound-enhanced images and churns a frenzy of emotions in response. Sometime in the next few days, this thought will tap her conscience. But for now she cannot quell her fascination. She notices how prevalently the city's name is mispronounced. The nasal stretching and dismembering of the capital begins to irritate her, the way the reporters and the so-called experts and the state department have snatched the song out of its syllables. They never heard it, she thinks, were never capable of hearing it, these tone-deaf gunks who spit exuberantly into their microphones.

She has lain here for fourteen hours straight, dozing through the night, like someone sitting by a hospital bed, jerking awake every hour to slip fingers across the loved one's forehead, willing the fever to subside. Like this she checked the status of the city on television. Now it is late morning. Her husband is at work and when he returns she will be where he left her amid bunched up cotton sheets, the stale smell of an unmade room, the dog bowl in need of a refill of water. She doesn't know the city on television; she has never visited this country. But she cannot wrench herself away. It is as if she has been there. The hushed streets; the stillness of its nighttime; the moon lingering luminescent, a timeworn sentry, God's eye: she cannot get enough of these pictures. They matter deeply. She reads her presence into the silence of the city on the TV screen. Only night and streetlights and a minaret; the leafy sway of date palms plied by a breeze. A slow, eternal rhythm: How many centuries of history are buried here?

Last night the muezzin's call had accompanied a wide shot of the city. Strong and willful and soothing, the azaan had sounded, in those moments before the first attack. But on the news channel, the anchor who could barely disguise her restlessness for the war to begin during her slotted broadcast time described the sound as ominous. The woman had sat up suddenly. As if she'd been struck; or as if someone had spilled a hot drink over her reclining body. In that moment she understood: the innocuous, taken-for-granted splinters of a heritage: how loaded they become in a foreign territory, when people persist in perceiving your ways as alien. The azaan was something that did not warrant comment. It had always been there, familiar as a bone; a necessary background sound; an ordering rhythm. When she recalls the moment now, anger curls about her thoughts.

In less time than it will take her to pull herself away from the television and make a half-hearted attempt to shower and dress and think of an excuse for why she is late to work, the western part of the city on television will be devastated. The reporters will not talk about death. Instead they will applaud the technology of an immaculate war. But she does not know this yet. A thought begins to form as she absorbs the accelerated speech of the television anchors and the experts whose agendas are becoming woefully transparent. They talk about preparing the ground for battle. They refer to the battleground as a theatre. They talk about a decapitation strike. In rapid succession they utter words: shock and awe, bunker buster bombs, deep penetration weapons, embedded media, mop up, tick tocky. This last one they repeat several times: tick tock. Tick tocky. They say shock and awe campaign, turning the phrase into an adjective and when they say we hope to shock and awe them, they twist it into a transitive verb, and the woman is stunned. She is absolutely amazed. She thinks, here is a dialect, a new dialect for a new war and she pulls out a notebook and starts jotting the words down as fast as they drop from the television. It is as though she is taking dictation. She doesn't know why she is doing it but she cannot stop herself. Then she decides she really cannot go to work today; it would be like walking out of a cinema before a movie had finished. For a fleeting moment she is ashamed at the comparison, ashamed she is succumbing to a habit that is sacramental in this country but one that she is disdainful of. How many times has she declared television to be the paved road to apathy? Abhorrent? But this is different. How can she disengage from the only thing that matters today—this live theatre, a dangerous parody of a Broadway production with its streaking lights, and its own crude script in its own crude dialect? Mouth agape, she monitors the incredible fluency of these television people; how quickly the new dialect appears to be gaining currency. She watches for their conscience to trip, to falter upon the murder embedded in this jargon. She decides she will make a conscious effort to not use these words because to speak them would be to give them life, to be complicit.

Again the city glimmers, magical on the screen. It is the combined effect of the lights along the river and the dome of the mosque in the backdrop. And the silence. A majestic serenity exudes from this nighttime shot despite the premonitory words of the television anchors. Despite everything, the city looks like a bride adorned. Not in defiance, but indifferent, detached, as if it does not have to, has never had to justify itself to the temporal.

Though she has never been to this city or visited this country, she believes now, after so many hours of watching over it, sitting by it in her room, invoking its spirit, she would know its textures. She thinks she knows now what it must be to stand beneath a widening sky and to sense the presence of the seeping desert nearby. What it must be to step into a cityscape with patches of lush foliage amidst so much sparseness, the eye's appreciation of green against a particular quality of light, the richness of this contrast. She yearns for a whiff of the salt breeze that washes the face of the desert, its ephemeral contours and nuances different each day. The city, in this glimmering shot, appears otherworldly and oblivious to pain. She looks away for a moment to pick up the phone, dial the number to her office, to leave a message that there has been an emergency. Then she decides she needs to get some air and thinks immediately it is a luxury to have such a thought, to be able to saunter into the street without threat.

Shoppers stream by her. What a privilege to live here, to tune out the world effortlessly. But when she steps out of her new favorite café with a large cup of black, sugarless decaf coffee into the busy street, a man from the local television station thrusts a microphone at her. He asks what she thinks of the boycott on French products and for a moment she is confused because she has left politics behind in her room. Then it spills out: It's the most absurd thing ever, the most ridiculous thing. He asks what she thinks of France's lack of support for the war. War? she finds herself asking. You can hardly call it a war! A war is when you have two armies fighting each other. War is not something orchestrated from the sky without warning, without a declaration. There is no dignity in terror. She knows she has not given the television man the light, airy sound bite that he had hoped for. To compensate, she raises the paper cup with its French logo and says salut! before walking off.

In the time it takes for her to order a large, decaf coffee, pick up paper napkins from the service counter, and speak her thoughts into the camera of the local TV station, the sanctity of a city will be destroyed. She will discover this only moments after she returns to the welcome of dogs, assumes her position on her bed and takes a sip of her drink. But first, her mind will wander briefly to the protests she has recently attended; it will pause on the vigil she joined the previous night outside the Federal Building after learning that a group of men who had undergone voluntary registration had been herded up to the tenth floor and shackled. She has never before been politically active. She has often thought it is a privilege to live here, to tune out the world effortlessly.

And she has spent her life indifferent to the lure of television. But when the campaign of terror begins, her gaze is entrenched. She takes a tentative sip of the hot coffee, sets it down, then brings the cup back to her lips in anticipation. It has been seconds only. But already it seems longer. The liberation of a people in progress. The camera that is feeding the image of the exploding city is fixed at a particular angle, offering a synecdoche of an unfolding trauma. Shock and awe. She will register this later, but for now she watches and watches. Afterward, or perhaps it has been happening all along and she doesn't know, her own shock will build in a gradient. Mathematical and precise like a well-wrought torture. The lid of her left eye twitches and she presses a knuckle over it. On the television, popping sounds accompany the plumes of orange and black; no human voice anchors the image. In the history of civilizations, when has hubris gone unpunished? she wonders as the western part of the city explodes before her eyes. What changes? As she lies here in this stagnant room, the world there, on the screen, the topography of what they know as home is being altered. She thinks: There are hallowed worlds beneath that ground, whole civilizations, histories and peoples. She cannot explain it. She doesn't know this city. But she has never felt so humiliated.

When it is all done and the first carnage has been unleashed, she will step out briefly onto her street for some air. She will notice the women who come out laughing from the chocolate shop. She will notice the light of the disappearing sun splayed on the cobblestones.

You—you who are so arrogant, she will whisper, you are only unearthing a past glory. You are only blasting us closer to what we were. She will mutter these words in anger. But for now she cannot take her eyes from the plumes of ripe color, the thundering sky, the city that is being broken.

Hanaan's House

~Amani Elkassabani

It was the American dream and it was coming true for Hanaan. "We bought a house," she told Maha that afternoon when the two of them met to shop at the Arabic grocery store near their apartment building. Maha congratulated her friend, kissing her once on each cheek, and Hanaan could smell the pungent aroma so distinctive of the mastic gum Maha chewed between meals.

"*Mabruk*!" said Maha. "Where is it?"

"Twenty minutes from D.C.," said Hanaan, her hazel eyes and honey complexion set off by her black headscarf. She had a fleshy nose and cheeks that took the shape of apricots when she smiled. Those who knew her described her as having a baby face, and those who met her for the first time expressed disbelief that she was married and had a child. Hanaan hadn't worked since Dina, now five years old, was born; but her husband Hisham had secured a job with a law firm in northwest Washington. They had looked for a place close to the District to cut Hisham's commute and they did not want to leave Maryland where Hanaan had grown up, so rather than settle, as many of her friends had, in the predominantly Arab neighborhoods of northern Virginia or the Pakistani community to the northeast of Washington, they bought a house in one of the Maryland suburbs west of the District. "In Brentwood Park," continued Hanaan.

Maha had removed the cellophane from an amber square of mastic gum and popped it in her mouth. Hanaan had always found the gum too bitter for her liking. "You're not serious," said Maha.

Hanaan nodded. "You should see the house. It's got a garage and four bedrooms. It even has a decent sized-backyard."

Maha's brown eyes widened and the smiled faded from her lips. "But Brentwood Park? Why *there*?"

"It's not just the house. The schools there are the best and you know Dina's starting kindergarten in the fall. Besides, it's a very safe neighborhood."

"Safe? For who? Muslims? Have you forgotten what happened to Dar-ul-Huda?" It was Maha's habit to ask a series of questions when she wanted to make a point. Her last question awakened a vivid memory of the day the two women, along with several of their neighbors, removed garbage that had been strewn across the lawn of the mosque near their apartment building and cleaned animal feces and rotten eggs from its doors and windows. It had taken longer to replant the azalea bushes that had been uprooted and to remove the words *DIRTY ARABS* and *MUSLIMS WILL DIE* that had been spray-painted across the white cinderblock of the mosque's entrance. And only weeks later did Hanaan feel comfortable enough to wear a scarf again in public instead of the beret she had used to cover her long black hair after the 9/11 attackers were described in newspapers and on television as Muslim extremists.

"I remember. I thought about it every time we looked for a house out there," replied Hanaan.

"And what about now? What they're doing. Taking away our rights, treating our men like criminals." Hanaan had heard Hisham talk about a new law that would require males from Muslim countries to be questioned and fingerprinted; she knew that Maha feared for her cousin, whose legal status was in jeopardy.

"Maha, the people in Brentwood Park are just people. They didn't attack our mosque; they didn't pass that law."

"It's enough that they send money to Israel." Maha pointed to Hanaan's scarf and continued, "Then they see you dressed like that, and they think you're a terrorist. They'll watch you all time."

"Maha, I'm not trying to prove anything to anybody. I found a house I liked and bought it. We move next week."

Maha eyed the cans of fava beans and the large jar of sesame paste Hanaan had put in her shopping basket. "You'd better stock up," she told Hanaan, placing a bag of pita bread in Hanaan's basket. "The stores out there probably only sell bagels."

When Hanaan returned to her apartment, she found a note saying that Hisham had taken Dina to the playground. It was a warm day in May and earlier that morning Hisham had promised Hanaan time alone so that she could finish packing. She sorted through the magazines on her bookshelf, deciding which, if any, were worth keeping. She leafed through an old issue of *Aramco World* that featured an article about the rise of Islam accompanied by a map of the Middle East. As she studied the arrows originating in Arabia and traveling across North Africa and Asia, she remembered seeing a similar map in her fifth-grade history book. On the facing page of her book was an account of Muhammad's political and religious life, including a paragraph that described how he had murdered hundreds of Jewish men and enslaved their women and children after the Battle of the Trench. She remembered showing it to her father, who had said the story left out that those Jews had betrayed Muhammad and that the book was probably written by Jews to make people hate Muslims. It wasn't until later that Hanaan began to understand how people she had never met could hate her because of who she was. The next year, when her class read *The Diary of Anne Frank*, her father said that Hanaan was only learning one side of a much bigger story. "Do you know what the Jews did to Palestinians?" he had asked her. Without waiting for an answer, he explained that Palestinian men and women were dragged into the street in the middle of the night, forced to watch their homes reduced to rubble, and sent to live in refugee camps. "The Jews," he had said, "wanted to take our land too."

In June of 1967, war broke out between Egypt and Israel. Hanaan's parents fled Ismailia with their infant daughter and drove into the Western Desert, where they stayed with Hanaan's grandparents until they could return home. The cease-fire did not end the tensions between the two countries and the next year, Hanaan's parents left Egypt. When she got older, Hanaan learned how her mother had fed Hanaan in the dark in the midst of the shelling that shook the ground like an earthquake and rocked her to sleep as explosions lit up the sky like fireworks. They were not, said her mother, the same kind of fireworks that had lit up the sky fifteen years before when Egypt was liberated from British rule. That was a time to rejoice, said her mother. The 1967 War was a time to mourn. They had come to America in search of a better life—leaving behind their apartment, personal things, friends and family—but they took with them their sympathy for the many who were suffering and their contempt for those who had made them suffer. Years later her parents shook their heads in disbelief when they saw men who had once been enemies grasp hands as friends. It did not matter, her father said, that a treaty declared peace between Egypt and Israel. Zionist Jews wanted only one thing: to confiscate the lands of neighboring Arab countries. It wouldn't be long before they tried to take Egypt again.

As Hanaan grew older, she found logical reasons to reject much of what her parents taught her, but she never completely forgot it. She had experienced moments of doubt about moving into an area with such a high Jewish population. She was feeling it now as she sat on the floor, magazine in hand, fingers tracing the outline of a place that seemed to exist within her. At this precise moment, she thought, a woman who dressed like her and spoke her language and touched her forehead to the floor when she prayed was mourning the loss of a son or a brother who had fought to regain his home. She felt at once guilty and grateful that she possessed a home of her own in Brentwood Park. Grateful won out, so she set the magazine in a box with others she would take with her and continued packing until the phone rang.

It was Maha calling to ask Hisham for legal advice about Maha's cousin. Apparently, Maha's cousin had decided to evade the Immigration and Naturalization Service, which had set a deadline for foreign nationals of Egypt, as well as 24 other predominantly Muslim countries to register their status with the U.S. government. Three years ago, Maha's cousin had entered the U.S. legally, but he had since overstayed his visa, deciding to risk deportation rather than return home to an uncertain future. Somehow, he had obtained a social security card, found work, and now he was a tax-paying member of society with a permanent residency application pending. Massive backlogs had delayed the processing of his paperwork, and until he got his green card, he faced the daily threat of being sent back to Egypt, especially if he were to appear before an INS judge. Hanaan told Maha not to worry, that she'd talk to Hisham and call her back.

Later that evening, Hisham furrowed his brow and smoothed down his black mustache as Hanaan retold the story of Maha's cousin. "If he doesn't register," Hisham finally said, "he'll probably get deported anyway." He sighed and dialed Maha's number. "Tell him to go in," he advised her, saying that obeying the law might gain him favor with the judge and that he could not be deported without a hearing. After Hisham hung up the phone, he turned to Hanaan and said, "Guys like him aren't who they want. How many terrorists are going to waltz into a government office and let themselves be questioned and fingerprinted?"

On the last Saturday in May, Hanaan and Hisham met the movers in Brentwood Park and carefully presided over the unloading of their belongings. Dina had spent the night with Hanaan's parents, who had offered to bring their granddaughter in from Baltimore the next day along with some things Hanaan didn't want to surrender to the movers.

The house sat on a quiet cul-de-sac. It was a two-story brick colonial with a modest yard and flowerbeds along the front walkway. The backyard, level with few trees, was enclosed by a low fence. Beyond the fence, along a row of cypress trees, ran a narrow sidewalk that led into a clearing where Hanaan could see playground equipment.

At first Hanaan had been elated, thinking how lucky she was to live near a park. But then the realtor told her the equipment belonged to a synagogue and, for a moment, Hanaan had felt strangely out of place. The house had appealed to her for reasons she could not logically explain. Maybe it was the way the sunlight poured into the kitchen from a skylight or perhaps it was her visions of family gathered in the dining room. She imagined a glow and crackle in the fireplace on cold winter nights and pictured Dina sitting in her lap as she read her a book in the family room. Her parents, who would finally have their own room if they chose to visit, would disapprove, she thought. Maha, who had once criticized Hanaan for buying lingerie made in Israel and cautioned her against befriending Jews, would not understand. But it was she—not her parents, not Maha—who would inhabit the house. And neither the synagogue next door nor the catechisms vilifying Jews she had learned as a child seemed like good enough reasons to abandon the dream of owning the home she had fallen in love with. Not even the memory of foul words spray-painted on her mosque or the pictures in yesterday's *Washington Post* of Arab men lined up outside an INS building were powerful enough to destroy her faith in the American dream.

Hanaan unpacked the last of the boxes marked FRAGILE and stacked dishes in one of the many cherry cabinets that lined the wall of her kitchen. Kicking aside the crumpled newspaper that littered the floor, she made her way to the center of the kitchen where she could better survey the contents of her cupboards and drawers. She was not entirely satisfied with the placement of her coffee mugs, which she had moved twice that morning already. She arranged her things by trial and error. Occasionally, her pots and pans and towels and linens fell into their cupboards and closets so naturally that she thought she had a knack for settling in. But now, thought Hanaan, it was no use to rearrange the mugs. Eventually all her things would find their proper places. So instead of emptying the cupboard completely and starting over, she took the mug she had gotten as a souvenir when she visited New York on a college trip, placed a tea bag inside it, and put a kettle of water on the stove. She hadn't used the mug in months and examined, as if for the first time, a series of painted vignettes of the city that decorated the outside of the mug. The vignettes included the Empire State Building, Times Square, and the Statue of Liberty. When she saw the twin towers in a World Trade Center vignette, Hanaan shuddered and set the mug down on the counter. Suddenly, she didn't feel like having tea anymore.

She gazed out a window at her backyard and visualized the flowerbeds of pansies and marigolds she would put in. Maybe she'd even plant a small vegetable garden in the corner that got good sunlight. She pulled on a plum-colored scarf and a loose-fitting button down shirt that extended well beyond the seat of her blue jeans and went to get a closer look at the yard. With arms crossed, she trotted barefoot out toward the fence and at the same time a procession of couples coming from the synagogue ambled down the sidewalk, returning, she guessed, from Saturday services. She glanced from the grass to the people passing by and back again, trying not to stare, not to scrutinize them even though she wanted to look directly at their faces, hoping to catch a glimpse of something she could point to that made them alien to her, something concrete that would justify Maha's warning to stay away from them. The women wore formal dresses and hats, making it difficult to see their faces. A few of them wore gloves, and Hanaan thought of her own mother, who not only wore gloves, but also covered her face, whenever she left the house. The men she saw wore suits and yarmulkes, mostly black. The boys and young men wore multi-colored ones and held them in place with silver barrettes. Again, she thought of her father, whom she couldn't remember seeing without a skullcap over his graying hair. Some couples were pushing infants in strollers, others held their toddlers' hands as they proceeded along the sidewalk just beyond her backyard. Most of the passersby conversed with each other, some looked straight ahead, a few looked in her direction and were expressionless; one woman smiled, and Hanaan smiled back.

She must have counted seven or eight families by the time the stream of worshippers tapered off and she had gone back into the kitchen. Her new neighbors, she thought, and suddenly she missed Maha and the smell of mastic gum on her breath. She searched for the tin Maha had given her as she was packing and found it buried in her pantry behind some boxes of instant pudding. Hanaan unwrapped a piece of gum, put it into her mouth, and let the saliva soften it before she started chewing. The medicinal juices washed over her tongue and for the first time she resisted the urge to spit out the gum. Putting her things in their proper places suddenly seemed much easier than making a place for herself in Brentwood Park.

By the time the doorbell rang that afternoon, Hanaan had cleared the newspaper from the kitchen floor. Maybe Hisham, who had gone to pick up some picture hanging nails from the hardware store, forgot his key, she thought as she opened the front door. A woman Hanaan did not recognize stood holding a covered dish. She had a fair complexion and blue eyes and Hanaan could see just the ends of her blond curls beneath the blue bandana she had tied around her hair. She wore a blue tank top, denim shorts, and brown sandals. Hanaan stepped back and quietly studied the woman's face, listening as the woman said she lived two doors down. "I saw your moving van this morning and I wanted to welcome you," she said.

Hanaan hesitated. The woman cleared her throat and Hanaan thought she had better say something to break the silence. "I'm sorry. I wasn't expecting anybody."

"I can come back later," said the woman, turning to leave. Hanaan did not know what to say next; she only knew she did not want the woman to go away.

"No, it's okay," said Hanaan, smiling. "Besides, I need an excuse to take a break."

"I'm Karen Sultan and this is Joel." She put one hand on the shoulder of the boy clinging to her leg and Hanaan noticed that, unlike his mother, he had brown eyes fringed with long black lashes.

"Hanaan Zakariah. Please, come in." The two women walked into the kitchen and Karen set the dish on the counter. Hanaan recalled the day she had moved into Maha's neighborhood. Maha's mother had brought over a tray of stuffed cabbage leaves and a roasted chicken when she introduced herself to Hanaan's mother. Maha had come too and given Hanaan three small pieces of chocolate wrapped in silver foil. The two of them ran into Hanaan's room and rummaged through the half-empty boxes looking for toys to play with while Maha's mother helped Hanaan's mother unpack.

"You really didn't have to bring anything," said Hanaan.

"I just brought a little of what I had."

Hanaan could see a mound of yellowish grain-like pasta mixed with pieces of chicken, carrots, and zucchini through the glass lid. "You just happened to have couscous?" she asked.

"We have it every Saturday after services. David loves it and it's the one thing I learned to make from scratch when we were engaged."

Hanaan pictured the boxes of dried couscous she picked up from the Arab grocery and imagined Karen pushing pasta dough through a sieve. "You *make* your own couscous."

"Only when David's mother comes over." They laughed. "It's still the best way to impress her." She gestured toward the dish. "This came out of a box."

"Mine does too," chuckled Hanaan.

Karen asked where Hanaan was from and Hanaan told her that her parents had emigrated from Egypt, but she had grown up in Baltimore. Karen exclaimed that she and David were married in Rabat and spent their honeymoon in Sharm el-Shaikh. "It's where I got this," she said, holding up a gold cartouche bearing a column of hieroglyphs.

Hanaan saw that Joel was still clinging to Karen's leg. "I have a daughter about your age," she said.

Karen beamed and said, "Hear that, Joel? You'll finally have someone to play with!" Hanaan saw Joel grin even as he hid his face in his mother's shorts. Karen explained that her older daughter Jenny had a best friend named Sarah who lived next door, but most of the neighborhood children were either too young or too old to make good playmates for Joel. "We'll have to get the kids together once you're moved in," said Karen. Hanaan agreed.

Hisham returned from the hardware store and saw two plates of vegetable couscous with chicken on the table. When Hanaan told him that a neighbor brought it over, he said, "And you were worried you wouldn't find a friend out here."

"We're hardly friends. She does have a son Dina's age and an older daughter. She seems nice enough."

The evening, Hanaan got a call from Maha. Her cousin had gone to Annapolis to register with the INS but didn't come home. The judge had ordered him detained and set a July date for the deportation hearing. "It was awful, the way they shackled his feet and hands and led him off to jail," said Maha between sobs. Hanaan tried to console her, and she composed herself long enough to ask, "How can they do this to him? Treat him like a criminal when all he was doing was obey the law? What about his rights? What about his freedom?" Hanaan admitted that the whole thing was horrible, and stayed on the line until she was sure Maha had stopped crying.

The next morning, Hanaan's parents pulled into the driveway, and Dina, full of energy, was the first to emerge from the car. Her auburn curls were tied back into a neat ponytail with a pink ribbon that matched her pink shorts and t-shirt. Hanaan squatted to hug Dina then stood up holding her, planting kisses on her cheeks. Hisham, who had come out to meet them, gathered Dina in his arms and Hanaan embraced her parents. They lingered in the yard and three boys who had been tossing a football in a neighboring yard paused to look at them. Hanaan was sure they had seen her in her headscarf earlier that day; she had been hauling empty boxes to the curb when her parents drove up. The boys had continued tossing the football as Hanaan made half a dozen trips to the curb. But perhaps seeing a man in wearing a long garment and a woman with her face covered surprised them. It wasn't their stares that bothered Hanaan. She got them often enough, especially after last September when she ventured out. What bothered her was that the stares now came from people in her neighborhood and she felt uncomfortable in her own front yard. "Let's go inside," said Hanaan.

After she gave her parents a tour of the house, Hanaan could see that her parents were happy for her. "There are so many Jews," said her father. "We drove by three synagogues on the way here."

"There were Jews in Baltimore too," said Hanaan.

"But we didn't live next door to them."

"Baba, this place has everything we wanted and it's so close to Hisham's office. The realtor told us the schools were excellent. And, Mama, look at the backyard. I can finally have a garden."

"There's a synagogue in your backyard!" cried her mother.

"Mama, it's a house of worship."

"Remember what they did to our mosque?"

"That was nearly a year ago. And the people in this neighborhood aren't responsible for that."

"They are all the same. Once an enemy, always an enemy."

Hanaan sighed and crossed to the window, where she could see the boys tossing the football. They were lucky, she thought, and though she didn't say so, she felt safe for the first time in months.

Soon after they occupied the house, Hanaan had unpacked all but a few things. The closets were smaller than she had thought so she decided to keep her winter clothes boxed up until the weather turned cold. The rest of the boxes contained things she didn't immediately need but knew she wanted to hang on to—papyrus paintings of Pharonic deities she bought on her last trip to Egypt, Eid decorations she would use later that year, Dina's old toys she could not bring herself to throw away.

Hisham's new job required that he spend long hours at the office, which meant that Hanaan and Dina were left to find ways to fill up their days. Hanaan occupied herself with settling in, dusting the dining room table and hanging curtains; cleaning out the fireplace and placing pillar candles inside it—just for now, she thought, until winter came and she could make a real fire. But the summer days seemed to stretch out interminably. In between phone calls to Maha, browsing through interior design magazines, and making lists of everything she wanted for the house, Hanaan's daily routine left her with time to become familiar with her surroundings. Karen Sultan, who had lived in Brentwood Park for nine years, was eager for Joel to meet Dina, and Hanaan was eager to know more about the neighborhood.

The visits started as casual encounters. While Hanaan planted flowers in her yard, Karen strolled over and struck up conversations. Hanaan was always surprised at how easy it was to talk to Karen. When Karen learned that Dina and Joel would be in the same kindergarten class that September, she was thrilled for them because Mrs. Shepherd would be their teacher. "Jenny had Mrs. Shepherd, too," Karen said, "and she loved her." Having an older daughter gave Karen the advantage of knowing which teachers at Valley View Elementary School were good and which were merely mediocre. The more Dina and Joel played together, the more often Hanaan and Karen saw each other. When their children weren't jumping on Joel's trampoline, they were running through Dina's yard. Soon Karen was inviting Hanaan and Dina to accompany them on outings—trips to a puppet theater, story time at the library. Sometimes the four of them rode the Red Line into D.C. and spent the afternoons strolling through the Smithsonian; other times they walked to the neighborhood swim club where Dina and Joel splashed in the kiddy pool. Karen's older daughter, Jenny, divided her time between her mother's outings and Sarah Levin's house. Occasionally, Hanaan saw Sarah at Karen's house, but the nine-year old never stopped running around long enough to meet Hanaan. It seemed to Hanaan that Jenny and Sarah, who were inseparable, were oblivious to Dina and Joel and were perfectly content to invent games that did not require the participation of a little brother and his new friend.

While Hanaan sometimes longed for the old neighborhood—the trips she and Maha took to the Arab grocer, the familiar streets and the comforting sights of seeing other women in headscarves instead of being the only one—she admitted that since moving to Brentwood Park a month before, she believed she had fit in better than she first hoped. Hanaan and Karen exchanged recipes and gardening tips; they talked about their children's loose baby teeth and fears of the dark; they shared memories of time spent on the shores of the southern Sinai peninsula and hopes that they one day might return. At times they made oblique references to terrorism and hatred and how so many things had changed since 9/11, but they stopped short of talking about any specific event. Hanaan had come to enjoy Karen's company, not just because they had children who got along, but because Karen never asked Hanaan about her faith or her politics, and Hanaan never felt as though she had to explain either one.

Hanaan wanted to tell Maha about Karen, but every time she tried, Maha told her to be careful. "They're always watching you," she would say. "They're watching all of us now. That's how they got my cousin." The deportation hearing for Maha's cousin was only a few days away and Maha was growing increasingly distraught.

On the morning of July 4, Hanaan rose to the sound of rain on her rooftop. Gray clouds darkened her usually sun-drenched kitchen. When Hanaan went out to retrieve the paper, she saw that nearly every house on the street, including hers, had a flag flying from its front porch. She mused that flags, which used to appear only once or twice a year on days like today or Veteran's Day, now remained in view week after week, month after month, a daily reminder of Americans' love for America and the values that it embodied. She recalled the days following 9/11 when red, white, and blue ribbons fluttered from nearly every car she passed, and flags were displayed on overpasses and outside homes and businesses. Even the Arab grocer near Hanaan's old apartment had hung one inside his window. Hanaan remembered seeing one of his most loyal customers spit on the flag and say she refused to set foot in his store until he removed it. The grocer told her that he did not want any bricks thrown through his window like those that had sailed through his brother's store across town.

The rain fell steadily all morning and Hanaan feared that she, Dina, and Hisham would get drenched if they ventured out to see the fireworks. But when the downpour became heavier that afternoon, Hanaan began to wonder whether there would be any fireworks at all. Dina had grown restless from having spent the morning inside and begged to be taken to Joel's house. When Hanaan stepped into Karen's foyer, she was nearly toppled by Sarah Levin, who was chasing Joel's older sister, Jenny. "She's spending the night," said Karen. "Her parents are out of town and I agreed to watch her. Jenny's loving it." Dina sat down beside Joel, who was sprawled on the floor surrounded coloring books, and surveyed his crayons before reaching for a purple one. Hanaan was amazed how the two of younger children could sit so still while Jenny and Sarah raced around the house, running from the den to the kitchen to the staircase that led to Jenny's room. "Jenny, Sarah, come say hi to Dina's mom," insisted Karen. The two girls paused at the foot of the stairs.

"Hi," said Jenny.

"Sarah, this Dina's mom, Mrs. Zakariah. This is Sarah, Jenny's friend." It was the first time Sarah and Hanaan had been introduced.

"Hi, Sarah," said Hanaan.

Sarah was silent, studying Hanaan's scarf and long-sleeved shirt.

"Mrs. Zakariah is from Egypt," said Karen.

Sarah looked at Hanaan with penetrating blue eyes and said, "That makes us enemies."

The girl spoke so casually that Hanaan nearly didn't believe she had heard the child correctly. "What did you say?"

"We're enemies. Because you're Egyptian and we're Hebrew." She giggled and darted off again, racing Jenny upstairs.

Hanaan felt an electric shock travel through her. She tried to contain her horror, but Karen must have seen the color drain from Hanaan's face. Karen's voice cracked as she called after Sarah, saying

"No, no, Sarah. We're all friends!" She cleared her throat and there was silence. Hanaan felt a knot in her stomach and her mouth went dry. All at once the intolerance that stemmed from childhood fear and ignorance surfaced and she thought herself naïve for having ignored Maha's warnings and rejected her parents' beliefs. A nine-year old girl who had never met Hanaan had placed her squarely in the category of an enemy. In a single moment, the girl had articulated centuries of theological and political history. Hanaan could almost hear the conversations at Sarah's house, her parents telling her who her enemies had once been, who they were now. And she thought of her own mother's words on the day she moved to Brentwood Park: Once an enemy, always an enemy.

Hanaan swallowed and turned to Karen. "No, we're not all friends. As much as I'd like to believe it."

"Trust me, her parents would be mortified if they knew what she said." But Hanaan was not reassured.

Hanaan returned home and sat by the fireplace with her head in her hands. Even though the room was dark, lighting the candles in the fireplace didn't seem worth the trouble. She knew that a film of dust had accumulated on the dining room table, but she didn't bother to clean it. She finally admitted to herself what she had known all along—the American dream was more than just owning a house and flying a flag from the front porch. She would be safe in Brentwood Park; Dina would attend the best schools, she would continue her friendship with Karen, but Maha was right. There would always be people who were suspicious and fearful of her because of who she was, especially now. Moving into Brentwood Park didn't change that. It only made Hanaan more aware of it.

When Hisham sat down beside her, she leaned her head on his shoulder. She told him what had happened and said, "Maybe I was wrong about this house, this neighborhood."

"She's just a kid. She probably didn't even know what she was saying."

"But she said it with such certainty, without even having to think about it."

That evening, Judith Levin called Hanaan to apologize. "I just want you to know how sorry I am for what Sarah said. She has a very vivid imagination," the mother explained. "When you showed up at Karen's house, you were a ready-made enemy."

"I don't understand."

"Sarah was just incorporating what she heard in synagogue into her game." It struck Hanaan as odd that within fifty yards of where she slept, children were learning who their historical enemies were and whether she liked it or not, she somehow fit that description. "But I took this opportunity to explain to Sarah that what happened 3000 years ago is very different from how things are today," continued Judith. "I want you to know that we are not raising our children to hate other people."

Judith insisted that Hanaan visit her when they got back in town, and Hanaan promised she would, if only for Karen, whom Hanaan knew must have explained the whole matter to Judith.

The rain continued to fall, but it didn't stop Hanaan from driving to Baltimore to be with Maha, who sounded awful when she called Hanaan to tell her that her cousin was going to be deported. In Brentwood Park, the storm had caused the fireworks to be postponed until the following night. As she traveled up 95 North, Hanaan searched the sky for some sign of celebration, but all she saw was darkness.

part six
PLAYS

An Afghan Woman

~Bina Sharif

I am silent. My silence is silent. Silent is my silence. You stare at me from your bedroom through your colored TV screen.

I can see you... I can see your face... anguished, shocked through the mesh on my eyes. We are both speechless. Silent.

Silently staring at each other through the colored TV screen... me in a burqa...

Me and my burqa in a permanent graveyard of Mujahdeen, Russia, America, Taliban, and now the bomb.

Power of the bomb is immense... It's the only power left to make us all speechless.

I wish they were fast and precise and killed all Taliban, the madman with the toys... AK47s, but instead of killing them, all my neighbors are dead... the children are dead. The children?

Children? Children?

I remember, I had children. I had a lot of pain when they were born. Where are they now?

And we, you and me are all made speechless. Power of silence is so immense that speech has been defeated. All sounds, all voices, all actions have been defeated by the silence.

I am silent. My silence is silent... silent is my silence, and now you are silent too.

You who always spoke.

Freedom of speech came from your part of the world. Freedom of speech is the gift of your world.

I depend on you. On your freedom of thought. Please speak on my behalf. Let me be silent.

Not you. Not you. Not you.

Let me be silent. My silence is my only power. The only power that I have ever known. I need to be powerful too. I am a human being too after all....

Or am I ? I think I am a donkey, or a monkey, or a sheep, a mouse, a cockroach....

I think I am a human being and a donkey at the same time. I am half and half. Half donkey, half monkey, a fly... half of a fly all covered up in a burqa... what an awful waste of fabric in such a poor, poor country of the dead. Dead and unburied… scattered on the roadside… a map for the invader… the conqueror… the death of the Afghan is the radar, surveillance which guides the winning army to the hidden devil… the precious geography. I am the living curse of my own destiny, my own geography.

But you? You are a powerful human being full of freedom and democracy. Your power is not in silence. Please speak for me.

How come you have taken so long to see me?

I have been in a burqa, beaten up, stoned, shot at in public in the roadside spectacle, a street fair arranged by the Taliban to celebrate the special effects of my brain being blown up in a cloud of blood.

All this has been happening long before september eleventh…

How come you have taken so long to see me ?

OH! YES, you are right. I wasn't shown on your TV screen for a long long time.

They were saving all the violent movies made about me for the right time… to be at the right place at the right time… that is important.

But thank God, now you have seen me… now… maybe you will speak on my behalf. I want to come out of this BURQA, and take a shower… my armpits are smelly… my hair has lice in it… my skin itches because of the accumulation of centuries of dirt and dust and poverty and disease and the stink of the dead bodies' rotten stench. I want to clean myself… smell nice and join you for a steaming hot, strong cappuccino in a café on a tree-lined boulevard exchanging ideas on the future freedom of our daughters and their destiny in any geography rich or poor.

The place of my birth is my tragedy and someone else's fortune… let's talk of ancient tales of KISMET, ALLAH'S WILL in a café full of freedom.

But the idea of a shower is a fantasy of course. AN AFGHAN WOMAN IN A BURQA ALSO HAS A FANTASY. Maybe through you, my companions of the TV screen… one day my fantasy and dreams will come true. Maybe one day you will speak on my behalf. I never wore a burqa before the Taliban took over.

We were professors, doctors, teachers, artists… imagine that! We were even artists here… right here in Afghanistan, now the modern grave of the modern civilization. Now even the inside walls of our homes are covered by heavy shades so the sunlight won't enter… even the sunlight is not allowed to see us… We don't see the sun the sun doesn't see us… I am so much in the dark for so long… but still not used to it. I trip and fall all the time. I feel embarrassed, so I don't go out much.

WHAT IS THERE TO SEE WHEN YOU GO OUT?

LOOK AT THE REMAINING STARVING CHILDREN BEING BOMBED?

Maybe it's good for them to die… so they won't have our fate or our country's fate.

Who knows which country will come next to bomb AFGHANISTAN'S RUINS after America kills TALIBAN. I wish they will hurry up so I can come out of the burqa and be finally free and take a walk in KABUL.

THE OLD, OLD KABUL. The Kabul of palaces, of fountains, of ancient statues, of pomegranates and grapes of CHAMAN… It was called, "Shaman Key Angoor," the best in the world, honey filled, melodious taste. The mouth would sing "ghazals" in Farsi and lanterns of light would dance in the belly of the mountains… now called cells of terror.

RAVINE OF LAND MINES. Maybe when I am free I should still not go out to walk… my limbs would be blown off. I should just stay inside this room, covered by the burqa and just sit silently till eternity comes and takes me.

Maybe that is the safest place to be. Maybe when I take my burqa off, you won't recognize me… you won't look at me any more. You will be too scared of my face.

Maybe there won't be any more eyes of mine on my face.

Maybe there will be two hollow sockets of a skeleton. There won't be a mouth or teeth or a nose.

I haven't been able to breathe for so long… of course my nose withered way.

You won't be able to take it. You are my only friends… my only companions through the TV screen. I don't want to frighten you.

I will just stay wrapped, engulfed in this burqa and just lie down on the floor… barefoot… or go out and lie down in a snowstorm covering the Hindu Kush mountains… colonized mountains of central Asia ready to be colonized once again.

I will just lie at the foot of the valley and never wake up again… why must a colonized person ever try to wake up? What is it to be discovered? You are a slave to the core once colonized… and believe me, I have been colonized… the invader was a mighty race. Very polite, very gentle.

Look at the results of gentility. Now the Americans are coming with their roar and thunder to get me out of this burqa. I am scared… of slavery… scared of liberation… you do not have this dilemma of destiny… you were never a slave. You are lucky, my sisters… the taste of liberation must be sweet… I am afraid to taste it… perhaps through your kindness, things will change… and I know from the depth of my silence that you have been kind….

Yes, I am confused. Yes, i am incoherent. Yes, i am chaotic. Yes, I am used to the burqa, my only private library of literature, science, art, music, mountains, snow, dirt, dust, dust, dust. Maybe I *do* want to be uncovered, but I do not want to sit on the roadside begging from the leftover soldiers of the winner army. How many more armies are out there to come to this land of Ghenghis Khan?

And now the Taliban. And don't you be fooled by the other…
the Northern Alliance.

Everyone is a power-hungry dog.

A piece of land, a piece of flesh, a pound of heroin, and a lot of dollars will do. "We are ready for the rape of all women while they are still covered by the burqa.

We can't wait… now we are rid of the Taliban… all you women line up for the mass rape. You are liberated and liberated by us.

Us!

The Northern Alliance—hey! come on! You have a debt to pay and we are here to claim it… lie down now, or do you want us to rape you standing up?"

I am exhausted by my destiny… by my geography… by the idea… that perhaps under the mountains of my birth… there is oil seeping through somewhere…

please tell me God… oh!!

I forgot… that I am a MUSLIM… I can't use the KAFIR language… I have to say the word, ALLAH instead of GOD. Please tell me, Allah, that it is not true… tell me that there is no oil here… no jewels here… no precious gems, topaz, and rubies—so the invaders can rest and stay home and our children can play freely… but children are dead and the remaining ones dying… so what difference does it make if the invaders come or don't come…

OH! I AM SO EXHAUSTED… STARVED… COLD… AND LONELY.

I CAN'T SPEAK EVEN IF I WANT TO. MY SILENCE IS IN MY BEING. IT BREATHES INSIDE ME. MY SILENCE IS USED TO BEING SILENT. I AM MY OWN DESTINY AND THAT DESTINY IS OF SILENCE.

Fear makes me rock. I will sit silently afraid in a corner of the world in a burqa and rock back and forth. Maybe I should smoke some opium… after all, I own the poppy seed, and soon it will be in the hand of the invader, the winner… a lot of profit… a lot of cash… I don't want cash… what will I do with it ?

I am still in a burqa. I am still smelling and I am still silent staring at you through the colored TV screen but perhaps you will speak on my behalf. Do not become silent observers of the rape, murder, hunger, oppression, the bomb, Taliban, death, and desperation. It does not resonate with your personality which breathes the free expression, a free thought, a free word, a free shout, a free argument, a free fight… you do not know how lucky you are… don't throw your fortune away… fortune of freedom is the only gift, the only freedom.

Why, all of a sudden have all of you become speechless? What happened to the march? What happened to the necklace of free thoughts strung like pearls? Let us, you and me, me in my silence, you in your speech, avenge all injustice done to you on september eleventh and to me for my eternal silence… let us mourn for your innocent dead and for innocent living dead.

I am so tired now. I want to lie down with my silence. I am silent. My silence is silent. Silent is my silence. But you are my pearls… pearls of words… words… words… words… perhaps you will speak on my behalf.

And when you do speak, don't forget to mention my dead children and my dead parents and my dead grandparents and my dead great-grandparents. Don't forget to mention the history of innocent death. We must never forget the history of innocent dead no matter where the tragedy struck them, in New York, Afghanistan, Ethiopia, Somalia, Iraq.

Sometimes the invaders think that no one with blood and bones and eyes and heart lives anywhere where their interests lie, but it's not the case. The human race is being slaughtered for this and that. It's amazing, even when everyone knows that the life will only last for a very short time, everyone's life has an end, a natural end planned by the almighty, and who are we to end it before its time? But the power to kill is a great power; I don't know it myself but it must be a great power; otherwise, why must a great satisfaction and pleasure come of it as a result? You will see when finally I am freed; there will be bodies with daggers piercing out of their eyes on the roadside. The highway to Kabul from Mazar-e-Sharif will be littered with dead soldiers, this time Taliban. It happened before—you didn't know it so I am telling you. Only a few years ago the ruler was Northern Alliance, who will soon be jubilant coming back with the help of mighty military powers of the world. Every few years some corrupt thugs are given power in this country, my Afghanistan, and according to the wishes of whoever rules that year we wear a burqa or not wear a burqa. "To wear a burqa or not a burqa, that is the question." And as far as the women of Afghanistan are concerned, that seems like the only question. With one leadership we are supposed to wear a burqa and be considered a slave and with the next not to wear a burqa and be free all of a sudden. Is freedom so limited for us? Will everyone happily forget about us after they help us take our burqa off and go have sessions of congress with a western woman senator to discuss the relationships of the first world with the third world concerning freedom of the underdeveloped while I continue to stare at you through the colored TV screen without a burqa this time but still as a deaf and dumb silent person silently staring... staring... silently? When I was born, God gave me a tongue, a brain, a mind to think and contemplate, and I have been contemplating my freedom for a long time, and when freedom comes finally I want to take it fully. I want to be a part of the bigger picture not only a ghostly, haunting pitiful picture standing still waiting for someone somewhere to make a choice for me to show my face or not and if I can then shut up as usual and go feed the children, but I have no children left. Remember the bomb that came to get me out of my burqa and killed my children on the way. Well, now my children are dead and I really have more time to be independent like a woman from the democratic world. I want to be the senator, the finance minister, the MP, the president, the philosopher, the thinker, the poet laureate. I want to talk to you, laugh with you, I want to be free in my own home, here in Afghanistan. No I don't want to be free in your country. I won't be free there. Not now. A foreigner is a foreigner is a foreigner. Sometimes their civil liberties can be mutilated.

Nothing like your own country even its rubble right now, always was rubble… always was… but I want to speak here. I want you to join me here, come here freely without any fear of being arrested. Come here to visit me when I am made free. Just like the whole free world goes to New York for an exciting visit. I want you to visit me, so I can take you sightseeing. I am sure there will be lots of sights to see. Many many dead bodies will stay on the mud roads of liberation for a long time. No burials for them. The liberated are never buried.

As a little girl I was very fond of pomegranates. Do you like pomegranates?

When you come to visit me in Kabul… I love the word, KABUL. My Kabul. I want you to visit me in my Kabul. Not the Kabul of Taliban, not the Kabul of Northern Alliance, not the Kabul occupied by the Allied forces showing you the map of it on TV… They had the map for so long but never showed it to you. Why not? Ask them. It's good to ask questions. You can. You are not speechless. You should never be. There would be no difference between you and me. Your land, your birth place, does not allow you to be silent, under pressure. It's the gift given to the subservient. They say the subservient has no choice but to agree with the powerful. That is the best weapon the powerful has. To call me subservient. It says it all. It's a complete word. A completely complete word. You don't have to say anything else. The whole world will understand. This word was created by the English dictionary for the whole world to understand. But I hate this word with a passion.

They can keep me silent because their guns are pointed at me but I'll tell you a secret. I hate the word "subservient." And I DO WANT TO HAVE A CHOICE NOT TO BE CHOICELESS. Would you speak on my behalf?

I will serve you pomegranate when you come to visit me in my "KABUL."

It's the greatest fruit. It's the fruit of kings and the prince and the princess. Its color is the color of bright burgundy red. The color of blood. Not the blood which spills on the dirt road but the blood which sustains a precious life with vigor and energy and joy. I will serve you pomegranate. A delicious fruit of the poet. When one eats pomegranate, one writes the greatest verses of beauty. Pomegranate comes from Kandahar, you have heard of the word, Kandahar? Haven't you? Your anchorman knows. Never spells it right. No one spells it right anymore. There are too many people involved in its liberation… the word has gotten confused… but you know what I am talking about. Now the city of pomegranates, "Kandahar," is fighting for its freedom and with it the gorgeous fruit itself.

You can get pomegranates in your city… yes, they smuggle them out for the rich and educated and fashionable. They're in Dean and Deluca. I read it somewhere. Yes, I am educated. I can read and write… I read it somewhere in a gourmet magazine where to find all the exotic fruits including pomegranatse, but some of the exotic things are still available in the graveyard of Afghanistan and one of them is me. Oh! well that's a joke. When I watch you my spirit lights up and I forget that the TV program in your bedroom is coming to its conclusion until tomorrow. I hope that the war in Afghanistan goes on for a long time so I can see you and you can see me. Once the war is over and all its reasons achieved I will be completely forgotten like before. I am sure and so are you: The war in Afghanistan wasn't fought to liberate an Afghan woman.

Forugh's Reflecting Pool: The Life and Work of Forugh Farrokhzad

~WRITTEN, TRANSLATED, AND DIRECTED BY
MARYAM HABIBIAN (2002)

The work and life of Iranian poet Forugh Farrokhzad (1935–1967) had inspired me for a long time already, devotedly reading and occasionally translating her work. When I was growing up in 1970s Iran, Forugh was a kind of personal icon for many educated young women, a symbol of artistic freedom and Iranian feminism. Her modern voice punctured the patriarchal Iranian intellectual establishment of her time.

It was now time for Forugh's legendary work and iconic life to influence and translate into my own research and artistic works. My recent academic presentations and theatre productions had concentrated on the self-empowered success of Iranian women performers and Iranian women directors, working under the Islamic regime of Iran yet simultaneously defying the stereotypical western views of oppressed, veiled women. The undaunted free spirit of these women in Iran today was a result of the path that Farrokhzad paved years before them. I would now pay tribute to this heroine and convey her contribution through my own production.

The idea for a tribute performance came to me after presenting a paper on Forugh Farrokhzad at a conference at the University of Edinburgh three years ago. I was excited to bring my research and study from the scholarly world into the world of performing arts, sharing what I had learned with a larger audience. In particular, I felt that dance and music could capture some of the rhythm and sensuality that enriches Farrokhzad's writing style—nuances that, despite the best efforts of the translator, inevitably get lost in another language.

On returning home to New York, I began to collaborate with a diverse group of musicians, artists, and dancers / actors. "Forugh's Reflecting Pool" debuted at a feminist bookstore and café in the Lower East Side two weeks after 9/11. The performance was enthusiastically received and the audience asked to learn more about this woman. The foundation was built for my new performance piece and my journey began.

I dedicate "Forugh's Reflecting Pool" to the memory of my parents.

—MH (2004)

Note: All the poems were translated by Maryam Habibian except for some parts of "A Poem for You," "O Jewel-Studded Land," "Only Sound Remains," and "He Understood," which were translated by Michael Hillmann; "The Sin," which was translated by Farzaneh Milani; and "The Solitary Moon," which was translated by Hamid Habibian.

(The stage is completely black. Forugh's voice is heard, reciting some parts of the following poem. An ensemble of dancers begin their dance with recitation and movement to the music with the video-images of Tehran and recitation of this poem by an Iranian girl in Tehran in the background)

Let Us Believe in the Beginning of the Cold Season

(Iman Biavarim be aghaze fasle sard, 1965)

And here I am
A lonely woman
In the beginning of a cold season
In the first glimmer of our understanding
of the contaminated state of the earth
And the simple despair and sadness of the sky
And the uselessness of these concrete hands.

Time passed
Time passed and the clock struck four times
Struck four times
Today is the first day of the winter solstice.

I know the secret of the seasons
And I understand the words of the moment
The savior is asleep in the grave
And the soil, the welcoming soil
Hints at the calm.
Time passed and the clock struck four times.

It is windy in the alley
It is windy in the alley
And I am thinking of the pollination of the flowers
The buds with their thin, bloodless stems.

And this tired tubercular time
And a man is passing by the wet trees
A man whose blue veins
slither like dead snakes
Along the two sides of his throat
Repeating the bloody words in his
worried temples
Hello
Hello
And I am thinking of the pollination of the flowers.

In the beginning of the cold season
In the gathering of mirrors for mourning
And the mourning society of pale experiences
And this sunset full of silent knowledge
How do you order someone to stop
Someone who is so
Patient
Heavy
Lost
How do you tell the man that he is not alive,
he has never been alive.

It is windy in the alley
The lonely crows
Wander around the old sick gardens
And the ladder
What an inadequate height it is.

They stole an innocent heart
And took it away to the castle of stories
And now
How can anyone get up and dance
And dip her childhood braids
In the running water
The apple that she has picked and smelled
Will smash under her feet?

Oh companion, oh dearest companion
What dark clouds are waiting for the sun's party!

As if it were in the imagining of flight that
the bird appeared one day
As if they came from the green lines of the imagination
Those fresh leaves breathing in the lusty breeze.

As if
That purple flame burning in the pure mind of the
windows
were only an innocent image of a lantern.

It is windy in the alley
This is the beginning of destruction
It was also windy
The day your hands were destroyed
Dear stars
Dear cardboard stars
When the lies start blowing in the sky.

How can one be comforted by the verses of failed prophets?
We will meet up like those thousands dead a thousand years
And the sun will judge our decaying corpses.

I am cold
I am cold as if I will never be warm
Oh companion, dearest companion "How old was that wine?"
Look here
How heavy the time is
And how the fish are biting my flesh
Why do you always keep me at the bottom of the sea?

I am cold and I hate the oyster shells
I am cold and I know
that of the wild poppy
nothing will remain
except for a few drops of blood.

I will leave the lines
And I will leave counting numbers
And among a few geometrical shapes
I will seek refuge at the expense of sensitivity.

I am naked, naked, naked
I am naked like the silences
between the words of love
and my wounds are all from love
from love, love, love.

I have rescued this wandering island
from the ocean's turbulence
and from the mountain's explosion
and being chopped into pieces
was the secret of that union
the sun was born out of its smallest pieces.

Hello oh innocent night!
Hello the night that will change
the desert wolves' eyes to deep bony holes
trusting
and near streaming water the willows' souls
smell the kind souls of the saws
I come from the world of indifference to thoughts,
words and sounds
And this world is like the snake's nest
And this world is filled with the footsteps
of people
who plot your execution
as they kiss you
Hello oh innocent night!

Between the window and seeing
There is always some distance.
Why didn't I look?
Like the time that a man
passed by the wet trees…

Why didn't I look?
As if my mother had cried that night
That night of my pain
when something was conceived
that night that I became the bride of the acacia's branches
that night that Isfahan was full of echoing blue tiles
And the person who was my other half
had entered my womb
And I would see him in the mirror
And he was clear and clean
like the mirror
And suddenly he called me
And I became the acacia's bride....
As if my mother had cried that night.
What an absurd light came through this closed window
Why didn't I look?
Those moments of happiness knew
That your hands would be destroyed
And I didn't look
Till the moment when the clock's window
Was opened and that sad nightingale struck four times
Struck four times
and I ran into that little woman with eyes
like the empty nests of the phoenix
and from the way her legs moved
it seemed that she was taking
the virginity of my glamorous dream
to her night bed.

Will I ever comb my hair
in the wind again?
Will I ever plant pansies in the little gardens again?
Will I ever put
geraniums in the sky behind the window?
Will I ever dance on glasses again?
Will the doorbell take me again to the sound of waiting?

I told my mother: "It is all over."

I told her: "It always happens before you even think about it
We should send an obituary to the newspaper."

The empty human being
The empty human being full of trust
Look how his teeth
Sing while he is chewing
And how his eyes
Eat alive while he stares
And how he passes by the wet trees:
Patient
Heavy
Lost.

At four o'clock
In the moment when his blue veins
slither around his throat like dead snakes
and repeat the bloody words
in his worried temples
Hello
Hello
Have you ever smelled
Those four blue poppies?...

Time passed
Time passed and the night
fell on the naked branches of acacia
Night slides behind the windowpanes
And with its cold tongue
drags the remains of the day inside

Where do I come from?
Where do I come from?
That I am so mingled with the smell of the night?
His grave's soil is still fresh
I am talking about the grave of those two green young hands....

How kind you were oh companion, dearest companion
How kind you were when you told lies
How kind you were when you closed the mirror's eyes.

And you would arrange the chandeliers
into brass branches
And you would take me to the pastures of love
in the cruel darkness
till that confusing dew that was the end of passion
would land on the sleeping grass
and those cardboard stars
would circle around the infinite.
Why did they talk?
Why did they direct everyone's attention to the lover's house?
Why did they shame the caressing of virginity's braids?

Look how here
The body of a person who spoke his mind
And flirted with his looks
And whose excitement was calmed by caresses
Has been crucified
by savage shots
And how your hand print
That looked like five true words
has stayed on his cheeks.

What is silence, what is it, what is it
oh dearest companion?
What is silence except for unsaid words
I am speechless, but the sparrows' tongue
is the tongue of nature's festivity.
The sparrow's tongue is: spring, leaves, spring
The sparrow's tongue is: breeze, perfume, breeze
The sparrow's tongue dies in the factory.

Who is this person
seeking enlightenment on this eternal road
and winding his perpetual clock with
precision of subtraction and division?

Who is this person
who doesn't recognize
the roosters' singing as the beginning of the day
as the smell of breakfast?
Who is this person
who wears love's crown
and has disintegrated among the wedding clothes?

So at last the sun
did not shine
simultaneously on the two disappointed poles
You became empty from echoes of the blue tiles.

And I will fly in such a way that they will pray
on my sound....

The lucky corpses
The disheartened corpses
The silent thoughtful corpses
The sociable, well dressed, well fed corpses
In the stations at the prescribed times
And under the makeshift lights
And the lust for buying the rotten fruits of absurdity...

Ah
why must people worry about accidents at the 4-way
intersections
And this sound of the traffic cop's whistle
when at any moment a man must, must, must
be crushed under the tires of time
A man is passing by the wet trees....

Where do I come from?

I told my mother: "It is all finished."
I told her: "It always happens before you think about it
we should send an obituary to the newspaper."

Hello to the strangeness of loneliness
I yield the room to you
Why are dark clouds
always the prophets of the verses of purity
And in the martyrdom of a candle
is its secret revealed through the last and longest flame?

Let us believe in
Let us believe in the beginning of the cold season
Let us believe in the ruins of our imaginary gardens
In the useless backward scythes
and in the imprisoned seeds.
Look how it is snowing....

Perhaps truth was those two young hands,
those two young hands
that were buried under the snow
And next year when spring
makes love with the sky behind the window
and they surge through his body
the sprouting of thin green branches
will blossom, oh companion, oh dearest companion.

Let us believe in the beginning of the cold season....

(The dance ends, and the narrator comes on stage.)

Narrator: Who was Forugh Farrokhzad?
The day she died, the newspaper headlines proclaimed, "Death of a great young poetess, death of the poetess of Iran's new generation." Forugh Farrokhzad, the poetess of "I committed a sin, a sin full of joy," died in a horrible car accident. But as one of her famous verses says: "Remember how to fly, the bird will die." Forugh's spirit lives on through her poetry. In tonight's performance we celebrate this spirit...

Only Sound Remains (Tanha sedast ke Mimanad, 1965)
Why should I stop, why?
The birds have flown toward the blue sky over blue water
The horizon is vertical,
vertical
and moving fountain-like
and at the limits of vision
shining planets spin.
The earth in elevation repeats its repetition
and air wells
change into tunnels of connection
and day in its vastness
does not fit into the narrowness of the newspapers' worms

Why should I stop?
The road passes by through the veins of existence
The quality of the environment
in the ship of the moon's uterus
will kill the rotten cells
and in the chemical atmosphere after dawn
there is only sound
melting the particles of time.
Why should I stop?

Sound, sound, only sound
The sound of limpid water flowing
The sound of starlight falling
On the wall of the earth's femininity
The sound of the binding of meaning's sperm
And the expansion of the shared mind of love.
Sound, sound, sound,
    Only sound remains.

FF: (comes on stage right) Who am I? To be honest with you, introducing myself is rather tiresome and ludicrous. Everyone who comes into this world has a birth date, comes from a city or a village, has gone to school, and has experienced a whole series of conventional events in her life. Like falling into the courtyard pool as a child, for example, or cheating at school; falling in love at a young age, getting married, these sorts of things. My story is as follows: I was born in Tehran into a middle class family of seven children in 1935. My father was a difficult man though he was my first mentor, and my mother was a good woman and a caring mother.

FF: Let's talk about love. Majnoon (the Romeo of Persia) who has always been a symbol of loyalty and constancy in classical Persian literature is actually quite a ridiculous character to me nowadays. When modern psychology rips him apart, analyzing him as a masochistic person who tortured himself with his love for Leyli, then the symbolism changes completely. Just think about it! When our Leylis drive fast cars and get ticketed by the police, then these Majnoons are not good for them anymore. So today's poetry should reflect today's reality/world, and its creator must be experienced and highly intelligent… Otherwise, her work will be just like everybody else's.

FF: I started writing poetry when I was 13. It just poured out of me in the kitchen and behind the sewing machine. I was quite rebellious, and I kept on writing and writing. I don't know whether they're good poems or not, I only know they present my "self" of those days. I was a teenager and curious about my body:

Ah
I remember the first day of my adolescence
when all the parts of my body began to open in innocent
amazement
to mix with that vagueness,
that muteness, that
uncertainty…
(from **He Understood**, Daryaft, 1965)

FF: Then came my foolish love and marriage at 16. Well, it's hard for me to talk about my husband, but I was too young and stupid to get married. Besides, he never understood me. And then came my baby boy. I was torn between being a mother and a poet. As much as I loved my child, I could not be satisfied leading a purely domestic life. Poetry, that blood-thirsty goddess, would not give up her hold on me. To deny her would have meant denying myself…

(Dancer(s) come on stage.)

The Captive (Asir, 1955)
I want you but I know
That I will never be able to embrace you
You are that clear bright sky
I am that captive bird in this corner of the cage

From behind the cold, dark bars
My envious eyes look at you in astonishment
I imagine a hand reaching toward me
And suddenly I long to open my wings to you

I imagine that in a moment of neglect
I might fly from this silent prison
To laugh into the eyes of the jailer
And begin a new life with you

I imagine these things, but I know that I don't dare
Leave this prison
Even if the jailer wanted to set me free
I wouldn't have the energy to fly

From behind the bars, every clear morning
A child's look smiles at me
When I begin a joyful song
His lips come toward me with a kiss

O sky, if I wish one day
To fly from this silent prison
What should I say to the weeping eyes of the child:
Forget about me because I am a captive bird

I am that candle that with the burning of her heart
Will brighten a ruin
If I choose silence
I will destroy a nest

FF: I was devastated to leave my baby, but I couldn't stay with him either.

Now I know from that desolate house
happiness is gone
Now I know that a baby is crying
sulking at his mother's departure
(from **The Desolate House**, Khaneye Matrouk, 1955)

FF: Don't think that I forgot, my boy, Kami. Every night I cried for you. They wouldn't even let me see you. Those wretched people, they demonized me to you, but I knew that one day you would find the truth for yourself:

I am composing this poem for you
one parched summer dusk
halfway down this road of ominous beginning
in the old grave of this endless sorrow.
This is the final lullaby,
at the foot of the cradle where you sleep.
May the wild sounds of my screaming
echo in the sky of your youth.
(from **A Poem for You**, Sheri baraye to, 1957)

FF: Yes, poetry helped me to express how I felt.

The sun, thirsty on the other side of the sky,
sitting in a censer of blood
day was passing
a melancholy girl sat by the window
and stared in alien thought
(from **The Girl and the Spring**, Dokhtar va Bahar, 1955)

FF: When my husband divorced me, a whole new world of getting to know other men physically and mentally opened up to me. I was very young and in search of myself, my body, and my womanhood. How dare a woman express her feelings about her body! But I didn't care. I made love with my body and my words and gave strength to my lover. (Dancers come on stage and dance to the poem.)

The Sin (Gonah, 1955)
Beside a body, tremulous and dazed
I sinned, I voluptuously sinned.
O God! How could I know what I did
in that dark retreat of silence?

In that dark retreat of silence
I looked into his mysterious eyes
my heart trembled restlessly
at the pleading in his eyes.

In that dark retreat of silence
I sat, disheveled, beside him
passion poured from his lips into mine
saved I was from the agony of a foolish heart.

I whispered the tale of love in his ears:
I want you, O sweetheart of mine
I want you, O life-giving bosom
I want you, O mad lover of mine.

Passion struck a flame in his eyes
the red wine danced in the glass
in the soft bed, my body
shivered drunk on his breast.
I sinned, I voluptuously sinned
in arms hot and fiery
I sinned in his arms
iron-strong, hot, and avenging.

FF: Of course, my father did not approve of my new life…

FF: Dear Papa,

I hope you're well. I bet you're hurt that I haven't written for a while and you think that I don't love you, but it isn't true. I wish I could write about my life, my feelings, my pain to you, but I can't because our ways of thinking belong to two different times. But I also won't feel satisfied as long as I keep these words locked in my heart and pretend to be someone else when I see you. Perhaps you still think of me as an empty woman whose thoughts are formed by silly romance stories. I wish it were true.... Then I would have been satisfied with that little house and the banker husband who was afraid of change of any kind. In short, I would be content with a thousand dirty, empty things. I wouldn't know the bigger, more beautiful world, and I would wriggle like a silk worm in my dark cocoon. But I can't. I want to be grand. I can't live like the thousands of people who are born one day and die the next without leaving any mark. I don't claim that everything I have done so far was right and that no one can criticize me. As the saying goes: "You have to live two lives/ One learning the experience/ the other using the experience." But I am not a bad daughter and I've never wanted to bring shame on my family. I want my family to be proud of me.

I remember when I used to discuss philosophy with the philosophy professor, you would mock me and say that I was a stupid girl and that my brain had turned to mush from reading nonsense magazines. Then I would break into pieces inside and the tears would fill my eyes. I felt like a stranger in my own house. You were always so rigid—it was as if you were afraid of losing your power, afraid we would not respect you otherwise. You should have known better. And after my divorce when I moved back into your house—whenever I remember that time, I get butterflies in my stomach. Why didn't you value me? And why did you force me to go abroad like a sleepwalker in a foreign country, not knowing where I was or what I was doing? Why didn't I dare bring my friends to the house so that you could meet them and tell me whether they were good people or not?

I am running away from these people
who when they hear my poems
smile to my face like fragrant flowers
but in private call me a mad person
with bad reputation
(from **Disillusioned**, Ramideh, 1955)

Only when I sit at my desk, reading and writing poetry and thinking, do I feel I truly belong to myself. No one looks at me with hatred or sympathy. No one tells me what to do or treats me like a stupid child. Perhaps it's best to close my lips and look at you with eyes that need love. When I think of my son, Kami, I want to scream and cry out loud. But I just want you to know that I am not a bad daughter and that I love you....

FF: In Tehran I found a circle of intellectual men whom I hung around with. The first man I adored was also my mentor. He helped me make my first documentary, the one about the lepers. I am a complex person, and so was he.

My beloved
like nature
has a straightforward understanding
by breaking me he proves the honest law of power

My beloved is a simple man,
a simple man whom I
in this sinister mysterious land
have hidden like the last trace of a great religion
in the folds of the bushes of my breasts
(from **My Beloved**, Mashoughe Man, 1964)

I wrote to him once:
I feel that I have lost in life. And I know much less than I should know at 27 years of age. Perhaps I have never had a clear goal. That foolish love and marriage at 16 destroyed the base for my future. I have never had a role model in my life. Whatever I have, I have learned it by myself and whatever I don't have is what I could have had. I want to begin again...
However, poetry has been my greatest guide in life.

Narrator/Interviewer: What do you think of today's poetry?

FF: Art is an expression of life. Therefore, it must have a different spirit in different times; otherwise, it is not right, it is not art. It is cheating. Today everything has changed. Our world bears no relationship to the classical world. I even think that my world has nothing to do with my father's world. I am talking about distances.

Interviewer/Narrator: Regarding "O Jewel-Studded Land," some so-called intellectuals didn't believe it was actually a poem.

FF: I never put limits on poetry. Wherever poetry is, one must find it and feel it. Look at all the volumes of classical poetry. These poems either speak of things so metaphysical that they are out of human reach, or they advise and moralize through flowery language... But we are going to the moon—not us, of course, but other people. You think that this is very scientific? Now come and write an ode to a rocket. "O Jewel-Studded Land" is about an inarticulate society capable only of cynical utterances. It is a poem composed entirely of rigid and rotting images. Not all poems should smell of perfume. Let some of them be so un-poetic that one could not write them in a love letter. Some people hold their noses as they pass this poem? Fine! This poem has its own vocabulary and form. I can't speak of the alley that reeks of urine by choosing the most fragrant scent from a list of perfumes. This would be pure trickery.

N: "O Jewel-Studded Land" echoes with irony. It's the title of a 1960s Pahlavi-era anthem, which begins like this:

> "Aye Iran, aye marze por gohar/aye khakat sar cheshmeye honar."
> [O Iran, O jewel-studded land/O your earth full of art.]

(The anthem music should be heard or a chorus should sing it. Video images of Tehran and Farrokhzad are seen on the screen, the music is heard and dancers/actors begin.)

O Jewel-Studded Land (Aye marze por gohar, 1962–63)
I won,
I registered myself,
adorned myself with a name, an identity card,
and my existence is now defined by a number.
So I say, long live 678, resident of Tehran,
long live 678, issued at precinct 5.
My worries are over now
in the homeland's loving bosom,
my pacifier: glorious historical traditions,

my lullaby: civilization and culture,
my toy rattle: the rattle box of law.
Ah,
my worries are over now.

Overjoyed,
I went to the window, and eagerly 678 times
inhaled air compacted with dung dust
    and the odor of garbage and urine.
And on 678 bills
and on 678 job applications I have written: "Forugh Farrokhzad."
It is a blessing to live
in the land of poetry and roses and nightingales, especially
when the reality of your existence
is acknowledged only after years and years,
where peeking
through the curtains for my first official look
I see 678 poets,
charlatans, all of them, a strange beggarly company,
searching in the garbage for rhymes and meters.
And at the sound of my first official steps,
suddenly from the dark slime, 678 furtive nightingales,
who, having transformed themselves,
for fun,
into 678 black crows,
fly lazily toward the edge of day.
And my first official breath
is impregnated with the odor of 678 stemmed red roses
products of the great Plasco factories.

Yes, it is a blessing to live
in the birthplace of [Sheik] Abu Dalqhak,
    the [opium addict] kamancheh player,
and [Sheik] Ay Del Ay Del, the lute-playing descendant of drums,
in the city of superstar legs and derrieres and bosoms
    and cover pictures and Art magazines,
cradle of authors of the philosophy
    "so what? what's it to me? forget it,"

cradle of IQ Olympics—Wow!
a place where, when you touch any transmitter of picture and sound,
the brilliant blare of a young genius blurts out.

And when the nation's intellectual elite
put in an appearance at an adult education class,
their chests are decorated with 678 electric kabob cookers,
and on both wrists 678 Seiko watches: and they are certain
that weakness derives not from ignorance but from empty pockets.

I won, yes I won.
Now in celebration of this victory
in front of the mirror, with pride,
I light 678 candles bought on credit
and leap onto the mantle so that, with your permission,
I might address a few words to you
    concerning the legal advantages of life
and to the resonance of enthusiastic applause
I break ground with the pickax on the part at the top of my head
for the lofty edifice of my life.

I'm alive, yes, like Zendeh Rud River that was alive one day
and from all that is exclusively
    the right of living people I will derive benefit.

As of tomorrow,
I can march in alleys
that are full of the nation's blessings
and among the shadows of telegraph wires
scrawl graffiti with pride 678 times
on the toilet walls:
"I wrote in such a way that even a jackass would laugh,
the writer's dick to the reader's ass."

As of tomorrow,
like a zealous patriot,
I'll have in heart and mind

a share in the great ideal which society
every Wednesday afternoon
follows with anxious excitement,
a share of those thousand-desire-nurturing 1000-riyal notes
which can be used for refrigerators, furniture, and curtains
or which for 678 natural votes
can be donated one evening to 678 patriotic men.

As of tomorrow,
at the back of an Armenian's shop,
after inhaling several snorts of a few grams of firsthand pure stuff
and consuming several not-so-pure Pepsis
and uttering several Sufi exclamations,
I'll officially join the association of prominent pensive
learned people and enlightened erudite excrement
and followers of the school of la-dee-da,
and scribble the plot outline of my first great novel
which around year 2678 AD.
will be formally submitted to a bankrupt press
on both sides of 678 packs of genuine Oshno Special cigarettes.

As of tomorrow
with complete confidence
I'll treat myself to one [velvet covered] seat for 678 sessions
in the assembly of assembling and guaranteeing the future
or the assembly of gratitude and praise
because I read Art and Science
and Flattering and Bowing,
and I know the correct way to write.

I have strode into the arena of existence
in the midst of a creative populace
whose great scientific strength has brought them
to the threshold of manufacturing artificial clouds
and inventing neon lights
of course in the research and laboratory centers
of chicken kabob stands.

I have strode into the arena of existence
    in the midst of a creative populace
who although they have no bread
have instead an open and spacious vista
presently bounded
on the north by verdant Tir Square
and on the south by historic Execution Square
and in those overcrowded neighborhoods reaching Cannon Square.
And in the shelter of the shining sky secure in its security
from morning till night 678 big plaster swans
accompanied by 678 angels,
angels made of mud and clay,
are busy advertising plans for silence and inaction.

I won, yes, I've won.
Therefore long live 678, resident of Tehran,
    long live 678, issued at Precinct 5,
who by determination and perseverance
has reached such a lofty station that
she now stands in the frame of a window
    678 meters above the ground
and now has the honor of being able
from that very window, not by way of the stairs,
to hurl herself madly down
    into the affectionate bosom of the motherland.

And her final will and testament is this:
that, for 678 coins, the honorable master Abraham Sahba
compose an elegy in sing-song, eulogizing her life. (Exit)

FF: Poetry is like a window for me, each time I approach it opens automatically. I sit there, I look, I sing, I shout, I cry, I become one with the image of the trees, and I know that on the other side of the window there is space, and one person hears me—that one person who will, perhaps, be there a hundred years from now—or perhaps already existed three hundred years ago, it doesn't matter. Poetry is a tool of connection with existence, with the self in its larger meaning. In my poetry I don't look for anything, but I find myself.

In "Someone Unlike Anyone," injustice stinks. No one wants to talk about it. The little city girl's desire for social justice connects her to the thousand little girls who have had the misfortune to be born poor. Her hopes are simple, but honest…

(Dancers begin to the recorded tape in Persian and music.)

Someone Unlike Anyone (Kasi keh mesle hichkas nist, 1966)
I have dreamt that someone is coming
I have dreamt of a red star
and my eyes keep twitching
and my shoes keep pairing off
And may I go blind
if I am lying
I have dreamt of a red star
I have dreamt when I wasn't even asleep
Someone is coming
someone is coming
someone else
someone better
someone who is not like anyone
Not like father
Not like Ensi
Not like Yahya
Not like mother
He is like someone he should be
and he is taller than the trees of the builder's house
And his face
is brighter
than the face of the Mahdi
And he won't even be afraid of
Sayyed Javad's brother
who now
wears the policeman's uniform
And he is not even afraid of Sayyed Javad himself,
who owns all the rooms of our house.
And his name, as mother
calls him at the beginning and end of her prayers,

O judge of all judges,
O savior of all saviors
And he can
read all the difficult vocabulary words of
the third grade
with his eyes closed
And can even deduct one Thousand
out of Twenty Million without coming up short
And can buy everything he needs from Sayyed Javad's store on credit
And he can do something so that the "Allah's" neon sign
that was as green as dawn
lights up again in the sky above the Meftahyian Mosque

O…
How great is the bright light
How great, the bright light
And how much I want
for Yahya
to have a cart
and to have a little lantern
And how I really want to sit on Yahya's cart
among the melons and watermelons
and ride around Mohammadieh square
Ah…
How fun it is going around the square
How fun it is sleeping on the terrace
How great it is going to Melli park
How great it is tasting Pepsi
How great it is seeing the films of Fardin
And how I love all the good things
And how I yearn to pull Sayyed Javad's daughter's braids

Why am I so little
that I can get lost in the streets
Why doesn't my father—who is not so little
and who does not get lost in the streets—
do something to speed up the arrival of the someone
whom I've dreamt about

And the poor people who live near the slaughterhouse
even the soil of their gardens is blood-soaked
And the water in their courtyard pond is bloody
And the soles of their shoes are bloody
Why don't they do something about it
Why don't they do something?

How lazy the winter sunshine is
I have swept the staircase to the roof
I have even washed the windows
Why should my father only dream of him in his sleep?

I have swept the staircase to the roof
and I have even washed the windows

Someone is coming
Someone is coming
Someone who is with us in his heart,
in his breathing, and in his voice

Someone whose arrival
cannot be stopped
and handcuffed and thrown in prison
Someone who has been born under Yahya's old trees
and grows up day by day
Someone from the rain,
someone from the sound of rain splashing,
from among the whispering petunias

Someone is coming from the sky at Canon square,
from the night of fireworks,
and sets the table
And divvies up the bread
And divvies up the Pepsi
And divvies up Melli park
And divvies up the cough syrup
And divvies up the slips on registration day

And divvies up the hospital waiting room numbers
And divvies up the rubber boots
And divvies up Fardin movie tickets
And divvies up Sayyedd Javad's daughter's dresses
And divvies up whatever is extra
And he gives us our share too
I have dreamt....

FF: A poem is born in the space between the moments of darkening and lightening. So life is always partially rooted in darkness, a darkness of which one should always be aware. It is like being aware of the secrets of puberty—it is not an ugly thing, it's natural.

I wrote to my brother once:

Dear Feri:
I am glad my hair is turning gray and there are lines on my forehead and two deep furrows between my eyebrows. I am glad that I am no longer a dreamer now that I am nearly thirty-two, even though being thirty two years old means having used up and left behind thirty two years of one's allocation of life. But instead I have found myself.

(The actor recites or sings and does some movement with the following poem.)

The Bird Was Just A Bird (Parande faghat yek parandeh bood, 1964)
The bird said:
What a scent!
What a sun!
Ah, spring has arrived
and I am searching for my mate.
Like a message
The bird flew away
from the edge of the balcony.
The bird was little.
The bird didn't think.
The bird didn't read the newspaper.
The bird wasn't in debt.
The bird didn't know people.

The bird flew over
the traffic lights
at the height of ignorance
and experienced
the blue moments
passionately.

The bird, ah, was just a bird.

FF: It's five o'clock, and I have returned from my trip to the north. My father gave me hell. I lie on my bed and watch the sun's dim light reflected on the dusty ivy through the half open window. There is a sense of suffocation, a feeling that I am not alone. As if someone is trying to scream from far away. I wish I could lift my head up and do the same.

But I feel that my voice doesn't carry. It gets lost among other noises, among them my father's hateful and angry voice as he screams and stamps his feet. Slowly raising myself on the bed, I listen to his words.

"This girl has no shame, no respect for family and social values. If you let her be, she'll bring that asshole over in front of my eyes."

I close the door and put my head on the pillow again.

What is wrong with being in love and bringing him over? Why can't anyone understand this? The world has become a ridiculous place, a world that would take away the right to love. I want to shout: "Don't worry! I would never throw myself on his bosom. It would be demeaning to my love. Even if you begged me to do it, I wouldn't do it."

I roll on my bed restlessly and grow silent and stare at the flight of the pigeons. Ah, how lucky the pigeons are! Under the sharp light of the sun they look like scattered white flowers on the lake and with any waves, or any wave of light, they go to different sides, and the ones who are in love lean on each other's heads and caress each other's beak. The sun, the clear sky, the wind and strange birds don't ever scold them and nothing will destroy their excitement and no one will scream: "Hey rotten pigeons! Hey slut pigeons! Have you ever thought about your family's morality and traditions? Have you ever thought what your bastard children would call themselves in the future? Are you even aware that you're committing acts of such evil lust? When I tell these things to my father, he looks at me enraged and says, "Stupid, stupid child! We're human beings, do you understand? Human beings! And there are many more important things than our instincts in our lives that we should think about." He might be right. I won't condemn him, but he repeated the word "human beings" so many times that I thought to myself: "We 'human beings' are so miserable that we can't even own our existence."

(Video images in the background.)

He mumbled the word "shame, shame, shame" and then he spat and ran to his bedroom. I could hear him scolding my mother for bringing up a shameful daughter like myself. I closed the door, but I could imagine that my mother after a long silence would sarcastically say, "You are absolutely right. What else do you expect in a country where a woman is no better than a piece of meat."

I knew she would come to me in the middle of the night and kneel down by my bed and caress my hot face with her hard hands and say kindly, "My poor child, I don't want to say anything. I don't know who is right or wrong. I just want to tell you that you're sick and you have to take care of yourself. This man is not planning to get married to you. So leave him and forget about him. Think about us a little bit.

FF: My dear mother, I am twenty-four years old and I hadn't lived till that moment. I only squeezed my life like jasmine flowers among my fingers and smelled its fragrance. I just drank every particle of oxygen and put the heavens in my bosom for only a week. Only for one week and you are so jealous about it.

How small this world is when it comes to loving! I felt this throughout my whole trip. People are jealous in spite of kindness. My mother believes that I have run away like a thief and my father says that he has never seen anyone so rude and shameless as I am. They expected me to get permission from them and say, "Dear father, dear mother, please allow me to go to the beach for a week with a man I love." I couldn't have told them because I left early in the morning and they would have created a war scene.

Behind the window, the night is falling like mist. As if night has crawled inside me, and I am sad. I don't want to open my eyes to the world that I have gotten to know. I feel that something is seizing my soul and I still stare at the pigeons in the sky.

I wish I was a pigeon. This world is too small for loving. Too small...!

Narrator: Forugh's car accident was a horrible one. The cemetery was filled with people. Forugh slept peacefully. There was no feeling in those excited, artistic hands.

(Video collage of the cemetery with my interviews of the young girl should be seen.)

As she grew up, Forugh became more and more silent. Her big eyes that were always so full of wonder started to change their shape and were filled with puzzled sadness. She always looked at the world differently from other people. And now, at her funeral, she was alone like her solitary moon and everyone was still jealous of her beauty...

(The dancers come on stage! Recorded voice of both English and Persian are heard at the beginning of the dance)

The Solitary Moon (Tanhaeeye Mah, 1964)
All along darkness,
the crickets cried:
Moon, ah, Great Moon.

All along darkness,

branches with their long arms
emitting a lustful sigh,

and the breeze
that had surrendered
to unknown secret gods,

and the thousands of hidden souls
in the secret layers of the soil,

and the glow worm
in its circling bright ring,
and the creaking
in the wooden ceiling,
Leyli from her tapestry,
frogs in the pond,

incessantly and in perfect harmony,
till dawn,
cried:
Moon, ah, Great Moon.

All along darkness,
the moon was aflame
on the balcony.
The moon was nothing
more than the heart
of her own solitary night.

All along darkness,
she sat sobbing
in her golden grief.

Forugh: Something is bothering me, something is getting under my skin and pushing me to dig in the earth and reach to the very depths of it. I belong to the soil of this world. My love is a place where seeds grow and spread their roots.... When I was away from home, I was like an orphan always thinking about my sunflowers. How much have they grown? Will you write to me as soon as they have flowers?

(Dancers begin dancing to the music that is made for this poem.)

On the Earth (Rouye Khak, 1964)
I have never wished
to be a star in the mirage of heavens
or to become the silent compatriot of angels
like the chosen spirits
I have never been separated from the earth
I haven't been acquainted with the stars
I stand on the earth
with my body like the stem of a plant
that sucks the wind, the sun, and the water
to live
filled with desire
filled with pain

I stand on the earth
 so the stars may worship me
 so the breezes may caress me

I am looking from my window
I am only the echo of a melody
I am not eternal
I am not seeking anything more
than the echo of a melody
in a joy that is more pure than the silence of a sorrow
I am not looking for a nest
in a body that is like a dew on my body

On the wall of my life's hut
the passersby have drawn memories with the black script of love:
a broken heart
an upside down candle
pale silent dots
among the crazy letters
any lip that touched my lip
a star was conceived
in my nights on the lake of memories
so why should I wish for the stars?

This is my melody
sweet and pleasant
there hasn't been anything more than this in the past

FF: There are some people whose daily lives are unrelated to their poetry, which means that they are only poets when they write poetry, then it's over. Poetry is a serious matter to me. It's a responsibility I feel toward myself, it provides the answers in my life. For me, being a poet means to be a human being.

(Parts of the video images of "Let Us Believe In The Beginning of The Cold Season" are seen at the end again.)

That Sara Aziz!

~Maniza Naqvi

Meet Ava, Sonia, Kulsum, and Shireen in four different levels but totally connected: from a sidewalk café where Ava who is a lawyer, is seated sipping her caffe latte, magazines scattered on the table in front of her, text messaging on her cellular phone. In a high rise building, somewhere down on Wall Street, where Sonia, an investment banker, is at her desk in an office seated in front of her computer emailing and next to her phone. In the suburbs of Westchester county where Kulsum, a housewife, is in her kitchen on a cordless phone. In a car, Shireen, stuck in traffic on the Triboro bridge, is a real estate agent and is also attached to her cellular phone by an earphone.

Let's give quiet Kulsum the opening line shall we? Scene opens. She's in her kitchen. She is mixing something in a bowl. Finishes, washes her hands, and stands looking out of the window drumming her fingers on the kitchen counter, and goes to the phone to dial. As the phone is ringing, she goes over to the stove and turns on one of the burners. Then reaches in the cabinet for a frying pan. (She continues with the motions of preparing and then frying pakoras through the following scene. The spotlight goes on at another part of the stage where Sonia is seated in front of her computer in the office.)

Kulsum: Hi Sonia, are you very busy?

Sonia: Hello my dear, never too busy to talk to you. What's up?

Kulsum: Oh nothing much, the usual. You know. It's so quiet, now that all the in-laws have gone home. Faraz is off on a business trip, to California, will be back next week. The kids are out with the nanny. So, finally, I have a moment to myself.

Sonia: Well I hope you're taking it easy, don't do anything, just sit back and relax.

Kulsum: Yes, relax, that's a good idea. No, yaar they're all very nice, they helped out and everything, everyone realizes this is not back home, you have to do things yourself over here. They are good sports; they said they actually had fun cooking-shooking, cleaning-sheening.

Sonia: Still, yaar, so many people, just relax.

Kulsum: Noooo-oh, what so many people? If we were back home I'd be living with them. No? So once in awhile if they come over, I like it very much…

Sonia: You don't always have to be such a goodie-goodie.

Kulsum: I'm not being a goodie-goodie. I mean it. It's so quiet now that they're gone, no one to talk to, no one to eat with. I mean it's just so different here, alone. The kids are missing everyone too. You know the grandparents and the uncles and aunts...

Sonia: Well, you're going home to Lahore for the winter holidays.... Anyway, how are the little favorite munchkins of mine?

Kulsum: Fine, just beginning to sound a bit too American for my liking. At 3 and 5 it's becoming why mom this and why mom that on everything and whining about everything.

Sonia: Well, that's going to happen. They were born here. Try to keep it to a minimum.

Kulsum: I keep telling Faraz we should go back. We have two daughters. I mean I don't want to raise them here. At least for a couple of years we should go back.

Sonia. You're sounding like a total jahil. What are you trying to say anyway?

Kulsum: Don't get me wrong. I want them to do all the things, get educated, work, everything, but growing up here, I feel worried.

Sonia: What are you worried about for god's sake!

Kulsum: I mean they are growing up alone, no relatives, no idea of sharing, no values.

Sonia: That's bull. They'll have your values and whatever else you want to teach them.

Kulsum: I can't teach them everything. The culture...

Sonia: Trust me on this one. Whatever you don't teach them, they don't need to learn.

Kulsum: I don't know yaar. I'm beginning to worry.

Sonia: You have nothing to worry about.

Kulsum: No honestly, yaar. Look, we weren't raised here.

Sonia: I know, I know what you mean.

Kulsum: I don't want them to lose out on that. That's all. Listen, why don't you come over. Yaar it's been weeks since we've gotten together, shouldn't we all get together? Why not come over for dinner?

Sonia: Tonight?

Kulsum: Yes, tonight, just catch the train and I'll pick you up at the station. Why don't you take the 7:05. It'll get you here at about 7:45. I'll meet you at the station.

Sonia: Can't tonight. How about tomorrow?

Kulsum: (Sighs) Fine.

Sonia: Don't sound so sad! We'll do dinner tomorrow. Why, what's wrong?

Kulsum: Nothing's wrong.

Sonia: Then why the deep sigh.

Kulsum: It's just so quiet here.

Sonia: You're just having the post-guests-from-back-home blues.

Kulsum: Guess so.

Sonia: We'll talk up a storm tomorrow night, and I'll stay over, go straight to work from your place okay.

Kulsum: Sounds good! Tomorrow is fine.

Sonia: Great.

Kulsum: Let's ask Ava and Shireen too.

Sonia: Okay.

Kulsum: Hold on let me get Ava. Ava?

Ava: Hi Kulsum!

Sonia: Hi, I'm here too.

Ava: Oh Hi, Sonia. Whatup?

Kulsum: Oh please Ava, don't start talking like a hoodlum.

Ava: Oh sorry dear, adab, how are you? What's going on?

Kulsum: Dinner. Tomorrow night at my place.

Ava: Sorry, Kulsum. I can't. How about the day after?

Kulsum: Another quick trip?

Ava: No, I'm suppose to meet a nephew of Faiza Khala, who works in the city.

All together: Ah huh?

Ava: Right. I suspect it's a major set up attempt.

Sonia: Suspect?

Ava: No, I know it is. But what the heck, I didn't want to let Faiza Khala down. I'll just go do dinner and grit my teeth.

Kulsum: Poor Ava.

Ava: I know yaar, this is really humiliating.

Kulsum: Okay, well then the day after tomorrow and we can have a post mortem of the nephew and dinner.

Sonia: Yes, Ava you can tell us how he tasted, whether you had him grilled or broiled or…

Ava: (Laughs) Yes, so day after tomorrow?

Sonia: Fine by me.

Kulsum; Okay.

Sonia: Kulsum, should I get Shireen on the line?

Kulsum: Would you? Thanks.

Shireen: Hello!

Sonia, Ava and Kulsum: Hi Shireen.

Shireen: Oh good, my favorite three, what's up.

Kulsum: Dinner day after tomorrow, my place, Kulsum and Ava can make it.

Shireen: Darlings! I'd love too. But what to do, can't, it's my yoga class night. But I'm free tonight or tomorrow.

Sonia: Can't. I have a blind date tonight.

Ava: Can't tomorrow night. I have my book group and then I have to rush for my tango class.

Kulsum: Can't we ever get together?

Sonia: Next week is all clear for me.

Ava: Can do Tuesday next week.

Shireen: Me too.

Sonia: Me three.

Kulsum: So dinner next week Tuesday. We're on, my place. But Sonia, come over tomorrow, too.

Sonia: Done. Ciao. Mañana.

Ava: Adios.

Shireen: Bye for now.

Kulsum: Khudahafiz.

Sonia turns to her computer. Reads for awhile. As she reads her email: "Fuck! I can't believe it! What the hell? This is unbelievable. She's really done it this time, the dumb fuck!" Picks up the phone and punches in the numbers.

The spotlight on Kulsum lights up, the phone rings and Kulsum frying something goes, picks up the phone, and walks back to the oven,

Kulsum: Hello. Siddiqqi residence.

Sonia: It's me again.

Kulsum: Look Sonia, I don't want to hear you can't come over tomorrow!

Sonia: No, not to worry. That's not why I'm calling. Guess what, you are not going to believe this.

Kulsum: He asked you and you're getting married.

Sonia: Don't you ever have anything else on your mind?

Kulsum: No, not where you're concerned, no. What else am I supposed to think about?

Sonia: Anyway, before you really get me angry, do you want to know what I called you for?

Kulsum: What? Tell me. I hope it's good gossip.

Sonia: Oh yeah, oooh yeah, this is a good one. And it ain't gossip.

Kulsum: Okay, yaar, I can't take the suspense.

Sonia: Guess what dear cousin Sara is doing?

Kulsum: She's getting a divorce? Oh no, not again. No wait, she's having an affair, Oh no, not again. She got drunk and was found naked in the garden in the hammock with someone else's husband? Oh no, not again!

Sonia: Oh no, much better than that. Much, much better. She's really done it this time. Are you ready?

Kulsum: Do I have to sit down for this, because I'm doing dangerous work right now. I don't want to hurt myself with the shock.

Sonia: Yeah, sit down. Are you ready? Dear, stupid, hypocritical, dizzy Sara, has gone into…

Kulsum: Labor, coma, business with the drug mafia, exile, convulsions, what, what?

Sonia: Hijab.

Kulsum: What?

Sonia: Hijab.

Kulsum: What?

Sonia: Exactly.

Kulsum: What? Where did you get that?

Sonia: Just got an email from Rehana, who saw her at a party last night. Dear, dear cousin Sara, walked in, covered in a Hijab. And Rehana said that she hadn't believed it either when people told her, because a lot of women had seen her around, you know picking up the kids at grammar school, etc., but last night at the fund raiser for the Heart Center, there she was, in Hijab!

Kulsum: So what?

Sonia: What do you mean, so what? It's ridiculous!

Kulsum: But many girls wear hijabs here, don't they, and in France and Germany and England?

Sonia: Yes, here. But not Pakistan. It's not our thing! It's not our culture. I mean it doesn't go with what we wear! It's western for godssake!

Kulsum: Malaysian and Indonesian women wear it.

Sonia: For god's sake, they're western... compared to us.

Kulsum: You're losing it.

Sonia: You're being stupid, and you know it.

Kulsum: Well you're just being silly.

Sonia: We're talking Sara, here.

Kulsum: So many other women in Pakistan are doing this now...

Sonia: She's not them!

Kulsum: Look Sonia, women need to wear the hijab because they're going out more to find jobs, working in offices, factories, taking public transportation. It's just a way of security for them and acceptance of their stepping out into the domain of men.

Oh wait, I have another call coming in. Hello, han, Ava. I've got Sonia on the line. You are not going to believe what she just told me. Hang up, I'll call you right back. Sonia, are you there?

Sonia: Yes.

Kulsum: I'm going to get Ava on the phone with us. Hold on. Ava

Ava: Hi!

Sonia: Hi again, Ava!

Ava: Hi Sonia!

Sonia: Where are you?

Ava: Bus yaar, finally an afternoon off! I decided to just take in the sun. I've had it with the deposition work. I hate the hours. I hate my bosses. I hate being on the partner track. I want to drop this whole thing. I'm telling you, it's just too much. I just got back from bloody Tokyo over the weekend only to find out I had to go for a day meeting to London. I just got back last night. I cannot understand why these things cannot be done through teleconferencing. I mean it's totally ridiculous. Okay, so one does chalk up the frequent flier miles, but frankly one doesn't need them (A) because one can never take a vacation and (B) because one has enough money to buy one's own tickets, thank you very much. And (C) again, because one never has the time to take vacations anyway! Then the first thing that happens this morning is that my client tells me he's having a panic attack, can't go through with the damn merger, and I'm saying go take a Prozac, calm down, do yoga, whatever, but I am not going to listen to not going through with the merger after I've sacrificed six months of my days and nights slaving over the bloody price earning ratios parity-bullshit. I'm really thinking about…

Sonia: Join dating.com.

Ava: What?

Kulsum: What?

Sonia: Dating.com. My blind date tonight, that's where he's from. I'm telling you, it's the best thing.

Kulsum: You're going to get killed by an ax murderer!

Ava: She's right, Sonia.

Sonia: Calm down! It's totally the thing. Since you're doing the "whatup" thing, you might as well do the dating.com as well.

Ava: Seriously Sonia…

Kulsum: Ava, shut up. Acha, shut up, we've got news for you.

Ava: (bored) What?

Sonia: You're going to love it.

Ava: What?

Kulsum: Sara was sighted last night at a charity ball in Karachi.

Ava: So? So what's the big deal? I thought news would be if Sara wasn't sighted at a charity ball in Karachi. Sort of like "man bites dog."

Kulsum: In a Hijab.

Ava: Excuse me?

Sonia: Sighted at the ball in a HIJAB!

Ava: I'm assuming it was a fancy dress ball and she was going as the Saudi Princess off to have her head chopped off, or the love interest of Mullah Omer.

Sonia: Good, very good. That was funny.

Ava: What the hell is she doing in a Hijab?

Sonia: This is just too good. Let's get Shireen on the line. Hold on, everyone. (She dials).

Shireen: Hello.

Sonia: Hi Shireen, I've got Ava and Kulsum on the line as well.

Kulsum: Hi!

Ava: Hi!

Shireen: Hi, Hi! Traffic is hell on the Triboro.

Sonia: What the hell are you doing on the Triboro at this time?

Shireen: Trying to get home to pick up the kids, yaar. Had a property I was showing in midtown. Acha Sonia, are you still interested in that loft in Tribeca, because you really need to let me know pretty soon.

Sonia: Next week, for sure okay?

Shireen: Is that a pukka okay?

Sonia: Yes, okay, next week, definitely.

Shireen: Fine.

Ava: How's the market?

Shireen: You tell me! You guys are the ones on Wall Street! I don't get it. It seems like people are just made of money. They don't know what to do with it. I just showed someone a place on West 72nd which can only be referred to as a walk-in closet, and the guy is putting down 750 for it. What is going on?

Sonia: What can I say, it's the stock market. It's the abouttoblow.com. It's crazy and it's about to blow.

Kulsum: You say that everyday Sonia. It hasn't blown yet.

Shireen: Well, until it blows I'm sure making beautiful commissions and that's fine for me baba. It's going to put the kids through college yaar. So don't say stuff that's going to jinx things or get the gods upset.

Ava: Shireen we've got some juicy stuff for you.

Shireen: Prada has a new design out in shoes?

Ava: Well, not as good as that.

Sonia: Well, almost as good.

Sonia: Dirt?

Ava: Oh yeah!

Sonia: Second that motion.

Shireen: It better be good dirt.

Sonia: Oh yeah, babe, like how!

Kulsum: Well, it isn't dirt.

Ava: Oh yeah it is, it's about Sara, not mother Theresa.

Shireen: She's not marrying again!

Sonia: Nope.

Ava: That's not dirt. That's recycled waste.

Kulsum: Whatever that means.

Sonia: Yeah Ava, what does that mean?

Ava: Don't know, just thought I'd say it.

Shireen: Okay, get with the program. Not an affair-shafair or anything?

Sonia: No such wimpy stuff.

Shireen: Oh my. This is going to be good. What is it? Naked again?

Sonia: Keep guessing, Shireen.

Shireen: Give up!

Ava: Hijabing it.

Shireen: Hijacking??? She's been hijacked?

Kulsum: (laughing) No! She's gone into hijab.

Sonia: She's gone no where. She's going everywhere as usual only she's wearing a hijab.

Shireen: Sara's in hijab?

Sonia: Yup.

Shireen: Hijab?

Ava: Yup.

Shireen: Unbelievable.

Sonia: Why? It fits in with all her other crazinesses.

Kulsum: It's not even part of our culture.

Sonia: Exactly.

Shireen: I mean what's happened to the place since we left. It used to be normal when we were there. Never heard of the hijab.

Kulsum: Of course dupattas…

Shireen: And chaddars and really if one was from the old city in Lahore then burqas, but what's with the hijab?

Sonia: It's totally Saudi, and our dear Sara is doing that hijab thang!

Shireen: Yet another one of Sara's fads!

Ava: Only this one's in our faces. This one is really making me throw up and get angry. How dare she do everything, break every rule, and then throw this morality in our faces, that bloody hypocritical bitch!

Kulsum: Hold on, she isn't doing this to you.

Ava: Oh yes she is. For her two days worth of whimsical trendiness copycatting somebody else I'm sure, she is causing a lot of harm.

Kulsum: Well…

Ava: Don't say she isn't! You know she's not capable of an iota of original thinking. I bet some rich woman out there that she hangs around with is in hijab suddenly and so Sara Begum decides to don it as well.

Kulsum: Maybe it's more than that.

Sonia: Why should it be? Over the time we've known her, how

many transformations have we seen, the remaking, the recreation of Sara Aziz? She went from long hair to short, from fat to thin, from brown eyes to green contact lenses, from brown hair to blond. From one husband to a fourth. From poor to filthy rich. I mean there is just nothing that you can say is constant about her.

Kulsum: That would make for an interesting person.

Ava: Or an extremely vacuous one.

Kulsum: Or perhaps there's some Mullah Omer in her life. She seems to attract men…

Ava: Oh for god's sake!!

Sonia: She thinks she can suddenly go into Hijab after all that she has done and become Ms. Saint. As if everyone is going to forget her past.

Kulsum: Well it's been known to happen.

Shireen: Well I think it's just in keeping with her frame of mind. Frankly, I think she's anorexic. Did you see how thin she was last time she was here? And she ate absolutely nothing, and she was on the treadmill all the time. A spoon of Ben and Jerry's god forbid, and she would spend the entire night on the treadmill at my place. Honestly baba, she drove me crazy. Tobah!!

Ava: Ben and Jerry was acquired by Unilever?

Sonia: Yes!

Shireen: Oh no! Does that mean my kids are going to make me boycott it? I mean years of not eating Häagen-Daz because they invested in South Africa, now this…

Sonia: It's history, Shireen. Anyway, coming back to the point: Sara, she's just selfish.

Shireen: Or you know what?

Kulsum: What?

Shireen: I think it may be she's getting older, and you know how obsessed she is about being young.

Ava: And the hijab covers the thinning hair, the sagging skin around the jowls and the neck?

Sonia: For god's sake we're all only 40!

Kulsum: But Sara stopped at 29. So she's 29. Hijab is so much healthier than Botox!

Sonia: Oh yeah, we're really 11 years older than her. Give me a break!

Kulsum: This year we are but next year, darling, we'll be twelve years older than her.

Shireen: No I think you are absolutely right. I was going to say the same thing. You know, I think she is really afraid of getting old and this is a good way to cover it up. But I think she's anorexic also. And then you know she really got a scare this year with the heart attack that Riaz had.

Sonia: Give me a break. Scare? My ass! It took her exactly one week after that to start planning her next trip to Europe.

Kulsum: What does that have to do with anything? Doesn't mean it didn't affect her.

Shireen: I think she really took it to heart. You know she really loves him.

Ava: Like she loved all the rest?

Kulsum: That is not very fair, is it?

Sonia: Ava, really, it isn't.

Ava: It's my opinion.

Shireen: Poor Sara.

Ava: Why poor Sara? She's a bloody hypocrite. *No so choaie kha key billie kerney challi haj*. The cat snarfs down 900 mice and heads off to perform haj.

Sonia: Haj! That's it. She went for her haj, didn't she? Maybe all the trips for umra and haj have done this.

Ava: Give me a break, haj and umra. You know I don't buy that at all. She goes there only to buy gold. It's the best place to buy gold y'know!

Kulsum: Don't be cruel. That's really unfair. She has always been religious. She has always done these things.

Shireen: That's true. That is one thing she has always done since she was a child. She has always prayed five times a day.

Ava: Well, you know what? I wish she hadn't. Because all her life she has done whatever she pleased, hurt whoever she pleased, broken every rule in the book, lied through her teeth, and made sure she absolved herself five times a day. So don't give me that shit.

Kulsum: I don't think we should sit in judgment of her that way. She has had a hard life. Seen a lot of pain.

Ava: Hard life? Hard life? She has caused endless suffering. She has lived for herself. Done only as she pleased, got her way in everything, and never given a damn about anyone.

Sonia: I second that motion!

Ava: How dare she? How dare she under the circumstances in this country do this!

Kulsum: What?

Ava: What do you mean "what," Kulsum?

Kulsum: What circumstances are you talking about?

Ava: The situation in this country!

Kulsum: What do you mean?

Ava: Kulsum, women are being killed in the name of honor!

Kulsum: What does this have to do with Sara?!

Ava: Everything! Women are being killed in the name of honor, for demanding a divorce or wanting to exercise their choice in marriage! All in the name of honor and chardivari. Women there work, just like they do here. They need to be able to move around, interact with other people. And she, she of all people, of all the people, Sara, should have the audacity to take this up as a badge. To actually become a part of that. Now that she has all she wants by doing exactly whatever she wanted all her life, she wants to take that away from everyone else.

Kulsum: She's doing it herself. She's not inflicting it on anyone else.

Ava: Oh yeah, if she walks into a room with all of us, and she is in a Hijab while the rest of us aren't, what does that say for us?

Kulsum: Why should it be about you or us? It's about her. Why are you reacting this way?

Ava: Don't you dare call me a reactionary to that bloody hypocrite. Don't you know what happened next door with the Taliban. Don't you read anything ever Kulsum?

Kulsum: Well, I do know my geography darling. It's not next door, next door is Scarsdale, quite frankly.

Ava: Do be serious!

Kulsum: Why don't you be less so? Do you really think I don't know what's happening in Pakistan or the world? But around you, I swear, I really feel like just giving it all a rest.

Shireen: Bibiyon! Bhainon! Hazrat!! Women! Girls! Kids! Dolls! For god's sake!

Ava: No, I can't let this just go. I can't let it rest. It has to matter. There is a country of women who are being buried alive in their houses, behind chaddors, even their footsteps cannot be heard. They are dying of suffocation. And this bitch thinks she can fool around with the Hijab because of whatever.

Sonia: Well, I think there's a bit of exaggeration there. And I'm not ready to condemn the Taliban. They've at least controlled most of the country, and if they can stop the fighting and the killing then let the women be in chaddar, for peace, so be it. And it can't last forever. It's only a phase. For peace, it's worth it.

Ava: Oh my god. I cannot believe what I'm hearing! Are you crazy? What's happening to everyone? It's all about the drug trade, the pipeline for oil. And women and children are paying the price.

Kulsum: Frankly, Ava, I don't think you want to hear anyone except yourself.

Ava: Frankly, Kulsum, I have something worth saying. It's hard to hear someone prattling on about with who, what, why all the time!

Kulsum: Well excuse me!

Shireen: Time out!

Ava: Why time out? Why should we try to even explain Sara's behavior. We know her. We know what she is all about. Suddenly this hijab should make her worthy of being above board, requiring our respect.

Kulsum: No one said that.

Ava: Sure, they did, maybe it's anorexia, maybe it's Riaz's heart attack. Bullshit. She is thin because she thinks she can attract the next fat cat with her sexy body and frankly should someone richer come along, Riaz dropping dead would only facilitate the matter.

Shireen: Don't be stupid, Ava. Watch your mouth. God forbid.

Kulsum: Really, Ava. Toba. God Forbid.

Sonia: Ava, cool it. Okay?

Ava: Fine. God forbid anything should happen to Riaz bhai.

Kulsum: I mean, if Sara, who has always been inclined toward religion all her life, should choose to do this, why is it such a terrible thing?

Shireen: We don't seem to have a problem with women wearing long skirts one day and short skirts in another season when the magazines dictate it so, so why be so overcome with anger over a hijab?

Sonia: C'mon guys, Sara has to manage her garment business. She does travel to the inner city areas, where people are conservative. All her workers are men and they are pretty conservative. She probably earns a lot of their respect by dressing that way and it probably allows her to stay around them for longer periods of time without question and without hassle.

Ava: I just cannot believe this shit. I cannot believe you guys.

Kulsum: And if you are going to follow the words in the Qur'an then…

Ava: Don't you dare say what you're going to say.

Kulsum: It's in the Qur'an.

Ava: It is not, it is not. This is exactly what an absolute ignoramus like yourself will say. You've never bothered to read anything…

Shireen: Ava, watch it!

Kulsum: Are you telling me that it isn't in the Qur'an?

Ava: I am telling you that the Qur'an does not say wear a hijab or to hide yourself. There is only one reference my dear: "O prophet tell your wives and daughters and the women of the faithful to draw their wraps a little over them. They will thus be recognized and no harm will come to them." That's it. In a state of war, it's in a contextual frame. Think about it, in a war, when men are animals…

Kulsum: Are you sure that's the only reference?

Ava: Positive.

Kulsum: Wow Ava, I didn't realize you were such an "Islamic."

Ava: See! For you that's an exogenous feature. I have to be something to do that. To me, reading the Qur'an is not a big deal! And in any case I have to, to be able to ward off fools like you!

Kulsum: Wow, I'm very proud of you. But are you sure? Can I quote you?

Ava: Of course I'm sure. I'm not you! And you're not quoting me, it's the Qur'an.

Sonia: Ava, I'm not so sure yaar, it's all over the place.

Ava: Where is it? Show me. Tell me. Where?

Sonia and Shireen: In Sura e Nisa.

Ava: I knew it! I knew it. You guys are so damn predictable. Women, in the section labeled women. You bloody affirmative action freak heads! Turns out gals, no. Not a word about any hijab, a whole lot though about sowing fields and guess what them fields are… us, us being the fields, but not a word about the hijab action. And by the way while I'm at it, that business about two women equal to one man, that is also bullshit. One reference only in the Qur'an… under a business transaction only, again contextual because women didn't deal with financial matters in those days.

Kulsum: Oh no you don't! Caught you! His wife Khadija was a

business woman!

Sonia: Yeah, but she did hire him to take care of her financial matters! Okay, so we've come a long way baby.

Ava: Exactly and again contextual. Although I wish we could be more like her. A forty-year-old marrying a 29-year-old guy and doing the proposing as well. Talk about a woman of the 21st century. You go gal. Love that gal.

Kulsum: Sonia learned something.

Sonia: If she were here, she'd be one of us. And Kulsum, do you think she was in a hijab when she did that? If she were here, I tell you, she'd be like us!

Shireen: Stuck in traffic on the Triboro, after closing a fabulous deal.

Sonia: Meeting Mohammad on dating.com.

Kulsum, Shireen, Ava: Toba, toba, god forbid.

Kulsum: Really Sonia!

Ava: I think she'd be sitting here sipping caffe latte, sitting here with me. She'd be the head of some corporation and right now would be appreciating the great abs that just walked by. Mmm-Mmm-Mmmm. Lord have mercy!

Kulsum: Tooba, tooba, tooba…

Ava: …and telling Kulsum to shut up and dialing Sara to tell her to get a life!

Sonia: Any second now we're all going to be struck down by lightning. I can feel it.

Kulsum: Please don't blaspheme Ava!

Shireen: Han baba, please, watch it. I think lightning travels and I certainly don't want to be zapped for you having a mouth on you.

Ava: Honestly. You guys are too much. Sara and her vacousness seems like holy devotion to you, while what I say is blasphemy!

Kulsum: She prays.

Ava: How the hell do you know what I do?

Sonia: Yeah Kulsum, Sara is not the only one who prays you know. She may be the only one who manages to be such a conspicuous performer.

Shireen: Yadan Aiyan, aiyan, loki panjwaley, usan her waley, yadan aiyan, aiyan. I remember you, everyone else remembers at allotted times, five times a day, me I remember you all the time.

Ava: Well sung darling.

Kulsum: Okay, everyone, bye.

Sonia: Ciao.

Shireen: Later.

Ava: Hasta la vista babes.

Sonia: Stay on the line Ava. I want to talk to you.

Ava: Okay. Look I'll call you right back okay. Bye everyone.

Sonia: Okay. Bye everyone.

Ava: Hi, it's me.

Sonia: You sound much better. Are you?

Ava: Yeah, I guess I'm much better. You haven't told anyone, have you?

Sonia: No, of course I haven't. But are you okay?

Ava: Well you can't really feel sympathy for me can you?

Sonia: You went into this knowing the full picture.

Ava: Yes. I place bets with myself that I'll hear from him the moment the weekend ends and he gets back to work. And so far I'm winning my own bet. I'm just one of his bad travel habits: cigarettes, quick gulp downs of bloody Marys; surfing the cable channels mindlessly.

Sonia: Ava, listen to me, you can't possibly be thinking of continuing this. There is nothing in this for you. What are you trying to do Ava? Why are you bent on hurting yourself like this?

Ava: I am amused that he now wants to be friends. Now that he has declared me a friend, does that mean I fall into the waste bin? His calling me a dear friend, I wonder why that makes me wince?

Sonia: Ava, what's the point? You knew there was an end as you were going into it in the first place.

Ava: I just don't get this. What an asshole. What a user!

Sonia: Look, leave it for what it was. Don't demonize him. You were both in this. Just leave it.

Ava: I can't. I can't disengage that way. What have I done here? There's no recognition of me. I need some recognition from him that this meant something to him. I feel like I'm walking in a silent invisible form.

Sonia: What is it that you wanted? What is it that you expected? He was going to leave you. You knew that going in. He told you that straight off the first time. You know the first thing men say is usually honest and truthful.

Ava: To not be acknowledged, that's what hurts. I've got to at least say this to him.

Sonia: No! Let go please. You've had two weeks of a break and he hasn't communicated with you during this whole time, so why even think of starting again?

Ava: No surprise there. I tested the hypothesis, and it tested positive. Pursuit, conquer, demolish, move on. All this is so pointless. POINTLESS.

Sonia: No, you needed to get that out of your system. It's done. Not pointless for that purpose. Pointless if you do anything more.

Ava: So for him it was just a continuation in a way of the big acquisition battle. So this must have been war all along? I wonder. I'm beginning to wonder if he really did consider me the adversary, the enemy all along. That it was him who had me pegged for the other, the one that needed to be defeated. I was the one who wanted to be a friend. I said that, we could be friends. He was so bent on "wanting."

Sonia: Be honest with yourself, Ava. You were doing the same thing as well! It was that whole merger thing.

Ava: But for him, wanting me translated into destroying and conquering, unraveling and unpacking. I even said that to him, don't unpack me, don't unravel me. But he wouldn't listen, just focused on wanting. How strange indeed that he should think that since now that he no longer values, no longer cherishes, he can be a dear friend. Now that the demolishing is done that he should think he could be a "dear friend." How does that work? It makes life like being at war. At war like this, engaging only to destroy, viewing the other as a danger, always despising the other as an enemy? Only able to deal with people on the basis of demolishing them?

Sonia: Ava, all you are doing is validating all the worst notions about yourself to yourself. Thinking his thoughts for him. Thinking everyone's thoughts for them. Validating your suspicions.

Ava: I get that from my therapist. I don't need that from you.

Sonia: Ava, it's true. This is one more reason for you to continue to be angry with yourself, with everyone! To remain an outsider; remain angry and cynical. He acted as you feared he would. And you acted as you feared you would.

Ava: And your point is?

Sonia: Break this cycle you're in. Ava, is this helping at all? Promise me you are not going to call him again.

Ava: It's over. Don't worry. I'm done.

Sonia: Promise.

Ava: Khuda ki Kasum. Okay?

Sonia: Okay, Ava, okay.

Ava: You have to admit though, Riaz bhai married Sara. She's lucky. Okay, she's his fourth wife. But he married her.

Sonia: Ava!

Ava: I'll give her that. I'll give him that.

Sonia: You're sounding totally ridiculous.

Ava: Perhaps.

Sonia: Trust me. Dating.com. Try it.

Ava: Don't be ridiculous!

Chocolate in Heat—Growing Up Arab in America

~Betty Shamieh

Note: This play sold out when it premiered at the New York International Fringe Festival in August 2001 under the direction of Damen Amir Scranton and performed by Betty Shamieh and Piter Fattouche. The same production was remounted for an extended and critically acclaimed run at Theater for the New City in 2002.

I. Need
II. Love
III. Ignorance
IV. Sex
V. Justice

Need ~ performed by Betty Shamieh

Education made me buy things I did not need and shoes that did not fit. The day before the Signet Society's Annual Ball, I found love in a pair of red stilettos my roommate, Jackie, picked out for me. Jackie didn't sponsor me as her guest for the ball because she liked me (though incidentally she did), but because I could play the part of the local exotique. The Society, as it was called by friends and foes, was initially created to facilitate the mingling of the best and the brightest with, as always, a few of the most beautiful in between. I was a scholarship kid, complete with a picture of me in my college's propaganda pamphlets that seemed to say, "See this face! Here's your proof we're making outcasts like this one overeducated enough to know that they'll always be underprivileged in this world!"

However, I had to be glamorously underprivileged and luxuriously poor or I was not welcome at the Society. I knew it and Jackie knew I couldn't afford it. Providing for me like a madam, Jackie took me to the local consignment shop to the dried up stars who could no longer afford to shine. There I found my version of the glass slippers with their red spikes. They were half a size too small. But I bought them and in a borrowed dress, I dressed and went, tapping my way to the marble door. Champagne all around and when a liveried butler offered me a drink in time, I exclaimed, "brink it and let me clink it" as I toasted every living soul taking up space in that room.

An old man, bearded like Father Time, watched me all the while. I asked, "Who is that?" and Jackie told me that he had won the Nobel Prize and came to all the Society parties. When I asked, "What for?" she answered irritably, "Something scientific. Who cares?" But I did and toasted his nobility, for the sake of science, as he beamed back.

There was an Arab prince there. Being an Arab myself, to me all Arab men are princes, but this one was an actual prince. The prince nodded to me politely. The prince was always polite. I said something nasty about his father's regime once, something I shouldn't have said, something I wouldn't have said if I had known he was in earshot.

Graham showed up with the cocaine. Graham wasn't a Society member, but since (in the words of Jackie) "his father owns the media and used it to buy the world," he was welcomed in the marble door by the aspiring and ambitious actors in us all, myself among the first and the last to see him that night (though the first is so rarely the last). As the roads made the rounds, I spilt more of the sand of heaven than I sniffed when no one stared. I preferred toasting champagne all night long, with making the tiny touch of my glass to yours more intimate than a kiss as I told all to "brink it and clink it with me." Soon the whole room caught on to my mantra, yelling, "brink it and clink it" then "brink and clink" and finally just "clink, clink, clink."

A thousand hands, quite a few more than necessary, lifted me on the carved oak table and asked me to make the traditional final toast as I towered and tottered above them. I raised my glass, like a Viking calling his comrades to war, and screeched, "To the most beautiful of the best and the brightest!" as the crescendo of clinks rose again only to descend into laughter. But after the denouement, all reached for their coats in one fell swoop, as I cried, "No! You can't go!" But we had finals coming up and the night, like the heavy curtain, was drawn to a swift close. "Let's beach it and brink it and clink it under the stars," I begged. But no one listened to the voice inside my head that said, "This night must not end. You'll never be this witty again!"

Someone yelled, "Graham will go with you. He'll take you for a ride," and the leer in his jeer made me realize I have a reputation.

So I, the woman of repute, go with Graham cuz the night can't end. He takes me for the promised ride in the car. And I'm not stupid. I know what follows, but I need the night not to end. It can't end. He doesn't speak, just drives, as if he's part of this machine doing his part, like the signal, like the shift, like the brake. He has a box of chocolates in the car. I want some, but don't dare ask. I'm working up the nerve to do so when the car stops at a lonely corner. I tell him, "This is no beach. Find me a beach in which to brink and clink." He hesitates, but does as I demand and drives till I can step out on sand. I look at night, and it seems that if I danced in space, my footprints would be the stars. "If I danced in space, my footprints would be the stars," I say and I go to show him how my heels could cut stars in the tar of night.

He grabs me. I know my part, but before we start, I need to show him. I know the drill, but how about in fifteen minutes? Fifteen minutes to look at the stars. No? Okay, five. One minute? Suddenly, a shooting star explodes like a white fist in my face and I am down for the count. He is spitting and yelling, "Wanna know why I can kill you and get away with it?!" I want to answer "yes, actually, I would appreciate it if you could explain to me why that's the case," but he's gallant enough to answer his own question by saying, "'cause you're just a brown piece of..." and I know exactly what that's about.

I flay and flip my fins like a fish caught on a hook. Knowing all the while all I have to do is get my sparkling red shoes together once and say "There's no place! There's no place!" and I will disappear from here, but it's kind of hard when he's got your-knee-bones-connected-to-your-shoulder-bones and his Adam's apple sticking out, obvious as a need, in your face.

O, my Wit! My wit! My wisdom for a whip, with which to watch him die from the stripes, slow and maddening as this feels. I'm about to stop struggling and number my way through it, just like how I get through the loneliness shade of darkness by counting each step to sleep. Until I hear my mother's voice telling me, "I named you Aiesha. It means: "She that lives." Bite the apple, bite into the seed till you reach the need" and I do so.

I stopped when I felt it bleed. That was enough for me to kick, kick, kick my way free as he clutched at me. He caught my spiked heel in his right eye, which I left lodged in him. For remembrance.

He howled to the wind, as I tottered homeward (moving forward somehow while back and forth between the height of the red heel and where my flat foot hits hard) till a woman of my complexion slowed to pick me up. She honestly did not mind that I bled on her clean cream carpet. I tried to impress her by making pleasant conversation though I lay bleeding in rags, with the fable of my superior education. Old habits don't die hard because they don't die.

I left school that day, leaving only one trace, but knowing I was safe. If Graham forces the only thing I left him on each girl in the kingdom, he won't find who he's looking for. That shoe never fit me.

Love ~ performed by Piter Fattouche

Mary Jane didn't call me to tell me that she didn't love me. She called to tell me there was no such thing.

"Love just don't exist, honey. It's all about positioning yourself in the world. You're a prince and all, but I don't want to move to Saudi Arabia."

"Jordan," I corrected her.

"That's right. Jordan. My mama says to think of almonds when I want to remember what country you're from. But if I took the time to think of something as random as almonds, I might as well take the time to remember a name as random as Jordan. Plus, I don't even like almonds."

I guess character isn't fate. Taste is.

"And he's a Kennedy. I mean his great-grandmother was Rose's cousin, twice removed."

"What does twice removed mean?"

"It means close enough that I've got to marry him when he asks me to. Being a Kennedy counts for a lot. Even in the South."

She hadn't been my first lover, only the first lover that mattered.

The entire time we dated I had her room filled with fresh flowers. I had fresh chocolates flown in every day from Belgium. I hid the gold boxes in the garden we planted daily there like treasures. I wanted her to eat chocolate. I mostly just wanted her to eat something besides celery and vitamins. But every time my bodyguards Riad and Ramsey removed the day-old chocolate, I noticed that she had left them untouched.

She was my only friend. The only one who spoke to me, aside from the streams of girls who break through the circle of my body guards and approach me in the dining halls with their eyes alive with excitement. Girls with a sense of vision, that makes them unable to see me. They can't look me in the eye without seeing past me to a future of riches and pomp in which every one says "her highness."

I don't hang out with the other Arab students either. They have a club—aptly called the Society of Arab Students. They get together for dinner every Sunday night in a dining hall room reserved for us. The president of the Arab society was a loud girl named Aiesha who visited her homeland only once. She was extroverted, always talking, always shouting, always laughing loud, acting silly, and trying to compensate for the deep-rooted shyness whose grip on her she was desperately trying to loosen. She sauntered up to me the day after Mary Jane dumped me.

"Hi. We're trying to get the Arab students to get together every Sunday for a meal. Please join us tonight." I said I would.

The few Arabic words she spoke revealed her family spoke the unmistakable dialect of a peasant. My bodyguards Riad and Ramsey teased me when she left, saying I traveled all the way to America to find a village girl. She had wide chocolate eyes that reminded me of my mother.

I arrived. I smoked a cigarette outside the door to calm myself. I was nervous. I wanted to make friends. I could hear what the students—this society of Arab students—were saying.

"Do you think the prince will come?" someone asked.

"I know the prince will come." I heard a voice ring out. It was Aiesha. "I asked him myself. Though I don't know why I chose to include him. His father might be an Arab king, but he certainly hasn't done much good for the Arabs."

"We saw you flirting with him," said another girl, her voice sounded so muted next to Aiesha's.

"I would never flirt with him. I'm Palestinian, and Palestinian women don't last long when they marry Jordanian royalty. Look at the guy's mother. The king killed his own wife. Sabotaged her helicopter. I bet his grandmother even knew and was in on the murder," Aiesha said.

"That's peasant talk, Aiesha. Conspiracy theories of village folks." It was an unmistakable dig. The prejudices of the old country were alive and well in America.

"If it would make you score as high as me on the SAT, then you'd wish you could have a little peasant blood in you too. They didn't want a Palestinian queen in Jordan. She became too popular. Jordan is seventy percent Palestinians who don't swear allegiance to any Jordanian king, so the King—his father—got nervous. He had to get rid of his mother."

"You shouldn't talk that way, Aiesha," said a girl in her thin voice. She probably knew Aiesha would be killed for saying such things in Jordan.

"His father's just a puppet of the U.S. anyway. Everyone knows he was on the payroll of the CIA. They got rid of his mother and I think his dad was in on it."

I stared at Riad and Ramsey, so brainwashed they were willing to die for me, and thought what I first thought when they wouldn't leave Mary Jane and me alone—are they guarding me or jailing me? Either way, I knew if I didn't stop Aiesha from talking, there is a good chance they would try with or without my knowledge or consent. I had to shut her up and all I could think to do was burst in. The room fell silent. Aiesha's brown skin paled.

"I just want you to know that I won't be able to attend dinner with you, but if you need funding, you can call on me." I said as Aiesha kept her eyes on the floor. I walked away and I knew from the stony look on Riad and Ramsey's face that it was clear to everyone in the room that we had heard what Aiesha said.

That night was the first time I snuck away from my body guards and wandered the streets alone. I ended up at the beach. I took off my shoes to wade in the water. A group of black men strolled by me. Each with a bottle in their hand except for one.

"The water's toxic, you non-English speaking motherfucker," one said to me.

"You're a motherfucker," I said and suddenly I was on the floor. He had hit me. I had never been struck before. It always seemed so exciting to me. A fist to the face had to prove that I'm alive and you're alive 'cause we're opposing. But in reality, it just hurt like hell. He pounced on me and raised his fist again. Now what terrified me, what you don't see on TV or film, is that when you're fighting someone, they are looking you in the eyes. They might be reacting to what a mother or father or teacher once said or did, but they're looking you in the eyes. They're watching their anger connect with your face. I watched his fist come toward me and suddenly halt, inches from my face. Another man had caught his arm.

"Leave him alone," the man said.

"Let go of my arm, Red."

"No," said the man who was called Red. "Leave this man alone."

Suddenly, I was alone, lying on the beach, wondering if I should be thankful for my life, and realizing you should at every moment be thankful for your life.

So, for the next three years I spent at school in America, I roamed the streets at night. Looking for random moments of connection, where someone crosses the ocean between us and says, "I will protect you, for no other reason except you deserve to survive."

I think of Aiesha sometimes. She left school. There was some scandal where she injured a rich boy and was either expelled or chose to go. I wonder where she is, this girl who said things I had never even heard whispered out loud. I wish I answered her that day, acknowledged that I had heard what she said about my family. I wish I told Aiesha the real question is not whether or not my grandmother or my father knew that the helicopter my mother boarded was going to blow up. The real question is: Did my mother know? That day the guards, who normally spoke so softly to her and adhered to her every wish, burst in and demanded that I not board the plane with her. "We have orders to keep the prince here," they said. "Your son will join you later." Did she know? Is that why she ignored the change in the guards' tone, didn't put up an argument, and forced me to go to my father though I always traveled by her side?

All I know was my mother was firm about me staying on the ground. She wiped my tears roughly as if it could erase the cause of them. She whispered, "I love you. I'll always love you," and left me alone.

Ignorance ~ performed by Betty Shamieh

The third time I got in a fight at school, I was taken to the high school counselor, Ms. Mann. She liked me and the feeling was mutual. She made sure I didn't get expelled, but in exchange she made me agree to participate in a new arts program for inner-city girls.

"I've signed you up for a painting class, Aiesha."

"Why painting?" I asked.

"You scratched your initials into the face of that girl. That shows that you have artistic tendencies. With your test scores, I can get you into one of the most prestigious colleges in the country with a free ride. Think how great your life would be then. You're a smart girl, Aiesha. You're not only smart enough to know you can get out of here, you're smart enough to know what it means for you if you do. But fight again and I can't help you. Don't fuck up." She swears with me because she thinks it will make me like her more. She's right.

"She called me a camel jockey. I had to fight her," I whined, "so people don't mess with me. Everybody's got a group and they stick to it. The Blacks stick together, the Latinos stick together, and the Asians hate each other in their own countries but here in America, they stick together too. I don't have anyone to stick to. I'm a rare bird, flying solo, and I'm not looking to become endangered anytime soon." It was a lie, though. I fought with that girl over a boy. All my fights with girls were over boys. Apparently, girls don't like it much when you deposit yourself in the laps of their boyfriends in the cafeteria, which I had recently made a habit of doing.

"I got one question for you, Ms. Mann. Would you try so hard to keep me in school if I didn't test so high?" Because she doesn't bullshit me and says no, I agree to take the class. I like drawing and stuff.

I'm sitting in painting class, staring at a white man in shorts stand still. It's the first day and we're already talking about perspectives. The model is wearing shorts because it's a class for teenagers. We're underage, shouldn't be exposed to the naked body, though I'm the only one who doesn't have kids in the room. Suddenly, a bass burst forth from below, a song I later learned was called "Night in Tunisia." Its rhythm was so strong you either moved to it or stopped moving at all. The beat punctuated through the drone of my painting teacher's talk. "No respect! No respect! Who will tell them to lower it?" He demands as I jump to my feet and with a backwards "I'll go" I'm out the door.

"No respect. No respect," refrained in my head as I tapped my way down the three flights of stairs, feeling the bass beat in my bones and on the dark basement floor. And what I saw there made me realize why some people have no respect and get away with it. The only light shone from the open double doorway of the dance studio, drawing me in. The dancers looked like figures of a painting in the frame of the doorway. But these figures were alive and spinning. I kept looking at a tiny girl in the front who looked like she weighed fifty pounds, and about forty-five of that was muscle. She had "it" if "it" meant she could do the same steps as everyone else and still stand out, as if she knew something you didn't, but might if you looked hard and watched long enough.

A tall black man stood still as a sculpture, one finger on his lips as if he had to stop himself from speaking. I knew I wasn't going back to that painting class that day.

"What did you think?" said the black man to me when the dance ended.

I didn't know what to say.

"Well, you can't just stand there and watch. Unless, of course, you plan on payin'. Can you dance, girl?"

"I've taken ballet," I said, not telling him I quit at age twelve when my breasts got too big for the costumes of our community center and I was told to try soccer.

"Good, then bring your butt to my class at nine."

"What level is that class?"

"The level of genius. Cuz Red will be teaching it."

"I mean, is it a beginning class? I'm a quick learner."

"Are you?" he said with a sidelong glance and the other girls laughed.

"I mean I'm probably an intermediate—"

"Ain't got no beginning, ain't got no intermediate, ain't got no advanced. I done told you all I teach is genius. You do what you can, till you catch up."

I later found out that Red was paid to teach four levels, which he combined into one. Most of the girls in the class weren't officially signed up, but were members of his dance company called the Red Jazz Dance Company. No one told on him.

I showed up the next day. Plopped myself right in front and began to stretch in the way that dancers do that seems more about psyching others out than really making your mind clear and your limbs long. I didn't know I was in the spot saved for the tiny girl called Nina. She gave Red a look that said, "don't expect me to take this!" He silenced her with a "let's see what she can do?" smile, a smile I would come to know well. She took a place right behind me and stretched furiously, mirroring any position I took but always reaching an inch further than I could have.

Red shouted out instructions. I thought I had it.

"Make it worth watching. Make your audience rather watch you than fuck you."

I didn't have time to think, "What the hell does that mean?" as he flipped the switch and "Night in Tunisia" blared as I took my first step in time.

I had it. I was warmth in the winter, I was balm in the desert, I was breath underwater. I moved in time with the internal tickety-tock of the high hot clock. Then, I lost the thread and stumbled about till Nina's foot smacked me in the nose. Light enough to show she saw me there. Not hard enough to break it, hard enough to show she could have.

"Sorry," I said, clutching my nose, expecting her to say sorry too. People who apologize too much expect everyone to do the same. She didn't. Instead, she smiled silently as I moved out of her spot. We could be friends now. I was forgiven.

"Baaaaah! Baaaaah!" Red bellowed like a sheep as he shut off the tape and hung his head. He proceeded to stand in front of each girl and scream "baaaah" then hang his head. Everyone except Nina and me. I held my nose and my breath.

"You followed her! Every single one of you except Nina," said Red to his company when he finally stopped his braying. "You've been dancing this number for weeks. It should be in your bones. This new girl learned it today. You don't know her. She don't look like no dancer. She ain't even in good shape. And you followed her! Trusted her more than you trusted yourself. Her! Wearing some aerobic gear with half her ass hanging out, looking like Jane Fonda on crack. If this isn't a case of the blind being led by the naked, I don't know what is."

I let out my breath, not meaning for it to sound like a sob. He finally looked at me. I had to save face. No dance teacher was going to make me cry.

"Cocaine," I said.

"What?"

"Jane Fonda is a star. She'd use cocaine."

Red looked at me. I felt my heart drop. Was I about to get kicked out of genius class?

"You're right. Now get your ass to the back of the room. And stay there till you can keep up. You did two dumb things today. One: wearing the outfit. Two: startin' off in front. Don't you ever step to the front before you know what to expect. You can always move up but…," he said, "it's a long road back to the back," the others chimed in as he pulled me to the back, where I stayed for many months.

I apprenticed for Red's company for longer than most, awaiting my chance to perform with them. One day I was dancing with the others and he shut off the music. "How could you? How could you?" Then he proceeded to lie on the floor, with his arm spread-eagle. He lay there, as if dead. The others held still in silence. Finally, he opened his eyes, turned his head ever so slightly, and fixed his gaze on me.

"Girl, what are you doing?"

"Dancing," I said. I had done all the steps right. Some girls in the row before me were even following my movements in the mirror. Girls in his company.

"You are so fine, sweetheart. You are so fine. You're so fine, you might be as fine as me. You probably get up in the morning and say, what's today? Oh, it's the day I get to be fine. Look at your watch. What time is it? It don't matter cuz I'm fine!"

There was no cool response to that, though I looked for one. I felt my cheeks grow hot. No one had ever talked to me this way.

"So if you're so damn fine, why are you going to go and do something so ugly?" as he proceeded to mimic the way I kept my hands in front of my chest and tried to cover myself with my arm. Everyone laughed, except him and me, and the ever-diligent Nina who used this time to stretch.

"They bounce too much."

"And they're gonna keep on bouncin', girl, till they get shriveled up and hang to the ground. They'll bounce till the day you die. What you got to lose, girl? There ain't a straight man in the audience who ain't gonna be thinking about whether or not he'd like to take you backwards or forwards. Your little arm in the way ain't gonna stop that from happening' and that's the absolute truth, baby. You either know it and use it, or you get your ass off the stage."

"Are you saying I should get a reduction?"

"I would never advise a lady to do that," he said with his sidelong smile. "Just don't put yourself on stage and expect people not to look at you. Or only at the parts that you want them to. That's not what it's about, baby. Okay, let's take it from the top."

I stood in the back and took it from the top. He smiled at me as I danced and said, "Big things are happening for you next year," and I smiled back.

When he told me to take ballet, I told him I would rather die. He nodded.

"But baby, you got to know how to fly before you can choose to slither."

I took ballet and he taught me how to slither.

"You free Saturdays?" Red asked me one day. I nodded. "I'm going to teach you my favorite dance, the one that's going to make me famous. I choreographed it for Nina, but I want you to do it." Simple as that, I was a soloist with the Red Jazz Company.

On Saturday I arrived earlier than Red did. He came in as I was eating my usual breakfast—a bar of chocolate.

"Girl, you shouldn't be eating that."

"I know," I said.

I stepped to the bar.

"Tummy in. Back straight. Booty under." I did so.

"Chin lower. Your chin up makes you look like you're reaching for something. Baby, you're already there."

He put his hand on my stomach.

"How old are you?"

"Eighteen," I lied.

I put my hand on his and slid it lower. He pulled away.

"Go home, child. Come next week ready to work."

"But—"

"I said go!"

I felt he refused me because he somehow knew I was a virgin and didn't want to be my first. So I cornered one of my fans from the freshman class, pulled him into the storage room at school, impaled myself upon him, and told him to go pound salt in the space of two short hours. Thus, I was rid of my hateful virginity all without getting myself an inch closer to becoming the woman I wanted to be.

I waited eagerly for Saturday to come. But my grandmother had to go and die on Friday, so I wrote a note explaining to Red I'd be back after the funeral later that day. When I arrived at dusk, the note was still on the door. I unlocked it and found Red inside. Furious, he grabbed my keys.

"No one keeps me waiting."

"I didn't want to. My grandmother died! My mother's not speaking to me because I left this early. I left you the note."

I said and saw it dawn on him that the chicken scrawl on a paper posted to the door was a message for him.

"Oh, Red. You can't read," I said. "I can teach you."

"Don't need nobody to teach me nothing. Too old. If I don't got it by now, I don't get it."

"But it's not like dancing, Red. There's no time limit. I can help you, like you help me. No one has to know."

"No."

"But..."

"Another word and you're out of my company. For good. You understand?"

"Yes, sir."

"And be here tomorrow. The only excuse I'll accept this time is your own death."

And since I didn't die, the next day he taught me the steps. I learned it, almost as well as Nina.

The day of our performance, Red still had to teach class to the girls not in the company. I came early to stretch and I overheard Red talking to the new girl, Jennifer.

"Since you're so fine, why you going to go and do something so ugly?"

Jennifer was far from attractive, by anyone's standards. I whispered such to Nina and she said offhandedly, "Aiesha, he says that to every girl." So that was just something he said to pump all the girls up. Because he knew it was a hard thing to dance, to ask people to look without touching. Because we each walked in his classroom with our own combination of weakness, shyness, and shame which he chose to unlock. Because we were beautiful, though no one told us so and, for most of us, no one ever will. It was the sweetest, most generous gesture I have ever seen a person do for others. And because it wasn't about only me it made me absolutely livid.

If I hadn't learned the truth right then, I probably could have dealt better with what would happen that later that night. I stepped out onto the unlit stage. Through the darkness, I could see a group of guys who sat in the front row. There was no way I could not smell the beer from the stage. I later learned our show was a precursor for a bachelor party of a shotgun wedding, someone's idea of joke.

"Hey, look at that pair," was shouted up at me over the melody and it went downhill. They just started saying, "Bounce. Bounce. Bounce" every time they saw my breasts move, till I could no longer concentrate on the beat of the drum, the depth of my breath, or the feel of the floor.

I knew what I should have done. I had seen Red fall short in class, his body aging, so he couldn't demonstrate everything he wanted so desperately to teach to us. He would slip into something else that was equally fabulous that he could do. It was a solo piece. I could have done some improv and no one would have known. But I was not the only fine one anymore, so I let everything be "bounce, bounce, bounced" out of my mind till I ran off the stage, the saxophone wailing a goodbye to me.

"Aiesha, where are you going?" he asked as I grabbed my stuff from the back room.

"I'm sorry. Send Nina. She knows the steps. I'm not a dancer. I'm not, okay? Red, I'm sorry I messed up your show. I'm sure Nina could do it."

"A half a dozen girls in the company could do it, but no one like you. Don't walk out like this, girl."

"I do what I want."

"No, you don't. You do what you got to do. Get out there and redo your performance. Do you understand me?"

"You don't know what they're saying!"

"Nothing that hasn't been said before and won't be said again." He had me by the arm and was dragging me to the stage at this point. I pulled myself free.

"I don't want to be a damned dancer, doing tricks with my body for money. I'm going to get a scholarship to college. I am going to be an intellectual. I don't want to end up like you. Working on rag-a-tag student productions that no one wants to see. Washed up at thirty-nine. Washed up and ignorant..."

At the word ignorant, Red stood up straighter and strode to the door, with his head held high though he shook with anger. And he paused, the light shining from the hall framing him in the doorway where he stood and asked me the question I ask myself every time I sell myself short for the sake of safety or gain or give up the chance to be a human being because of cruelty or shame, a question I finally understood never had anything to do with looks.

He asked me, "Why would a person who is so fine do something so ugly?"

I still don't have an answer for him.

Sex ~ performed by Piter Fattouche

"What do you do when sex sells and you're sexy?" Liza said, answering my question of why she's a prostitute with that question.

I met Liza on a lonely corner in Alphabet City a few months ago and she charged me twice what a blowjob cost to talk for twenty minutes. We saw one another every Monday at four, and she charged me for every session.

You'd think prostitutes would be surprised when I tell them that I don't want to sleep with them. I just want to talk. I'll pay them to talk. They're not surprised at all.

Like Liza tells me, "More often than not, the part of my body that customers are most interested in is my ears. Most johns have sex as a formality, use it as an excuse to talk to us. Or rather to make us tricks listen. Almost never does a john come, do his business, and go. They always want more than they pay for. If I really like a customer, if he's a nice guy with problems, I'll try to convince him to see a psychologist. They never do. They don't want to seem abnormal, so I guess they go to prostitutes instead."

I'm convinced there are worse things than loneliness. I just haven't found them yet. I'm hoping I never will.

I'm talking to prostitutes for research for a book I'm writing—"The Different Kinds of Rapists (dash) How To Never Be A Victim" by me, Ahmed El-Far. It's a book for women. I've begun by profiling victims of rape, sexual violence, and prostitutes. I want to find out how people contribute to their own demise. I know my work is important. As a man, I feel like I can offer special insight into the subject, because to be a man is to understand the urge to rape. I would never act on that urge, but I understand it. With my book, I'm giving women an insider's view. I dip into my own resources, my own understanding of a predator, and every once in a while excavate truth. Once you understand your predator, you cease to be prey. I want to help women understand.

My first chapter is called "Ignore Your Instincts." They can be wrong, you know. It's better to think rationally. People can be reduced to types. Know the type of predator you're dealing with. Memorize the characteristics of each type of criminal. Know their weaknesses, capitalize upon them, and you can survive. For example, if you're dealing with the angry aggressive type, act like you are in more pain than you actually are. This type of criminal feels no control in his own life, usually is married or lives with a woman. Any unexpressed aggression he has toward her, he takes out on you. If he tries to rape you and your first instinct is to pretend that you enjoy it, ignore that instinct. This will not endear him to you, just the opposite. He will feel you are taking control and this will anger him.

When the AIDS epidemic began, it changed everything. I thought it would change crime along with it. I was wrong. The nature of human beings is to adapt to every circumstance and a criminal is still a human being. Initially, I thought it was wise to advise women that, if a man tries to rape you, tell him you have AIDS. But that was before I learned how a prostitute in Chattanouga died when she did that, killed by a man on a suicide mission, who tried to drink her blood.

Liza never listened to me as I told her about the different types of rapists and sex offenders. She should have, since prostitutes and strippers are most often the victims, because the victimizers don't think they count as much and neither does the law.

"You're paying to listen to me and you're doing all the talking," she would say to me in between chews when I tried to explain to her the different profiles I came up with. For our sessions, we would meet at McDonalds. She ate with her mouth open. One time she told me, "You keep going on and on about the different types of men. How long do you think your book will be?"

I tell her the latest estimate, feeling like I have to physically restrain myself from shouting, "chew with your mouth closed!" "It'll be roughly five hundred pages," I tell her.

She says while stuffing McNuggets in her mouth, "Well, I want to write a book about the different types of men too. You open the first page of my book and all it will say is "bastards." That'll be it. The entire book will consist of one fucking word. It'll be a two syllable masterpiece. Bas-tards. But it won't be a thin book. Oh no! There will be about a hundred blank pages after that. So you'll keep turning page after motherfuckin' page and looking for more kinds of men till you get to the end, which is really the beginning, where you see the only type—the one category—every single man very comfortably fits into is bastards." She burps really loud.

"Women are not exactly flawless creatures themselves," I counter.

"Bastards."

"Stop saying that."

"Bastards. Bastards. Bastards."

"Okay, I know you had a hard time in your life. Your dad messed around with you. But at least you can talk about what happened. Imagine being a boy who is molested. There's no room in this society for men to ever admit…"

"What's your point? When boys are molested, they are molested by men."

"Not necessarily. You think your life is so hard. Imagine dealing with, say, a mother whose husband dies a protracted death. Maybe that mother has one son who she sleeps in the same bed with on the night her husband dies till the day she does. I'm sure there are mothers who hold their sons too closely and say, "This is not damaging you. This is not damaging you," till the words melt into pants. Imagine if that woman thought feeding her son whatever he wanted in the morning made up for what she made him do in the night. Maybe it was even worse to feed the kid whatever he wanted, because he'd only choose chocolate till it made him sick, since no one would make him stop…"

"So you slept with your mom?"

"No, of course no. I was just saying… hypothetically…"

"Don't worry. I won't tell anyone. Besides, according to your research, I shouldn't be alive much longer anyway."

That night I took Liza home with me to the house my mother and I once lived in. I've been meaning to move, but I've been too busy with my book to really have the time. I put Liza on the couch. In the middle of the night, she came into my bedroom and said she would do it with me for charity, which is a pretty clear indication that she was my girlfriend, right? Well, she was the closest thing to a girlfriend I ever had. I loved her, but I only wanted to make love to her when she was nowhere to be found. When she was there in front of me, when any woman is there and ready, it's very hard for me to… well, it's just very hard for me.

I sold my parent's property in the old country and have been living off that for years. I needed more to support the research for my book. Prostitutes are expensive to talk to. I started working for my Uncle Lou in his liquor store on the afternoons I have off. Lou speaks hardly any Arabic. I thought during the long hours in his liquor store, I could teach him a few words here and there. He only liked learning how to cuss. Liza started stopping by the store and Lou befriended her. He endeared himself to her by offering her free food. It's his tactic. Give a little, expect a lot. I work with the man and, if I take a bar of chocolate, he makes me pay for it. Retail. I don't understand why women like men like Lou. I'd like to write a book about it. I think Liza is starting to sleep with Lou, for next to nothing, which is worse than doing it for free.

Every Sunday we play "tawlet zaher." Six or seven of my relatives gather at a different home each week. We gamble on the game, betting on ourselves and each other. Lou breaks the rule of "no women" and brings Liza. When Lou loses and he always loses, he takes Liza in a back room with him and we hear her giggling. I realize I'm going to have to listen to them together. Suddenly, she starts to scream, "No, no, no." The other men pretend they don't hear it, they roll the dice, and I don't move. The dice rolls again and I don't move. "God! Somebody help me!" I can't take it anymore so I knock stupidly and then bust down the back room door and see Liza and Lou sitting on opposite sides of the room. Lou is laughing. I see it's a trick, a joke, and I am the butt of it.

"What took you so long, Mr. Hero, Mr. I'm-going-to-help-all-women-with-my-stupid-book?" Liza looks at me, challenging, angry at me for a reason I can only guess at until I realize it was a test and I failed. I want to beg her forgiveness, explain I was too shocked to move, but I can't get words out of my mouth. "I said, what took you so long, you *motherfucker*?!" Lou stops laughing when he sees the look on my face. Lou's my mother's brother. "Shut up, bitch," Lou says in his gravelly voice. She calls me that name again and Lou slaps her. Liza leaves in tears. I can't look at her and she doesn't look at me. Lou and I go back out to the living room to watch the game that continued to play outside the whole time. Humiliation is like white noise. You can choose not to focus on it, get used to it, ignore it, but it will always be there.

It's the day after and a little girl comes into Lou's Liquor Store to buy a chocolate bar. Lou gives it to her for free and feels her up and I don't stop him. Because last night I figured out what Liza must have known a long time ago—that I can't write a book that will prevent women from becoming victims. No one can. There's no way to teach or learn how to survive. You either do…

Justice ~ performed by Betty Shamieh

I would watch men watch my mother, as she carved her curves through the thick air of Spanish Harlem, where we—one of the only Arab families—lived. She would pass, oblivious to the noise and rumble and its hush, as the world held its breath with her every step. The stares and catcalls from cars did not penetrate her mind. None could catch her eye, because she looked through people like one looked at walls or rocks. But they certainly caught mine, since I made a game of glaring up at her admirers, the angry imp at her side, till they looked away sheepishly. She was probably thinking of my father's disappearance, like I did almost all the time. The dark boot stains he left as his only trace were etched into our white carpet and the smooth sheets of our minds. With time, the footprints faded but left us smudges of gray that shaded the backdrop of our lives.

"Get what love you can, but never trust a man," my mom's clients would say to her, their eyes wide and unblinking as fish, wanting to swallow tidbits of her story while avoiding the hook of intimacy that is always attached. She was the local seamstress. When they questioned her about her history without asking questions, she would simply respond by telling them how much their bill would be. "That will be five dollars," she would say even if a moment before the price had been four. If they argued, they were shown the door. That was their punishment. Those that stayed knew not to try to ask without asking again.

My mother only went out for necessities. In fact, for as long as I could remember, my mother only went out on every other Saturday for sewing supplies and food. At the end of every Saturday trip, I would beg my mother to let me buy candy at Lou's Liquor Store. She usually said no, but sometimes said yes. Her responses were as inexplicable as they were unpredictable, like rain. You couldn't argue with it. And one Saturday, one Saturday that was not in any way special, she for some reason said yes. I knew she liked to buy milk from Lou, because he sold hot goods for cheap.

Normally, I went to Lou's with my friends. He would scowl at me, because I would carry seven or eight bars of the same brand of chocolate to the cash register. I would weigh each chocolate bar against the other in my hand before selecting one. I wanted to make sure I got the best and biggest bar and I knew that, though things came in the same packaging, what was on the inside could be very different. I didn't understand why he would yell at me, since I would put the unwanted bars back into their carton even neater than how I had found them. He often tried to tell us girls that the quarters we had given him were nickels. I would give him the look my mother gave her clients who complained about her prices. He knew he wouldn't get away with that trick with me.

But when I went with my mother on that Saturday, Lou was all smiles. Lou's real name is Lotfi. He's an Arab too. He greeted my mother loudly in Arabic, "Salamah aleykum." My mother greeted him not at all and headed straight for the refrigerator. Lou followed us and watched my mother compare dates on the milk. Lou patted my head and asked, "Is this your daughter?" though we knew he knew exactly who I was. He was speaking to her breasts. They didn't answer and neither did she. My mother continued to compare dates on the milk, ignoring him. "She's beautiful... like her mother." No response.

She selected the milk bottle she wanted and went up to the register with me and him in tow. "One thing, Aiesha," she commanded. "Yella." "Yella" literally means "hurry up" in Arabic. It figuratively means "you better fucking get a move on now." Listen to an Arab woman speak to her child and you'll notice every other word will be "yella," but there are different kinds of "yellas." Something in my mother's tone makes me choose quickly, the first time I bought a candy bar without weighing it against its sisters.

At the register, my mother and I placed the milk and chocolate down in sync. It took Lou a minute to step up behind register where he ought to have been. We waited. The sun blazed through the glass window behind the register, so I could only make out the dark outline of his bald head and pointed ears that towered above us.

"How much?" my mother asked.

Lou said, "It's on me this time. You being a woman all alone, raising a child..."

"No," she responded in a tone that said "I mean it" clearer than if she had said it. He told her the price, she paid it. Waiting for change, I saw her tug on the back of her blouse at the base of her spine, a nervous habit I later developed when I felt even my husband's eyes on me. "At least let me give the girl this," he said in a voice somewhere between a groan and a growl, while offering me the expensive Toblerone chocolate he kept behind the counter. As I reached for it, my mother smacked my open hand, making rosy imprints on my wrist and dew in my eyes spring forth.

"Where is your money to pay for that, Aiesha?" she asked sadly as I looked up at her, questioning.

"It's free, a gift, so the girl can grow up sweet like her mother," Lou groaned and growled at us. "Everything has to be paid for sooner or later, Aiesha," and though she addressed me, it was clear her words had a message marked for him.

As the glass door slammed shut behind us and we were out in the bustling street again, my mother took my red wrist and rubbed it. She was sorry. "Aiesha, we don't go in there alone. Not you or me without the other, do you understand?" I nodded, realizing it was the first time she laid down a commandment that applied to us both. It made me think of her better-alive-than-sorry speech she sometimes screeched at me, like the time I lost track of time in the library and she had called the police. "You can't say your mama never warned you that it is a hard cold world, that there may be men waiting for you behind every open door. If you end up with your legs broken in some ditch, you'll have no one to blame but yourself because I warned you. You can't say your mama didn't warn you."

And I couldn't, but I loved chocolate. My mother never seemed to notice that I stole quarters out of the forbidden drawer, where she kept change for her customers, though I later realized she must have known. Money was tighter for us than I could have ever conceived of. And I spent all the money I stole in Lou's Liquor Store.

On the first day of fourth grade, I went alone to Lou's. There was another man behind the counter playing backgammon with Lou, a man I later found out was Lou's nephew. They huddled over the board, reminding me of the picture of the Fates at their knitting that hung in the public library. I was quick at picking my usual chocolate bar that day, afraid I would be late and my mother would get suspicious. Against my better judgment, I was beginning to believe with the blind faith of adults that things that come in the same packaging can't be that different. Bar in hand, I rushed up to the register, but Lou didn't look up from his game.

"Pretty girl," Lou's nephew said as he threw down his dice, made his move, and won the game. I felt Lou let out his breath in one angry gasp of disbelief.

"Ahmed, You know whose kid this is?" said Lou still staring at the board, forlornly mourning his strategy that had ceased to matter. Unlike my mother, I did not need to ask the price of what I wanted in Lou's store. I offered my money for the candy with my eyes averted. I couldn't see which faces the voices were coming from.

"Whose?"

"I forgot her name... but you know her. The Arab woman who lives around the corner. You know, Amira," said Lou making the groan-and-growl sound again. At the sound of my mother's name, I raised my gaze to notice his hands cupped around his chest as if he were a woman holding her heavy breasts. Lou laughed. "The woman who Yusef Habib left to go to Arizona with that hot red-haired waitress, the one who worked nights at Sam's. Some men have all the luck. We've known your parents, little girl, since before you were even a twinkle in your daddy's eye," said Lou.

I felt all eyes turn on me, the remnant of that twinkle, slow and deliberate as sunflowers follow the light. I offered my twin quarters again, watching them watch me, feeling that they could see through my skin to my quick-beating heart.

"It's free, little girl," said Lou, but I knew it was not and I shook my head. "I said, it's free," he repeated with force as I pressed my quarters down. They clanged on his smoothed-down steel counter, echoing louder than I intended, the way things of the same substance often sound when they meet. I held my chocolate bar tight to my chest and had my free hand on the steel bar of his glass door when Lou cried, "Wait!" I stood still as he snaked up close to me, all the while unwrapping a Toblerone in his thin veined hands. "You have to take this. I can't sell it because it lost its wrapper" were his words as he wrapped my free hand with his around the chocolate. The more I tugged away with all my weight, the harder he squeezed my hand around the chocolate bar. Then I felt his thumb press upon my left breast quick as a hammer hits a nail. As he let my hand go and I soared backwards against and out the glass door, I heard the roar of his laughter rush after me like a river, as Lou said, "Take it, so you grow big tits like your mama."

I could still hear his laughter, babbling like a brook within me, as I ran through the streets. Only when I stopped in front of my empty schoolyard did I realize I had let out a stream in my school clothes. Suddenly, I felt the need to find a swing and swing. But when I got to the playground, I saw that someone had wrapped the big swings around the bar, too high for even the tallest man to reach. But still I jumped up and reached for the wound swings that swayed in the wind, that looked like shining black birds tugging at chains. I had seen kids make a game of harpooning the swings over their bars at the end of recess. It was as if keeping the swing from others was somehow possessing it forever.

So I forced my way into the swings for babies and, though my hips were too wide for the seat, I could float back and forth if I kept my knees bent. And I did so till the eye of the sun shut and it was dark, all the while with the two chocolate bars, one unwrapped, melting in my clenched hands. When the clock from the nearby church struck seven, I went back to Lou's and smeared the words "I hate you" a million times in melted chocolate on his window.

Then I went home. I ran to the bathroom and changed clothes before my mother, who sat sewing, could speak. When I emerged in my pajamas, my mother asked me where I had been and I told her at the library. "No books?" she questioned. When I told her none had interested me, I knew she knew I was lying. It was the first lie I told that she didn't dig into and expose the roots of its untruthfulness to the light. She knew no matter how much she asked me without asking, she could never make me tell what happened to me and how it made me feel, because I had learned from her how not to.

I listened to the wind howl its secret curses and the rain fall noisy as wet kisses throughout the night. I welcomed the rosy fingers of dawn, knowing that they would point Lou to a place where he would see the black words of my hate written on a clear wall. I was going to storm that store and stand silent before him. He had one of two choices: apologize or kill me.

But when I got to his store, the wind and the rain had swept the chocolate words away, so that only I could see the outlines of "I hate you" in my reflection in the glass.

The day I got my period Lou died alone of a stroke in his store and somehow I felt that was justice.

AFTERWORD

Shattering the Stereotypes in a Post-9/11 World: A Conversation with the Playwrights

~Conducted by Fawzia Afzal-Khan (October 2004)

I wanted this anthology to conclude with a section that represents the recent work of Muslim women playwrights because drama to me is the genre par excellence where personal and political conflicts are dealt with in their rawest, most immediate form: on stage, where audiences are confronted with humanity in the guise of characters observed at their most vulnerable, naked moments, confronting those difficult questions most of us prefer to shove to the background most of the time. Certainly, in the plays published in this section, we see reflected many of the most important issues of our times.

In Maryam Habibian's one-woman play, gender and class oppression are experientially observed through a chronicling of the radical poetry and life of Iran's first major feminist poet, Forugh Forrokhzad. Betty Shamieh gives us a taste of what it's like to grow up Arab and female in America through a multiplicity of perspectives, thus helping shatter monolithic myths about Arab women. Bina Sharif forces us to confront the plight of Afghan women as they struggle for freedom from the twin yokes of religious and patriarchal oppressions on the one hand and imperialist aggression against their homeland on the other. And in "That Sara Aziz!" by Maniza Naqvi we begin to see subtler, internal critiques taking shape against mental and emotional conditioning of women that reproduces cultural oppression with, at times, the willing consent of the women, forcing us to ask the question—are they victims or survivors, particularly when class privilege and material comfort is part of the package deal? What gives the world the right to brand you as "oppressed" if you don't see yourself that way? Or do we revive Marx's concept of false consciousness as an apt one?

As a means of putting some issues I had been struggling with regarding Islam, women, and art to rest—or not!—I decided to assemble a list of rather basic questions, which I posed to the playwrights represented in this volume. I asked them what they thought of the label, "Muslim Woman Playwright," how they felt about living and working in the USA post-9/11, and particularly how free they felt to work in their chosen medium, what some of the literary influences in their lives had been, how supported they felt by their families, what they felt about the role of Muslim men in their lives as creative female artists, and what their views were on the relationship between art and politics.

I received fascinating responses—fascinating to me because, despite the differences in their choice of subjects for their plays, despite obvious differences of style, approach, and temperament observable in their work and personalities, the answers I got back to my questions were almost identical, if differently inflected. While most of them (except one) understood and maybe even appreciated the possibilities of "being heard" in the present with the label "Muslim Woman Playwright" attached to them, none of them wanted to be stuck in that ideological or artistic box. One of them was very clear that she saw herself as a person—not a label. Their desire to distance themselves from what they perceived as the confinement of labels, while being aware of the need for representation, made me think back to the early days of feminist literary debates in this country and elsewhere when women were conflicted about being called "women writers." Betty Shamieh summed up the two sides of the debate best when she pointed out that "if your culture or religion is demonized, which is the predicament of Arab and Muslim Americans in this country, I think it is particularly important to identify yourself as an artist from that background. Of course, worthwhile art ultimately will transcend the culture of the artist who creates it. But, I think it is important to represent yourself because it complicates the views of the people who are exposed to your art." Thus, while she and the other women in this section do wish their work to transcend geographical, ethnic, gender, and religious labels and boundaries, they are cognizant of the fact that at certain times, identifying with a label, particularly one that has acquired a negative aura, may be a revolutionary gesture, necessary to break through the very stereotypes engendered by that label.

While they all expressed their sense of freedom as far as the ability to write, live, and work in the U.S. post-9/11, most admitted to feeling their new work was more scrutinized, often becoming a lightning rod for critics from the left and right. Bina Sharif in particular expressed a sense of unease taking her work out into the public domain, telling me, "I feel anxiety. I feel fear. I feel unfree because my work is very strong and my sense of creativity is honest and edgy. It makes people nervous especially after 9/11... They are taking everything personally and they have a limited knowledge of Islam." Yet she, like the others, admits that there is simultaneously a real hunger on the part of most American non-Muslims to learn more about the world of Islam and how Muslim artists see the world.

For these playwrights working with issues brought to the surface in the wake of 9/11 in a very immediate way, there is then the possibility of being heard by more people than ever before. Habibian, for instance, informed me that when her play, scheduled for a preliminary reading at the Bluestocking Café a couple of days after 9/11, was about to be postponed indefinitely due to the café owners' unease regarding its timing and subject matter, she put her foot down, insisted on the reading being held, and lo and behold!—it attracted an overflow crowd with more than 120 people wanting to get into an 80-person capacity room. In fact, it was the reaction of the audience to her material, their eagerness to learn more about this radical feminist poet from a Muslim land, that prompted Habibian to embark on turning her project into a full-length script, which would result a year later in a full-length production performed at the CUNY graduate center and later at the William Carlos Williams performance space in New Jersey.

Maniza Naqvi came right out and said to me that she was offended by the question about Muslim and Arab men and their relationship to ideas about culture and progress and women's rights. By its very nature, the question to her implied that "our" men are incapable of appreciating women artists, that they are opposed to culture and progress, the assumption being put forth that "creativity," "progressiveness," and "muslim" are mutually exclusive terms. As such, Muslim women who are artists and creative are aberrations, whom Muslim men—and also most women—cannot appreciate! Of course, put that way, it becomes obvious how the very idea that we might think to ask about whether Muslim men "support" women as creative artists and autonomous beings does indeed reveal the stereotypes about Muslim cultures and Muslim men that we have ALL internalized, to a greater or lesser degree.

The other playwrights, while admitting that women in the Muslim countries or the communities they grew up in (Pakistan, Iran, Palestine) are often stigmatized when they step out of "traditional" roles by men and women alike, also underscored the ways in which these cultures at the same time support and value strong women, women who often defy conventions. Admittedly, there are many contradictions and paradoxes that surround not only the term "Muslim Woman" but also "Muslim" or "Islam" in general. These terms apply to societies in constant flux, where "female oppression" is but one way of looking at an ever-shifting kaleidoscope, a concept that obscures as much as it reveals about male-female relations in Muslim cultures and societies.

It is to reveal, as much to themselves as to their readers and audiences, the nuanced myriad realities of their many worlds and multiple allegiances now simply and simplistically being lumped under the monolithic label "Muslim Woman," that these women write their essays, their poems, their dispatches from the field, their plays. Is their art political? Should it be? Naqvi sums it up nicely: "All art is political." If indeed, taking up the pen is a political act, then these women writers are all political beings. Their work serves as a warning of where our world is headed. Their work shapes our perceptions of the world and shows its inhabitants to be infinitely more complex than any label suggests.

NOTES

Introduction

1. Sergeldin, Samia. "Mediating Identities in Crisis: American Muslims Post-9/11." Unpublished paper.

2. *Unholy Alliance*. Rushdie, Salman. Editorial. *New York Times*. 2 November 2001.

3. Goldberg, Michelle. "Osama University?" www.salon.com/news/feature/2003/11/06/middle_east

4. Hilton, Isabel. Review of *Terror in the Name of God: Why Religious Militants Kill*, by Jessica Stern. *New York Times Book Review.* 16 November 2003.

A Letter to India

5. Manto, Saadat Hasan. "'Chacha Sam ke Nam Chutha Khat' (fourth letter to Uncle Sam)." *Manto Rama*. Lahore: Sang-e-Meel, 1990. 393–394. All nine letters written by Manto in this vein have now been translated; see Khalid Hasan. *Letters to Uncle Sam*. Lahore: Alhamra, 2000.

6. Manto, Saadat Hasan. "'Chacha Sam ke Nam Teesra Khat'(third letter to Uncle Sam)." *Manto Rama*. Lahore: Sang-e-Meel, 1990. 386–387.

7. Manto, Saadat Hasan. "'Chacha Sam ke Nam Panchwan Khat' (fifth letter to Uncle Sam)." *Manto Rama*. Lahore: Sang-e-Meel, 1990. 401–405.

8. Manto, Saadat Hasan. Preface. *Untitled in Baqiyaat*. Lahore: Sang-e-Meel, 1998. 411–414.

Where Is Home?

9. I use this term with reluctance, because of the negative connotations it has in the Palestinian context.

Rachel's Palestinian War

10. This paper was first delivered at a conference entitled "Responding to Violence," held at Barnard College of Columbia University in the fall of 2001.

11. Some lines (mainly the lines in italics) were taken from emails Rachel Corrie wrote to her parents while she was in Palestine.

12. *Debke*: A traditional Arabic dance.

CREDITS

"Adventures of a Muslim Woman in Atlanta" by Nadirah Sabir was first published in the online *Atlanta Journal-Constitution*, Sept–Oct 2001.

"Am I a Muslim Woman? Nationalist Reactions and Postcolonial Transgressions" by Minoo Moallem was first presented at the Practicing Transgression Conference, celebrating the 20th Anniversary of the Publication of *This Bridge Called my Back,* U. C. Berkeley, February 8, 2002. The author wishes to thank Norma Alarcon for inviting her to be part of the conference.

"Billy Bush Sam-ton" by Fawzia Afzal-Khan was first published in *Poets Against the War*, ed. Sam Hamill, Nation Books, 2003.

"The Burden on U.S. Muslims" by Azizah al-Hibri was first published in the Boston Globe, September 11, 2002, A23.

"The Conflict" by Nathalie Handal first appeared in *Scheherazade's Legacy*.

"Expert" by Sham-e-Ali al-Jamil was previously published in *Mizna*.

"Fragments From a Journal" by Zohra Saed was first published on www.tehelka.com, September 20, 2001.

The interview with Riffat Hassan was first published in *Dawn* in January 2003.

"Letter to Uncle Sam..." is reprinted with permission from *Economics and Political Weekly* Nov 8–15, 2002.

"Muslim Women's Rights in the Global Village: Challenges and Opportunities" by Azizah Yahia al-Hibri is reprinted with the permission of the *Journal of Law and Religion*.

"Must We Always Non-Intervene?" by Afsaneh Najmabadi was drafted for the colloquium "Responding to Violence," October 24–25, 2002, Barnard College, The Center for Research on Women.

"Unholy Alliances..." by Fawzia Afzal-Khan first appeared in *Counterpunch*, Dec. 2003.

"Where is Home? Fragmented Lives, Borders Crossings, and the Politics of Exile" by Rabab Abdulhadi was presented in different versions at the following conferences, lectures, and symposiums: "All I have is a Voice: A Teach-in on War and Peace" at Hunter College-CUNY; "Globalization and Resistance" at CUNY Graduate Center; "Guadino Lecture" at Williams College; and "Women, War, & Displacement: The Gender Dimension of Conflict" at Hofstra University. It was published in *Radical History Review*, special volume on National Myths in the Middle East, March 23, 2002.

AUTHOR BIOGRAPHIES

Rabab Abdulhadi

Rabab Abdulhadi works in the Center for the Study of Gender and Sexuality at New York University.

Humera Afridi

Humera Afridi is a *New York Times* Fellow at NYU where she is completing her MFA in Creative Writing. She is currently working on her first novel. Originally from Pakistan, she has taught English in Saudi Arabia, Dubai, and Dallas, and creative writing in New York. She was a staff feature writer for the *Gulf News* in Dubai from 1997 to 1998.

Wajma Ahmady

Wajma Ahmady is a poet and memoir writer. Her poetry appears in the forthcoming anthology *Drop by Drop We Make a River: Afghan Writings of War, Exile, and Return*. She received her BA in literature and writing from UC San Diego and is completing her MFA at the New School University.

Azizah al-Hibri

Azizah al-Hibri is a professor at the T. C. Williams School of Law, University of Richmond. She is a former professor of philosophy, founding editor of *Hypatia: a Journal of Feminist Philosophy*, and founder and president of *KARAMAH: Muslim Women Lawyers for Human Rights.* A Fulbright scholar, she has written extensively on issues of Islam and democracy, Muslim women's rights, and human rights in Islam. She guest-edited a special volume on Islam for the *Journal of Law and Religion*. Her recent articles include "An Islamic Perspective on Domestic Violence" (*Fordham International Law Journal*, December 2003) and "Redefining Muslim Women's Roles in the Next Century" (*Democracy and the Rule of Law*, Congressional Quarterly, 2001). She is currently completing a book on the Islamic marriage contract in American courts. Dr. al-Hibri is a member of the advisory board of various organizations, including the PEW Forum on Religion in Public Life, the Pluralism Project (Harvard University), and *Religion and Ethics NewsWeekly* (PBS).

Sham-e-Ali al-Jamil

Sham-e-Ali al-Jamil is a Muslim woman of South Asian decent. Raised in both the UK and the US, she is a poet and writer whose poetry has been published in *SALT Journal*, *Mizna*, and *Roots and Culture Magazine*. She currently works and writes in New York City.

Barbara Nimri Aziz

Barbara Nimri Aziz is a Syrian-American journalist who has most recently been reporting from occupied Iraq. She is also a veteran print and radio journalist and founder and host of WBAI's weekly Arab talk-show radio program *Tahrir.*

Amani Elkassabani

Amani Elkassabani was born in Alexandria, Egypt, and came to the US when she was two years old. Her work has appeared in the journal *Mizna* and in *Azizah* magazine. She won the QALAM Award for Short Fiction in 2000 and the RAWI Creative Prose Award Contest in 2002. She is currently a high school teacher in Maryland, and working on a collection of short stories. She is member of the International Women's Writing Guild and the Radius of Arab American Writers and Friends.

Maryam Habibian

Maryam Habibian received her Ph.D. in educational theater at NYU. Her most recent effort has been an NEH scholarship to the Research Institute on "Cities and Public Spaces in Comparative Cultural Contexts"; with the support of this fellowship, she traveled to Iran and made a documentary based on Forugh Farrokhzad's poetry and the city of Tehran. She has given presentations on Farrokhzad's poetry in both Europe and America, as well as several presentations on "Women in the Performing Arts in Post-Revolutionary Iran" at different colleges in New York City. Her latest directorial credits include *Theater of the Reflecting Pool*, performed in NYC and New Jersey, and *Forugh's Reflecting Pool*. Dr. Habibian has also directed and co-translated (with Lois Becker) *The Invitation* and *Blessed Are The Meek*, both performed at the Expanded Arts Theater. *The Ugly Older Sister*, which was written and directed by Dr. Habibian, was performed at NYU's Black Box Theatre.

Nathalie Handal

Nathalie Handal is a Palestinian poet, playwright, and writer. Named one of the ten Arab writers of note by the *San Francisco Chronicle*, she has directed and is the author of numerous plays and books, most recently *The Lives of Rain,* which was shortlisted for the Agnes Lynch Starrett Poetry Prize/the Pitt Poetry Series. She is the editor of *The Poetry of Arab Women: A Contemporary Anthology*, an Academy of American Poets bestseller and winner of the PEN Oakland/Josephine Miles Award. Handal is poetry editor for *Sable* (UK) and development executive for the production company, the Kazbah Project. She teaches at Columbia University.

Riffat Hassan

A Pakistani-American feminist theologian, Riffat Hassan is chair of the Department of Religion at the University of Louisville.

Suheir Hammad

Suheir Hammad's work has appeared in over a dozen anthologies and numerous publications. Her own books are *Born Palestinian, Born Black* and *Drops of This Story*, both published by Harlem River Press. Suheir has won several awards for her writing, including the Audre Lorde Poetry Award, a Van Lier Fellowship, and the Bernard Cohen Short Story Award. She recently starred in "Russell Simmons Presents Def Poetry Jam on Broadway."

Ayesha Jalal

A professor of history at Tufts University, Ayehsa Jalal obtained her BA from Wellesley College and her doctorate in history from the University of Cambridge. Dr. Jalal has been Fellow of Trinity College, Cambridge; Leverhulme Fellow at the Centre of South Asian Studies, Cambridge; Fellow of the Woodrow Wilson Center for International Scholars in Washington, D.C.; and Academy Scholar at the Harvard Academy for International and Area Studies. Between 1998–2003, she was a MacArthur Fellow. She has taught at the University of Wisconsin-Madison, Tufts University, Columbia University, and Harvard University. Her publications include *The Sole Spokesman: Jinnah, the Muslim League and the Demand for Pakistan* (Cambridge, 1985 and 1994) and *Democracy and Authoritarianism in South Asia: A Comparative and Historical Perspective* (Cambridge, 1995). Her most recent book is *Self and Sovereignty: The Muslim Individual and the Community of Islam in South Asia Since c.1850* (London/New York: Routledge, Delhi: Oxford University Press, and Lahore: Sang-e-Meel). She is currently working on a new book-length project entitled *Partisans of Allah: Meanings of Jihad in South Asia*.

Mohja Kahf

Mohja Kahf's first book of poetry, *Emails From Scheherazad*, was a finalist in the Paterson Poetry Prize (2004). Her scholarly book, *Western Representations of the Muslim Woman,* examines medieval and Renaissance European literature. She writes for "Sex and the Ummah," a column on MuslimWakeUp.com. Two short stories by Kahf appear in *Dinarzad's Children: Fiction by Arab American Writers*, ed. Pauline Kaldas and Khaled Mattawa, and one of her essays appears in *Scheherazade's Legacy: Arab and Arab American Women on Writing*, ed. Susan M. Darraj. Kahf's second book of poetry, *The Hagar Poems*, and first novel, *Girl in the Tangerine Scarf*, are forthcoming.

Faryal Khan

Faryal Khan is a Pakistani-American freshman at Carnegie Mellon University, with a passion for singing and poetry.

Nadia Ali Maiwandi

Nadia Ali Maiwandi is an Afghan born in New York City in 1969. She is a writer and editor and has worked with publications including afghanmagazine.com, *Afghan Journal*, *The Oregonian*, *Willamette Week*, alternet.org, *Newsday*, and the anthology

Another World Is Possible. She has also worked with such groups as Afghanistan Relief Organization, Middle Eastern Women's Empowerment and Resource Center, and Afghan Solidarity, among others. She holds a BA in English/Creative Writing and currently lives in Portland, Oregon.

Anisa Mehdi

Emmy Award-winning journalist Anisa Mehdi is an internationally renowned expert on Islam. Her commitment to broadening Americans' understanding of Muslims and the Middle East has led to unprecedented access to people and places around the world. Mehdi received critical acclaim for producing and directing "Inside Mecca," a National Geographic Special premiering on PBS in 2003, and for her three-part series on the Hajj for PBS's *Religion and Ethics Newsweekly* in 1998. She won the 2002 Cine Golden Eagle Award as executive producer of the PBS *Frontline* special "Muslims." She has also produced for ABC News *Nightline*. For over two decades Mehdi has been an on-air correspondent, program anchor, producer, director, and writer. She has received numerous awards as arts and culture correspondent for the New Jersey Network News (PBS). Anisa Mehdi has an MS from the Columbia School of Journalism and a BA from Wellesley College.

Minoo Moallem

Minoo Moallem is professor and chair of the Women's Studies Department at San Francisco State University. She is the author of *Between Warrior Brother and Veiled Sister: Islamic Fundamentalism and the Cultural Politics of Patriarchy* (forthcoming from University of California Press, 2005). She is also the co-editor (with Caren Kaplan and Norma Alarcon) of *Between Woman and Nation: Nationalisms, Transnational Feminisms, and the State* (Duke University Press, 1999). She is the guest editor of a special issue of "Comparative Studies South Asia, Africa and the Middle East, on the Iranian Immigrants, Exiles and Refugees."Trained as a sociologist, she writes on postcolonial and transnational feminist cultural studies, cultural nationalist and religious fundamentalist movements, and Iranian cultural politics and diasporas. Her publications are in Farsi, French, and English.

Nirmen al-Mufty

Nirmen al-Mufty is a journalist based in Iraq. In recent years she has been working for US TV networks as well as writing her weekly column in an Iraqi paper. Her English language articles relating to developments in Iraq are frequently carried by *Al-Ahram* weekly from Cairo. She was a frontline reporter during the Iran-Iraq war and since 1991 has been reporting on developments inside Iraq. She speaks Hungarian, English, Turkoman, and Arabic. She lives in Baghdad with her 19-year-old son, Ali.

Afsaneh Najmabadi

Born in Iran, Afsaneh Najmabadi received her BA from Radcliffe College (1968) after attending Tehran University. She has an MA in physics (Harvard 1970) and a Ph.D. in sociology (University of Manchester 1984). Her publications include *Women with Mustaches and Men without Beards: Gender and Sexual Anxieties of Iranian Modernity* (University of California Press, forthcoming January 2005), and *The Story of Daughters of Quchan: Gender and National Memory in Iranian History*. She has been a fellow at the Institute for Advanced Study, Princeton (1994-95); the Women's Studies in Religion Program, Harvard Divinity School (1988-1989); the Pembroke Center for Teaching and Research on Women, Brown University (1988-1989); and a Nemazee Fellow at the Center for Middle Eastern Studies, Harvard University (1984-85). After nine years at Barnard College, Najmabadi joined Harvard University in 2001 as Professor of History and Studies of Women, Gender, and Sexuality.

Maniza Naqvi

Maniza Naqvi was born in Lahore, Pakistan, and lives and works in Washington, D.C. on poverty and conflict. She is the author of three published novels, *Mass Transit* (Oxford University Press, 1998); *On Air* (Oxford University Press, 2000) and *Stay With Me* (Sama, 2004). She is currently working on her fourth novel, *A Matter of Detail*.

Farrah Qidwai

A Pakistani-American writer based in New York City, Farrah Qidwai holds an MFA in creative writing from the New School and is an MA candidate in media studies. She is currently working on a novel.

Nawal El Saadawi

Nawal El Saadawi is a medical doctor, writer and militant advocate of Arab women's rights and the rights of the oppressed masses everywhere. She served as Egypt's director of Public Health under Anwar Sadat, until she was summarily dismissed, and later imprisoned, as a result of her political activities and views concerning women's rights over their bodies and sexuality. Despite political harrassment by the Egyptian authorities, the banning of her books and a recent fatwa against her, Nawal Saadawi continues to write, publish, and give talks the world over.

Nadirah Sabir

Nadirah Sabir, who holds a BA in journalism from New York University, is currently an online editor and columnist with the *Atlanta Journal-Constitution*. Her online column, tagged "The Adventures of a Muslim Woman in Atlanta," is read worldwide. In it, she writes about daily news and lifestyle issues, travel, multiculturalism, pluralism, Islam, and a variety of other topics. She may well be the first Muslim woman in America to have such a column.

Zohra Saed

Zohra Saed was born in Afghanistan and lived in Saudi Arabia before immigrating with her family at the age of five to the US. She is co-editing the forthcoming anthology *Drop by Drop We Make a River: Afghan American Experiences of War, Exile and Return* with Lida Abdul. Saed received her MFA in poetry at Brooklyn College (2000) and is a doctoral student in English at the CUNY Graduate Center. She serves as a cultural consultant on Afghanistan and Muslim-Americans for film and theatrical scripts. She teaches at Hunter College's English Department and has initiated courses on the West Asian Diaspora.

Shahzia Sikander

Sikander's work has been exhibited at the Museum of Modern Art (MOMA), Smithsonian Museum, Whitney Museum, San Diego Museum, National Gallery Museum, Istanbul Biennal, Johanessberg Biennal, MOMA Paris, and many other international venues. Recipient of the Joan Mitchell and Tiffany awards, Sikander was recognized by the city of New York for pioneering the revival of miniature painting, for advancing the debate on multiculturalism, and for preserving and promoting the heritage and culture of South Asia. In 2004 *Newsweek* listed her as one of the most important South Asians transforming the American cultural landscape. Her painting appears on the front cover.

Betty Shamieh

Betty Shamieh is a Palestinian-American playwright and actor. Her play *Roar* was presented off-Broadway and was selected as the *New York Times* Critics' Pick for four consecutive weeks. Her play "The Black Eyed" will premiere at the Magic Theatre in 2005. She is a graduate of Harvard University and the Yale School of Drama.

Bina Sharif

Bina Sharif is a playwright, actress, director, visual artist, and poet. She has had 22 plays produced in New York, Europe, Pakistan, and across the United States. *Afghan Woman*, her one-woman play, was written shortly after 9/11, was initially produced at the Theater for the New City in NY, and since has been performed throughout the world. *Afghan Woman* is now part of a trilogy that includes *Democracy in Islam* and *Muslim Glitter*. Since 9/11, she has also published a collection of prose poems entitled *War Folios*, and other short plays related to the tragedy in Iraq, such as *Comedy of Terrors*. Her ongoing project, *Manhattan Days*, consists of writing and visual art. Bina is a Joseph Jefferson Award Nominee actress from Chicago's Goodman theater. She has received awards from the NYSCA and the Jerome Foundation, and has won a Franklin Furnace Award and the award for best performer for the Gay and Lesbian Theater Festival. Bina is a medical doctor but does not practice, and has a master's degree in public health from John Hopkins University. She is originally from Faisalabad, Pakistan.

Mahwash Shoaib

Mahwash Shoaib is a Pakistani-American poet. As a poet and scholar, she is interested in avant-garde, experimental, political, and multilingual forms. She also translates contemporary Urdu poetry into English; her translations of the Urdu poetry of the Pakistani poet Kishwar Naheed have been featured in the journals *Connect* and *Chain*. She is an English doctoral candidate at the CUNY Graduate Center and also teaches at Queensborough Community College in New York. She is currently working on her dissertation on the transnational poetics of twentieth-century American and Asian poets.

Eisa Nefertari Ulen

Eisa Nefertari Ulen responded to September 11th with "Muslims in the Mosaic," which originally appeared in *Essence* magazine and was anthologized by Robert Atwan in *America Now*. Her essay "Tapping Our Strength" was included in Lee Gutkind's Living Issue Project on CreativeNonFiction.org. Other essays have appeared in several anthologies, and Eisa has contributed to the *Washington Post*, *Ms.*, *Health*, and *Azizah*. *Essence* nominated her for a 2002 National Association of Black Journalists award. She has also received fiction-writing fellowships from the Frederick Douglass Creative Arts Center and the Provincetown Fine Arts Work Center. A member of the English department faculty at New York City's Hunter College, she was awarded a 2004 Presidential Award for Teaching. Eisa lives with her husband in Fort Greene, Brooklyn.